CARGO, CULT, AND C

CARGO, CULT, AND CULTURE CRITIQUE

Edited by
Holger Jebens

UNIVERSITY OF HAWAI`I PRESS
HONOLULU

Printed in the United States of America
09 08 07 06 05 04 6 5 4 3 2 1

Library of Congress Cataloging-in-Publication Data

Cargo, cult, and culture critique / edited by Holger Jebens.
p. cm.
Includes bibliographical references and index.
ISBN 0-8248-2814-3 (hardcover : alk. paper) — ISBN 0-8248-2851-8 (pbk.)
1. Cargo cults. 2. Nativistic movements. 3. Melanesia—Religious life and customs. 4. Melanesia—Social life and customs. I. Jebens, Holger.
GN472.75.C37 2004
306.6'99925—dc22

2004003470

University of Hawai'i Press books are printed on acid-free paper and meet the guidelines for permanence and durability of the Council on Library Resources.

Cover and interior design, and composition by Teresa Bonner.
Text in Goudy Old Style and display type in Agenda.
Printing and binding by The Maple-Vail Book Manufacturing Group.
Printed on 60 lb. Sebago Eggshell, 420ppi.

Contents

Acknowledgments

The texts collected here are revised versions of papers presented at a workshop bearing the same title as this volume and generously sponsored by the Volkswagen Foundation (and supported by the Aarhus University), which was organized by Karl-Heinz Kohl, Ton Otto, and me and held in November 1999, in Aarhus, Denmark. The workshop, whose title was suggested by Ton Otto, simultaneously marked the conclusion of a three-year research project, which was also generously supported by the Volkswagen Foundation, was supervised by Karl-Heinz Kohl, and in which Otto and I took part. Personally, I wish to thank Karl-Heinz Kohl, without whom neither the research, the workshop, nor this volume would have been possible.

CARGO, CULT, AND CULTURE CRITIQUE

CHAPTER 1 Introduction
Cargo, Cult, and Culture Critique

Holger Jebens

Cargo cults might be very like omnivorous but servile chamaeleons. They gobble up positivist and mechanistic social theory and have plenty of spit left over; they are very good at appearing as any one might imagine them to be.

—*Kenelm O. L. Burridge*

In Western writings on Melanesian cargo cults, authors point almost routinely to the vastness and heterogeneity of the relevant literature. Indeed, from the "invention" of the term "cargo cult" itself in 1945 (Lindstrom 1993: 15) until the present day, the phenomena labeled by it have exerted a remarkable attraction on "the West," that is, on academia as well as the general public. Doug Dalton gives one reason for this fascination in stating that the topic "raises the most basic issues regarding assumptions about the interpretation of history and cultural difference," which, in his view, "need to be understood and debated in contemporary post-colonial anthropology" (2000a: 292). As Lamont Lindstrom (2000: 294) and others have stressed with reference to Lévi-Strauss, cargo cults are "good to think." They are, one might add, good to think with and good to think against, not only for "us," but also for their alleged adherents.

As is the case with other topics in the history of anthropology, however, the fascination with cargo cults has been subject to change, being more fashionable at some times than at others. Thus, the late 1950s and the 1960s, in particular, saw a proliferation of "cargoist" writings, among them now classic accounts by Peter Worsley (1957), Kenelm Burridge

126). Similarly, Michael Rutschky associates demonstrations in the German Democratic Republic prior to so-called reunification with cargo movements (1992; cf. also Kohl, present volume), whereas Roy Wagner refers to contemporary Western beliefs concerning unidentified flying objects as "our very own cargo cult" (2000: 370, 372).

The more Western cargo discourses were dissected, the more the term "cargo cult" turned into a highly contested label, with some authors even stating "a need to reconsider the advisability of its use at all" (Hermann 1992b: 69). Indeed, as particular aspects of cargo cults are generalized into features of Melanesian culture at large, the term tends to lump together different ideas and practices that actually may have very little in common (Read 1958). Accordingly, cargo cults have more or less been proclaimed not to exist, at least not as a group of analytically distinct phenomena (McDowell 1988). Moreover, as Melanesian culture is constructed as a kind of "cargo culture," the term potentially exaggerates the distance between Melanesia and "the West," thus falling into the much-criticized trap of "othering" (cf. Hermann, present volume). In addition, authors have long pointed to the negative connotations of primitivism and irrationality derived from the term "cargo cult" first being coined by planters, colonial administrators, and missionaries in order to denote and dismiss whatever they saw as obstacles to their respective intentions.[5] These negative connotations are also characteristic of indigenous discourses in that they can be detected when Melanesians talk about cargo cults themselves.[6] Accordingly, Stephen Leavitt speaks of a "pejorative understanding of 'cargo cult' that is codified in Papua New Guinea law (it is illegal to engage in cargo cult activities)" (2000: 322).

The very existence of indigenous cargo discourses, however, can also be employed to argue against those who might be dubbed the "cargo critics." If we as anthropologists find our hosts and informants appropriating and making their own use of the term, who are we to try to take it away from them? If we eliminate cargo from our vocabulary, how can we understand its role in peoples' lives? Such an elimination, it is claimed, would mean missing the chances that the term has to offer. According to Dalton (2000b: 352), the "destruction of the category 'cargo cult' ... precludes the critical self-reflection and examination of Western culture and social scientific rationalism" that understanding this category as a Western creation makes necessary. For Otto, the combination of "cargo" and "cult" even constitutes "a felicitous conceptual match" (1999: 97) because it provokes us to think about our separation of economy (cargo) and religion (cult) as distinct cultural domains, and it makes sense "that cargo cults concern also our image of ourselves."[7]

To some extent, "critics" and "defendants" of the contested label both agree that the way we name, describe and interpret "cargo cults" appears to have a great deal to do with our own culture. In Dalton's view, this is also true of the phenomena themselves, since he sees them as "a parodic enactment" (2000b: 348) through which Melanesians try to make sense of the fact that Westerners claim "to have grasped universal truths which transcend the limits of mortal men," while they simultaneously "continue to take from those to whom by all rights and proclamations they should be giving" (2000a: 290). "Western culture," Dalton argues, "is in this way nothing if not extremely confused and therefore also confusing," and this confusion, by virtue of being enacted through them, is precisely what makes cargo cults "strange" and "odd" in Western eyes.[8] Therefore, in order to comprehend cargo cults properly, Dalton claims that it is necessary to examine "the irrationality of the Western views Melanesians mimic in what appears to be 'cargo cult' type behavior" (2000b: 352); in other words, "to investigate the 'cargo cult' phenomenon entails studying not only scientific phenomena but also ourselves as subjects."[9] According to McDowell, however, this is exactly where Western authors have failed so far: because anthropology as a discipline is basically about discerning cultural differences by way of intercultural comparisons, interpretations of cargo cults have, in her view, tended to "focus on difference and ignore similarity" (2000: 374). For McDowell, this constitutes a "failure to do genuine comparison" (2000: 378) that not only "allows us once again to distance ourselves from the 'other' in ways that imply hierarchy,"[10] but also causes us to "miss an opportunity to use the 'other' to understand ourselves as well as to provide an impetus for our own cultural critique, so eloquently called for by Marcus & Fischer (1986)."[11]

Dalton's and McDowell's writings can both be seen as typical of much of the recent "cargoist" literature in that, whether interpreting cargo cults as a "parodic enactment" or perceiving a "failure to do genuine comparison," they concur in stressing—and demanding an elaboration of—the self-reflexivity inherent in the deconstruction of the term and in the concomitant revision of the perception of the Western Self.

II

The first set of chapters in this collection presents three authors who already have established identifiable and influential positions in the critique of Western cargo discourses. Building on his earlier deconstruction of such discourses, Lindstrom analyzes the term "cargo cult" itself, the listings of things allegedly desired by cargo cultists, as well as "four possible narrative types" within the "cargoist" literature in order to suggest that there is an "affinity of modes of desire" between Melanesia and the West and to call for "a genealogy of desire."

Elfriede Hermann discusses Western "cargo cult" constructions regarding the Yali movement of Madang Province (Papua New Guinea), which was described by Lawrence (1964). She focuses on how "cargo cult" has itself been reconstructed by the inhabitants of Yali's home village, who adopted the term in all its negative connotations and now adamantly deny "cargo cult" in their own regard. Thus, she writes, "The indigenous activities so promptly dismissed as 'cargo cult'" appear "rather as reverberations of Western cargo discourses and various Western cultural practices" and, in this regard, "the Western Self can in no sense be divorced from the indigenous Other." For Hermann, however, continuing to use the concept of "cargo cult" means insisting on such a "Self-Other dichotomy" rather than to attempt to overcome it. Therefore, she suggests that, if the term must be used at all, it should only be written *sous rature* (i.e., "under erasure"). The problematic, if not damaging, effects of Western discourses are also brought out in Martha Kaplan's examination of Fiji's colonial and postcolonial history. Taking as an example the so-called Tuka movement, which was "first fearfully imagined and then made real in colonial perception and then, in many cases, in Fijian practice and self-definition" before scholars such as Worsley and Burridge had "reified the category of cult," Kaplan argues that to move "beyond definitions and reifications" and to replace "an analytical framework using 'cargo cult' ... by a dialogical account" would allow us to gain a less distorted and perhaps more sympathetic view of indigenous agency.

The second set of chapters can be seen as answering recent calls for self-reflexivity and expanding the general framework of the contemporary debate on cargo in at least two ways: by referring to the widespread phenomenon of Christian millenarianism and by, so to say, pushing the conventional geographic boundary of existing "cargoistic" literature westwards, that is, by also including data from Papua and eastern Indonesia.[12] Karl-Heinz Kohl describes the rumors evoked by his presence on East Flores and an indigenous myth that people took to be substantiated by the picture embossed on the reverse side of a German coin he had shown to one of his informants. Stressing that "the process of anthropological 'othering' can also have some advantages for the one who has been othered," and thus contradicting critics such as McDowell, Hermann and Kaplan, Kohl views the myth allegedly associated with his German coin as "an integral part of East Florinese indigenous anthropology," which leads him into an analysis of the relationship between money and religion in the West, as well as to an assessment of the postwar history of Western societies in general and of the German mark in particular. Interpreting the development of the German currency as "a 'money-cult' issuing from the very heart of a modern capitalist society," Kohl concludes, building on Lindstrom's insights, that "cargoism was a kind of behavior dominating Western societies in the first postwar decades" and that it was only the concomitant and "very similar kind of materialist orientation and desire" in the West that made it possible to reify diverse (and multifaceted) indigenous movements as cargo cults.

With respect to the eastern Indonesian islands of Maluku and Halmahera, Nils Bubandt examines indigenous millenarian ideas and suggests that they "not only reflect local tradition or Christianity but are also part of a discourse of mimicry of the 'cargoism of modernity.'" This application of the term "cargo cult" to the concept of modernity results from Bubandt's claim "that modernity itself is a millenarian project and that this millenarianism is often turned into a cargo cult of modernity by third world states." In eastern Indonesia, however, modernity—and "America" as its "icon" or "simulacrum"—proves to be highly ambivalent, because, according to Bubandt, people associate it not only with commodities and Christianity, but also with violence and destruction. Jaap Timmer provides another example of the connection between cargo and millenarianism postulated by Bubandt, as he records and analyzes a case of millenarian critique that the Imyan of Papua direct against their own government and church and that, though sharing many similarities with so-called cargo beliefs, leads to the emergence of a new "tradition of knowledge"—*agama*. Here, unlike in the eastern part of New Guinea, local forms of Christianity play an oppositional role, facilitated by Papua's continued incorporation into the Muslim-dominated Indonesian state.

The three subsequent chapters represent a return to Melanesia, the "heartland" of conventional "cargoism." This move is introduced by Robert Tonkinson, who simultaneously continues Bubandt's and Timmer's engagement with Christian millenarianism. Drawing a historical comparison between Melanesian and Aboriginal reactions to the arrival of Westerners, he identifies millenarianism in general and cargo cults in particular as a response that is characteristic of Melanesia but absent from Australia. Tonkinson's account does appear to have some bearing on the recent deconstruction of the term, for, if "cargo cult" merely constitutes a function of the Western imagination, one wonders why this imagination has not been applied to ideas and practices from Aboriginal Australia as well. This invites the conclusion that there might in fact be a correspondence between the term and the Melanesian ethnographic reality. It is the latter that is foregrounded in my own and Stephen Leavitt's contributions.

My own chapter documents and interprets indigenous cargo discourses from West New Britain Province (Papua New Guinea) with respect to images of Westerners and the cultural Self that are articulated in their context. These images exert a mutual influence, being as ambivalent as Bubandt's eastern Indonesian concepts of modernity and "America." In my view, this ambivalence mirrors a basic dialectic of passivity or self-alienation, on the one hand, and of activity or self-affirmation, on the other. Drawing on his own fieldwork in East Sepik Province (Papua New Guinea), Leavitt stresses the religious and "deeply personal" character of cargo beliefs, focusing on the fact that Melanesians are known to have associated Westerners who are often believed to live in a world without anguish, pain, sickness, hunger, or conflict with their own ancestors. Thus, Leavitt both claims and demonstrates that in general a "more enhanced understanding can emerge from the more intimate features of cargo ideology as revealed in the personal narratives of individual actors." Accordingly, he urges anthropologists to ground their interpretations on single cases, that is, to pay close attention to what specific persons actually say in equally specific situations.

The concluding set of chapters brings together indigenous and Western discourses as well as the categories of the cultural Self and Other expressed in their context. This is done by arguing for an approach that is both comparative and critical, as it takes up McDowell's insight that "genuine comparison," in the sense of not focusing on differences and ignoring similarities, provides us with both "an opportunity to use the 'other' to understand ourselves" and "an impetus for our own cultural critique."[13] Dalton illustrates this combination of comparison and critique when, in his contribution, he views the phenomena termed "cargo cults" as "the Melanesian physical enactment of historical context, which is provided by Western colonial culture," and, by the same token, as "an accurate mirror of the exploitative self-contradictory ideology of Western bourgeois culture." Here, Dalton both elaborates on his arguments against abandoning the term and sustains his call for self-reflexivity; in other words, for a thorough interrogation of "the most basic premises of Western culture."

Ton Otto refers to the well-known Paliau movement of present-day

Manus Province (Papua New Guinea)—in his view "an example of mutual attempts at interpretation between Melanesians and Westerners"—and compares indigenous and exogenous notions of "work," "wealth," and "knowledge." As "Western and Melanesian concepts, values and practices" are used "to mutually illuminate each other," Otto argues that a "sustained comparative analysis" of this sort can form the basis for "a culture critical perspective" that, in turn, he sees as "an intrinsic part of the anthropological method of comparative-ethnographic research as well as a raison d'être of the discipline as such." Vincent Crapanzano understands hope to be "an emotionally and morally toned descriptor of an existential stance or attitude" that is common to both Westerners and Melanesians, and he calls for a consideration of its role "in cargoism" at three "never fully independent levels of consideration": "the linguistic (or grammatical), the cultural (or ideological), and the social structural." Finally, Joel Robbins compares the anthropological critique of concepts such as "totemism," "kinship," and "cargo cult" with millenarian practice in both the Papua New Guinea Highlands and South America as another form of critique. Thus, the anthropology of cargo cults and other varieties of millenarianism becomes "part of a comparative anthropology of critical practice." For Robbins, however, millenarian critique must not be restricted to one's own cultural Self, because he assumes that "finding new ways to open ourselves to the understanding of other cultures" would allow these cultures to "critique our concepts in ways that allow us to continually develop them."

III

The various key positions outlined and developed in the present volume prove to be quite divergent: whereas some authors suggest that, problematic or even damaging for a variety of reasons, the term "cargo cult" should be written only "under erasure" or abolished altogether, others claim that "there is, however, a danger, too, in turning away from the central concept of cargo" (Leavitt) and that, precisely because of its troublesome nature, it could profitably be used for self-reflexive purposes. Nevertheless, other contributors do not appear to be particularly committed to the contested label, because they quite comfortably apply the notion of millenarianism as well—paralleled perhaps by the fact that in some accounts "cult" and "movement" are almost used alternately.[14] This terminological heterogeneity, if not uncertainty or even confusion, appears

3. See Bodrogi (1951), Worsley (1957), and Mühlmann (1961). In viewing cargo cults as "'proto-national' formations of a transitional kind," Worsley (1957: 255) follows Jean Guiart (1951a), who has termed them "Forerunners of Melanesian Nationalism." Andrew Lattas's work (1998) constitutes a more recent version of the "resistance to colonial oppression type of interpretation," because for him cargo cults take place within the context of a continuous struggle in which subjugating Westerners and subjugated Melanesians struggle with each other for power (cf. Jebens 2002: 194). See also note 16.

4. In Lindstrom's words: "What used to be Melanesian culture becomes cargo cult writ large" (1993: 42).

5. See Hempenstall and Rutherford (1984) and Kaplan (1990b, 1995b). Accordingly, in the 1940s planters and missionaries blamed each other and the colonial administration for causing cargo cults (Lindstrom 1993: 15–25) so that, as Dalton notes, "explanatory emphasis shifted toward the West and away from the Rest" (2000b: 351). In this sense, one might add, the self-reflexive turn in the interpretation of cargo cults is not entirely without precedent.

6. See, in this volume, the contributions by Hermann, Otto, and me.

7. Otto (1999: 96). Similarly, Lindstrom (present volume) notes that "a combination of the words cargo and cult can make us prick up our ears," and for Dalton (present volume) this combination "expresses an essential critical nature through the tension between the terms 'cargo' and 'cult.'"

8. Dalton (2000a: 290). Thus, Dalton locates cargo cults neither solely in "Melanesian culture" nor in the Western mind alone, but sees them rather as a kind of "co-production" or, in Stewart and Harding's phrase, as "an artifact of entwined practices" (1999: 287).

9. Dalton (2000b: 347). In a similar vein, Wagner, having claimed that "cargo cult has grown into something of a Loch Ness Monster," states the following: "It looks like we will never figure out what it is until we have made some more progress in figuring out what we ourselves might be" (R. Wagner 2000: 372).

10. Thus, for McDowell, not to compare cargo cults genuinely leads to "othering," just as the term itself does for some critics.

11. Here, McDowell seems to see cause and effect as mutually dependent: the "failure to look at our own culture(s) and its (their) complexities in the light of the 'other'" is brought about by overexaggerating differences and ignoring similarities, but at the same time this failure also "engenders naive comparison" (2000: 376).

12. Most of the data in this collection, however, come from Papua New Guinea, the Seaboard (Hermann, Leavitt), the Highlands (Robbins), and the adjacent islands (Jebens, Otto). In addition, Kaplan and Tonkinson, whose chapters both have a rather historical orientation, refer to Fiji and Australia, respectively.

13. A comparative approach is already implicit in the contributions by Lindstrom and Hermann, since Lindstrom calls for a "comparative genealogy of desire," whereas Hermann examines how differences between Self and Other are constructed in both Western and indigenous cargo discourses.

14. A connection between cargo and millenarianism is drawn here by Bubandt, Timmer, Tonkinson, and Kohl, the latter two quite explicitly understanding cargo cults as a form of millenarianism.

15. In this sense, a distorting function is shared by both the phenomena and the term itself because, according to Otto, cited here by Dalton, the "very word 'cargo cult' has provided us with a mirror in which we have failed to recognise ourselves" (Otto 1992a: 5).

16. Consider, for example, the images of "us" and "them" expressed in indigenous cargo narratives (cf. my own contribution to the present volume). By contrast, to interpret cargo cults or

millenarian movements as expressions of anticolonial or counterhegemonic resistance seems to presuppose the existence of a fundamental opposition between Self and Other. This interpretation is rejected here by Bubandt and Dalton, on the grounds that it may be the result of a Western projection (Bubandt) or that one rather "needs to adopt a view of Melanesian 'cultures' which does not see them as separate from the European global capitalist domination, and sees them as neither its victims nor its resistance" (Dalton). See also note 8. My own position resembles Dalton's, because I suggest that there is a dialectic of passivity and self-alienation, on the one hand, and of activity and self-alienation, on the other (present volume).

17. Although I agree that there are similarities between Western and indigenous cargo discourses and that the former do indeed have an impact upon the latter, in my view, talking about "reproduction" invites the potential danger of underrating selection, transformation, and creativity in the way Melanesians appropriate and make use of the term "cargo cult." Thus, missing what might be only apparently similar or what might be "essentially Melanesian" under a "Western surface" would amount to ascribing to Melanesians the role of merely passive recipients of external influences. (I am aware that I am here reversing McDowell's critique by implying that one should not focus on similarity and ignore difference.)

PART I

AGAINST CARGO

CHAPTER 2 Cargo Cult at the Third Millennium

Lamont Lindstrom

We have reached a new millennium. This is an apposite time to rethink South Pacific cargo cults—social movements that often reached for the millennial. Thanks to the relentless calendar, we have moved forward into a time that cargo cultists desired, at least nominally. Cargo cultists, notoriously, looked to their horizons for signs of newness and change. Standing at the cusp of the third millennium, we, too, can look both backward, to consider what the noise was all about, and forward into the twenty-first century, to wonder whether cargo cults have much of a future.

Cargo cults blossomed in the postwar 1940s and 1950s throughout the Melanesian archipelagos of the southwest Pacific. People turned to traditional or innovative religious ritual to obtain "cargo." Cargo, or *kago* in Melanesian Pidgin English, is rich in meaning (see Otto, present volume). Sometimes the word meant money or various sorts of manufactured goods such as vehicles, packaged foods, refrigerators, guns, and tools. And sometimes, metaphorically, cargo represented the search for a new social and moral order that would ensure local sovereignty and the withdrawal of colonial rulers. In either case, people worked for and expected a sudden, miraculous transformation of their lives. Cargo cult prophets commonly drew on Christian millenarianism, sometimes conflating the arrival of cargo with Christ's second coming, often called "Last Day."

But has this Last Day come and gone? Or might we look forward to future cargo culting? Will cargo cults continue to erupt, or will they prove to have been a twentieth-century reaction to colonial inequalities and the disruptions of a world war? A number of successful movements now ongoing will certainly survive in the twenty-first century, institutionalized today as political parties and churches in Vanuatu, the Solomon Islands, and Papua New Guinea. These parties and churches, however, are no longer the cargo cults they once may have been.

Within the history of anthropology, the cargo cult—as a seductive puzzle—emerged at the point when the discipline reoriented its interests to tackle problems of modernization and development. Following the Second World War, anthropological concerns with documenting disappearing cultures or discovering the natural laws of social organization faded. By the 1950s, problems of economic development, social change, and innovation and diffusion instead became foregrounded. Cargo cults attracted considerable attention, either as maladies of creeping modernity or misguided, although understandable, local reactions to global economic and political transformation.

Anthropologists and cargo cultists alike wrestled with the same problems: the effects of global forces on local communities, economic and political inequalities and how they might be redressed, and the search for effective models of social change. Roy Wagner noted this shared orientation in 1975, when he suggested that "anthropology should perhaps be called a 'culture cult' for the Melanesian 'kago' is very much the interpretative counterpart of our word 'culture.'"[1] Postwar cultural anthropologists and cargo cultists worked to make sense of each other's horizons.

Previous investments in changing modernization have faded away, replaced by new interests in globalization, world systems, hybridity, diaspora, and the like. Colonial Melanesia is no more; all archipelagos but New Caledonia are independent. We never made it to the Last Day, so perhaps we should bury cargo cult, not praise it. There are, however, signs that cargo cults won't so easily disappear in the third millennium. Cargo cult stories are strangely appealing. They continue to pop up in tourist guidebooks, on the Internet, and in tabloid journalism, as well as in introductory anthropology and comparative religion texts.

I once suggested that, whatever their ethnographic reality in Melanesia, we relish cargo cult narratives because they are parables about our desire (Lindstrom 1993). We find reassurance in strange tales of people who are madly in love with what they cannot have. Cargo cult stories function to naturalize the mode of desire that will continue to dominate the third millennium. This reading focused on *narratives* of cargo cults—on stories that anthropologists mostly have told to one another. I was not interested in any cargo text's ethnographic truth but rather in its repetitive story elements, narrative structure, and popular uses. I confessed that I would not say anything about Melanesian reality in that my concern instead was "solely with the stories we tell about cargo cult, not with their historical and ethnographic accuracy" (1993: 12). Cargo cults are Melanesian, but cargo cult accounts belong to us.[2]

I will try again to make a case for this reading of cargo narratives—that these fundamentally are tales of a mode of desire that we know well. I recognize that I use the word "desire" promiscuously to label any condition, or feeling, of want. English vocabulary is rich in this area and one might differentiate desire from other lexical categories such as want, covet, yearn, need, crave, require, demand, long for, like, and love (see Crapanzano, present volume). But whatever one calls this condition, cargo cult stories suggest a kind of forlorn, sometimes mad, state of insatiable wanting. The strength of this anticipation and longing in the face of hopeless, even irrational, odds is where I think we should begin.

The Fascination of Cargo

Attention to cargo cult spills outside anthropology. Unlike much of our discipline's product, there is a popular market for cargo tales. Though the market may be small, it is profitable. One strange place cargo cult occupies today is the tourist brochure. The mad cargo cultist who once alarmed administrators and panicked missionaries, now entertains passing tourists. Cargo cults, like other sorts of conspicuous cultural practice, have been repackaged for sale in the international cultural tourism market. One such brochure, "Destination Vanuatu," features among its tour packages information about Tanna Island's John Frum movement:

> It all started in 1940, when John Frum came along from the sea claiming that there would be a wealth of goods and money if only the Europeans would leave the island. Soon after that, the arrival of American troups [*sic*] landing with planes, jeeps, refrigerators, radios and cigarettes gave credence [to] the myth.... Nowadays this religion which has attracted numerous supporters, is celebrated through prayers and dancing every Friday at Sulphur Bay....Visitors and members of the congregation gather around the Red Cross in the sacred clearing and lay flowers to the sound of singing and praying, waiting for John Frum to return with a white cargo laden with riches. (Destination Vanuatu: n.d.: 56)

Like fire walking, or hula dancing, or cannibal forks on display at various Pacific hotels, cargo cults signify the exotic South Pacific and reassure tourists that they have properly spent their recreation dollars. Tourist interest in cargo cults as spectacle follows along behind the earlier

Whose Cargo?

Some cargo stories about John Frum cultists are *too* strange. When I first lived on Tanna in 1978 and 1979, people I interviewed were either vague or cagey about what sorts of goods, exactly, they hoped that John would someday arrange to be shipped to them. Cargo cult writers, however, are often moved to identify just what it is that Melanesians want. (One can imagine that we readers—expert shoppers ourselves—desire to know.) These cargo lists, one can suspect, record our own desires as much as they do what Melanesians may actually have wanted, and also *how* they wanted what they wanted.

I collected as many cargo "shopping lists" as I could find in the literature and added them up (Lindstrom 1996). Heading my meta-list are various sorts of foodstuff, clothing, tools, weapons, and refrigerators. Here are some examples of things that John Frum people on Tanna have been reported to desire:

- "Highly exciting things like calico and electric torches and refrigerators" (Priday 1950: 67);
- "Enough food for everybody, prefabricated houses, washing machines, refrigerators, and blondes for the chief men" (Cameron 1964: 224);
- "Jeeps and refrigerators and canned food" (Coates 1970: 278);
- "Icebox, a pair of trousers, and sewing machine" (Illich 1971: 50);
- "Fabulous shiploads of refrigerators, jeeps, bulldozers, bottles of Coca-Cola" (Hermann and Bonnemaison 1975: 92);
- "Radios and refrigerators" (Gourguechon 1977: 312);
- "Material goods such as refrigerators, television sets and washing machines" (Shears 1980: 105);
- "Canned food, axes, cameras, and refrigerators" (Hamilton 1983: 1);
- "Radio sets, refrigerators, cartons of cigarettes" (Pouillet 1992: 38);
- "The liberating cargo of trucks, jeeps, houses, fridges, tables, chairs and cigars" (Evans 1992: 130).

Cargo cultists, so we are told, particularly long for refrigerators.[4] Refrigerators also dominate visual representation of cargo cults. An illustration from Harold Goodwin's *Cargo* (1984), a novel for children, depicts Melanesian children inspecting the innards of a wonderful fridge (figure 2.1). Refrigerators similarly anchor a depiction titled "John Frum and his white cargo plane arrive on Tanna"—an illustration from Grolier's *New Book of Knowledge: The Children's Encyclopedia* (1969: 564) (figure 2.2).

Figure 2.1 The cargo refrigerator (Goodwin 1984).

Figure 2.2 John Frum and his white cargo plane arrive on Tanna (Grolier 1969).

This strangely frequent appearance of refrigerators on Melanesian cargo lists helps naturalize the peculiar status that they occupy within our own social and household economies. The refrigerator has a powerful double impact as both metonym of technological progress and the focus of family sociability and commensalism. Solid white, gently humming refrigerators

		Cargo	
		Good	Bad
Cult	Good	1. Prophecy	3. Carnival
	Bad	2. *Bildungsroman*	4. Horror

Figure 2.3 Four cargo storylines.

nor culting is wrong. Rather, both the objects of desire and the ritual to obtain these are good, correct, and happy. These unproblematic cargo stories are local accounts, for example, the prophecies of cult leaders.

Box 2 in figure 2.3 contains storylines that approach cargo as fundamentally a good thing. Cargo—which represents modernity, technology, Western civilization, or progress—is a proper object of Melanesian desire. Everyone understandably wants access to the bounty of modernity. Of course Islanders should demand refrigerators. Who, save the savage or the depraved, does not prefer to drink his beer cold? The problem, however, is with those cults. Islanders have naturally joined the hunt but they are barking up the wrong tree. In a sorry state of ignorance, confusion, and desperation, they turn to false prophets and bizarre rituals in the mistaken belief that this will bring cargo. The true "road belong cargo," however, is education. Islanders need schooling in modernity. They must learn hard truths about work, technology, industrialism, capitalism, global markets, and so on. Eventually, though, light will dawn. Education, work, and better opportunities will guarantee the people's cargo. Mad cults will at last disappear from the islands.

We might call this the bildungsroman storyline in that it accentuates education and moral development. Cargo cultists may be irrational and childish, but eventually they will grow to join the global order of adults. The heyday of bildungsroman cargo narratives was certainly the 1950s and early 1960s. The storyline clearly resonated with modernization theory, with the cold war, and with the escalation of international development programs.

We can take Kenelm Burridge's cargo classic *Mambu,* first published in 1960, as a useful example of cargo bildungsroman.[7] Burridge is exquisitely sensitive to the painful condition of Papua New Guineans distressed by colonialism and racism. They long to be New Men because Australian overlords have mostly treated them as animals or children. They have lost grasp of their self-worth, and their cosmology now fails to satisfy their needs. They either hypervalue tradition in resistance to repugnant Australians or devalue it as useless rubbish. Like Franz Fanon writing during the same years, Burridge is acutely aware of the body aches of colonialism. Burridge, however, comes to a different conclusion. Neither revolution nor the self-assertion of *Négritude,* Burridge's solution is that elusive cargo will be acquired only by means of native education and better-behaved Europeans. Islanders need to reject their past and transform themselves. Only this will bring cargo home.

Burridge's modernist conclusion is that Melanesians were perfectly correct to be cargo cultists, only they were going about things the wrong way in light of an unfortunate but understandable interference from their culture—what Burridge called their "myth-dreams." Nonetheless, education will indeed transform the islands, if gradually. "Largely as a result of mission education, the young men are beginning to make the necessary transference out of their own understanding into the technical idiom of Europeans. If the right means can be found they will have access to manufactured goods and they will gain access to cargo" (Burridge 1960: 228). Eventually, old myth-dreams will fade as people wake into the bright light of economic rationality.

Perhaps worried, and rightly so in the late 1950s, that this enlightenment and enwhitenment of Melanesians could well encounter still European resistance, Burridge proposed a new colonial personage—that of the good white man. This new cargo protagonist is the moral European—either the wise missionary or the boyish administrator who assumes the role of cargo prophet to bring wisdom and, eventually, manufactured goods to the people. Europeans must themselves assume the powerful position of cargo prophet—elbowing aside competition from Mambu and other local pretenders who have gotten things all wrong: "The implication of this analysis is that moral European and charismatic figure can be one; that if missions and administration could follow out the proposals of the myth-dream they would themselves fulfil the role of the charismatic figure" (Burridge 1960: 265). Education and charity will at last ventilate and evaporate those burdensome island myth-dreams. The boys will become men. Premodern Islanders still act "in accordance with the dictates of their emotions rather than their intellects, from what they feel rather than from what they have thought out" (Burridge 1960: xviii). But good Europeans will in the end teach people to intellectualize and rationalize their powerful desires and ambiguous emotions. When we reach the end of the cargo story, everyone is grown up and goes happily off to work.

The Marxist version of cargo bildungsroman is somewhat less hostile to culting. Cults, although irrational, may be a necessary evolutionary stage along the way to modernity. Melanesians are cultists because they are yet unable to organize effective political parties. For example, Marvin Harris—who drew on Peter Worsley's (1957) influential appreciation of cults as a form of resistance—argued that cargo desires "had to become the idiom in which mass resistance to colonial exploitation was first expressed. ... By repressing any form of open agitation, strikes, unions, or political parties, the Europeans themselves guaranteed the triumph of cargo."[8] Or there is Pem Buck who concluded, "Cargo thinking is a call to practical action, just as was Martin Luther Kings's [*sic*] 'dream'" (1988: 167). Cults are a form of political juvenilia, but eventually will give way to real politicking and the resulting global redistribution of cargo.

Bildungsroman narratives worry little about the psychological and social consequences of achieving modernity. Cargo, albeit sometimes elusive, is good—good for civilized European and good for developing Melanesian alike. On into the 1960s and 1970s, however, the preference for cargo over cult became unsettled and shifted and happy bildungsroman collapsed into dark carnival. A growing suspicion of the socially erosive effects of wealth, and of modernity in general, coupled with a likewise growing admiration of the creative and liberating potential of cults—an appreciation of protest and revolt, resistance, third world independence, and black, women's, gay, and sundry liberation movements worldwide.

We might call this third storyline the carnivalesque. These narratives typically involve a critique of modernity; revelers who must foreswear meat—the carne of carnival—should lay off the cargo, too. This type of story celebrates the positive political and psychological effects of cults. Whereas in the bildungsroman tradition, cults were dangerous madness or, at best, a regrettable if understandable misstep along the path to adulthood, in carnival storylines they are the main event. The moral cultist took the leading role away from the modern European hero-prophet. Trance, dance, free love, drugs, cult communitarianism, the New Man, the New Age, living the myth-dream—all this is the human solution and not the problem. Real cargo emotion trumps false materialist reality. Deep cult truths impugn corrupt and immoral economic systems.

Philosopher monk Thomas Merton, in the late 1960s, explored this notion of cargo culting as liberating. He wrote a cycle of blank verse that celebrated cults as a vehicle of freedom. The poems, in part, praise the resistance of John Frum cultists:

I Neloiag
Am John Frum King
I level the mountain
Where my planes will come
I am King of American Flyers
I can arrest the British
With my telegraph
Though they declare me insane (Merton 1968: 106)

Nicol came with twenty police and tied John Frum to a tree
But everyone said it was not the real John Frum
For John the True
Had gone to America
To confer with Rusefel
To get a Black American Army
And Liberator Planes
All flown by Blacks
And full of dollars
To let out every man
In Nicol's prison. (Merton 1968: 115)

Merton also celebrated the ritual of earlier cultists on Malekula who in 1923 had attacked and killed a plantation owner named Clapcott:

We sing this nightletter against you Mr. Clapcott and tomorrow
All the bodies riding on the winds of resurrection
Shall have white skins because you are gone
So for you Mr. Clapcott we sing this message
Fine special delivery bullets in the chest tomorrow
And then our ship will come from America
Where there is no more death
Repeat nightletter Mr. Clapcott sir you sonofabitch you notice
Ghost wine has blown down your coconut trees
And your beach is very red. (Merton 1968: 113–114)

Carnival cargo culting challenges invidious economic and political orders to liberate the human potential trapped therein. But cults succeed to the extent that they fail. They are noble human endeavors only so long as real cargo does not arrive. Actually succeeding in modernizing themselves with cargo would corrupt the essential humanity of cultists. Merton returned to this theme in his 1979 collection of essays, *Love and Living,* to argue that cargo culting is indeed an honorable and universal human characteristic, but cargo is not its truest aim: "Man wants to go through the Cargo Cult experience and does so repeatedly ... all of us find the Cargo experience, in whatever form, vitally important.... The deeper function of a Cargo Cult, then, is not to get cargo, but rather to bring a community together" (Merton 1979: 86). Carnivalesque storylines celebrate liberating culting but mistrust the mutagenic effects of cargo itself on humanity. Culting can liberate without finding any cargo. The New Man is a possibility. A community may come together.

More recent employments of cargo cults read as horror stories. *Neither* cargo nor culting is redemptive. This fourth storyline feeds on the fundamental pessimism of 1980s postmodernism. Despite people's best efforts, there is no escape from painful states of internal subjugation and external domination that are inherent within human societies everywhere. Cargo horror stories share carnivalesque suspicions of capitalist modernity—of cargo—but they lose faith in the liberating potential of cults. People's cargo desires lead inexorably to their doom, or at least to the dissolution of a one-time happier, more humane way of life. Cargo and culting alike turn out not to bring what one expected but instead, often in horrible irony, cause injury and suffering.

This storyline is a direct descendent of the plot of *Frankenstein,* the novel that Mary Shelley finished in 1817. Exactly what is horrible about Frankenstein's hubris and his monster has been variously understood. Readers of the story have found therein a horror of biological science run amok (e.g., Turney 1998), of the uncivil working class (O'Flynn 1983), and of subject races and miscegenation (Malchow 1996). The horror story emerged with modernity, reflecting new fears of a world that appeared increasingly out of control. Whether the roots of horror were dangerous new technologies, the mutinous working class, or threats to European racial purity, the storyline typically linked this causally to the withering of traditional social relationships and happy families.

Frankenstein's anguished monster, for instance, cannot achieve his desire for family and sociability. The doctor refuses to make him a mate. And the monster's "sense of displacement from a home base and from nature is fundamental to the modern sensitivity. The monster belongs to our age of moral and ecological chaos; and he roams the wild with a grotesque impassivity and disorientation altogether familiar in the myths and files of contemporary alienation" (Ross 1972: 3). A more abysmal horror, though, afflicts the hapless doctor. His clever plans apparently achieve his goal of controlling life itself—his cargo, we can say—but this accomplishment brings tragic death, anguish, and the destruction of his family.

H. L. Malchow argued that Frankenstein and similar gothic horror introduced "a *language* of panic, of unreasoning anxiety, blind revulsion, and distancing sensationalism" (1996: 4 [original emphasis]) that partly drew on nineteenth-century anthropology. A gothic marriage took place between the languages of horror and anthropology; both dealt in the primitive, barbaric, uncivilized, and taboo (Malchow 1996: 5). Gothic anthropology's fear of monsters reappears in our time in the fourth cargo cult storyline: cults have monstrous consequences for island societies and cargo—even should this miraculously be delivered—also leads to a bad end.

Harold Goodwin's children's novel *Cargo* has a horrible ending of this sort.[9] In the text, Islanders want refrigerators, boomboxes, disco music, and beer (as represented in a striking example of cargoist art, figure 2.4).

Cargo desire also motivates the story's American characters, who include television producers scheming to film the cargo cult in order to sell refrigerators and other appliances, a shady anthropologist who steals a traditional feather headdress to decorate his apartment, and an avaricious New York art collector who exports back to America the contents of the local men's house. Melanesian culture—including cargo cults—has become part of the cargo of the West. The village's young men, after selling off their carvings to the collector, sing as they load up the cargo plane bound, this time, back to New York: "We are cargo people now. ... We don't want old stuff anymore" (Goodwin 1984: 114).

But the newly acquired cargo, swapped for carvings, leads to horrible consequences and the unhappy ending that just one load of cargo will not satiate desire. After drums of diesel used to fuel shiny new electric generators burst into flames and burn down the village, the bedraggled survivors and their frightened pigs huddle around a now silent refrigerator defrosting in the men's house. An angry elder smashes one still-chugging generator with his club and a chorus of weary men and women sing: "Nothing lasts forever, nothing lasts forever" (Goodwin 1984: 123). Meanwhile, back in New York, the primitive art collector has so encumbered his

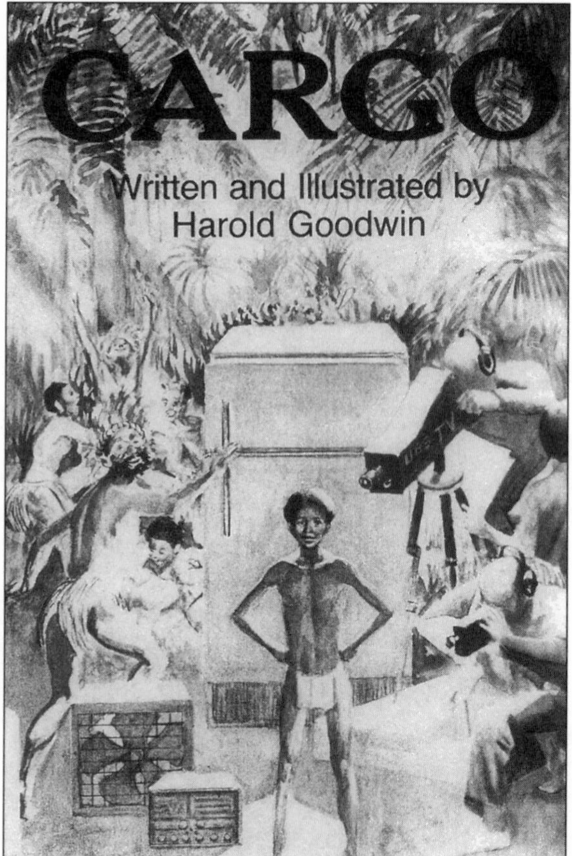

Figure 2.4 The cargo arrives (Goodwin 1984).

apartment with dark smoky carvings that he confesses, "Since there is no room for anyone to sit down here anymore, or even stand, I am much alone" (Goodwin 1984: 127).

The horror of cargo is that it fails to satisfy. Cargo does not satiate desire that is unremitting. And cargo culting has unforeseen and terrible consequences—the destruction of village lifeways, or the end of New Yorker sociability. Just as Dr. Frankenstein's monster destroyed the doctor's family, so does the modernity's cargo erode happy kinship with our fellow human beings. It turns people into monsters. Modernity's mad developmental projects must ultimately fail in Papua New Guinea and in New York City alike.

The cargo horror storyline also animates recent anthropological analysis, including some of Andrew Lattas's accounts of Kaliai cargo culting on New Britain (see also Jebens, present volume). Lattas offers an awful take of the economic, political, and psychological circumstances that have driven the Kaliai into cargo culting. Instead of alleviating their world of pain, however, this culting leads to even deeper suffering and degradation. The cultist Kaliai suffer a doubled self—their cargo beliefs are "part of the process of making one's race morally responsible for the conditions of its own subjugation" (Lattas 1992d: 32). True, most of this self-alienation originated in traditional beliefs about personhood and, more recently, in the colonial experience, but cargo culting has made it all worse. The Kaliai elaborate a series of cargo beliefs to resist their painful situation, but these just accentuate the horror: "the techniques of colonial domination come to be localized and 'indigenised' as they become part of the local institutions which resist colonialism" (Lattas 1992d: 51).

And cargo, too, causes injury insofar as differences in material wealth are internalized bodily as a sort of moral, as well as economic, weakness (Lattas 1992d: 35). Cargo cults turn people into monsters. The Kaliai blame the victim, in this case themselves, for the crime. Cargo culting both creates and manages the "space of suffering and pain formed out of the alienation of a self from its double" (Lattas 1992d: 37). Monstrous Kaliai: Lattas has, in a way, retold for the South Seas the horrible tale of Dr. Jekyll and Mr. Hyde.

Of course, anthropological accounts of cargo cults are about a lot more than simple bildungsroman, carnival, or horror. Still, cargo cult storylines have strangely, even suspiciously, shadowed major intellectual traditions of the past fifty years: from modernization theory's bright optimism to the celebration of resistance and liberation to the gloomy pessimism of post-structuralist dread. We might at least wonder whose storylines these are.

Whose Desire?

Oscar Wilde's *The Picture of Dorian Gray* (1891) is another high-modern horror story about the tragic consequences of wanting gone wrong. A year later, in 1892, Wilde's *Lady Windermere's Fan* introduced what has become one of the most famous epithets of modern desire: "In this world there are only two tragedies. One is not getting what one wants, and the other is getting it." At the dawn of the third millennium, this is by now an old, comfortable cliché. But we might begin with Wilde's irony to identify cargo stories' implicit mode of desire.

Wilde's joke fingered a central quality of modern desire—that this is never stilled. Desire is unceasing either because the cargo never arrives, or because, if it does arrive, it soon fails to satisfy. I have speculated that a similarity in structure between cargo cult stories and Western romances might explain cargo's curious place in popular culture today (Lindstrom 1993). Both kinds of narrative present desire as ultimately insatiable although nonetheless inescapable and pleasurable. Cargo cultists will not give up. They keep searching the skies, no matter the fact that no cargo has arrived, or is likely ever to do so. Like us, islanders suffer wanting ceaselessly.

The sort of endless desire that popular cargo narratives trade in is also the sort of desire that nourishes our own romances and love. It is the sort of desire that makes ongoing shopping an integral component of identity construction. This is the mode of desire that justifies affairs and divorces. It accounts for Imelda Marcos and her 3,000 pairs of shoes. It drives art collectors. It fills the shelves of bookstores and supermarkets with romance novels. It haunts the shopping mall. It animated the restless Bill Clinton and Monica Lewinsky and the public hunger for their spectacle.

It is this affinity of modes of desire that makes cargo cult such a slippery and productive term. Cargo cultists are Melanesians, but we happily assume their cultist identity, if often only to decry cargoism among ourselves, too. We, too, can see ourselves as victims of desire, of modernity at large. We are tormented by need for love and commodities both, and these desires are so pleasurable we see no way to give them up despite the injuries they cause. We easily feel ourselves to be cargo cultists because unrequited cargo love makes good sense for us, in view of fundamental understandings of how desire works and feels. And, moreover, this mode of desire seems even more real insofar as Melanesians appear to suffer it, too.

I am not going to return to this argument here. Instead, I conclude by looking ahead beyond 2000. Is our persistent curiosity about cargo cults nowadays merely antiquarian? Are cargo cult studies today just ethnohistory, redolent of anthropological interest in the Ghost Dance or the Boxer Rebellion? True, some cargo cults, in a way, still operate in Melanesia, transformed into local churches and parties. And millenarianism continues to animate much of the region, although this nowadays usually takes the form of Holy Spirit and Christian revival movements. And, perhaps, as people everywhere are absorbed into a world system where economic inequalities persist, and even deepen, resistance movements similar to cargo cults might break out anywhere. Conversely, it may be that cargo cults were a unique mid-twentieth-century phenomenon and we will see no more of them.

Whatever happens in the third millennium, I suspect that cargo cults will continue to demand attention, both analytical and popular, because they highlight questions of desire. Anthropologists find cargo cults good to think about because they demand we undertake a comparative genealogy of desire. Otto (1999: 96) has called for such a genealogy, noting that my previous reading of cargo cult stories as romances had failed to provide one. I am not going to offer one here either. Instead, I will point to some obvious places where a history of desire 2000 might start.

It is at least an open question if human experience of desire has been the same at all times and in all places. If unending even though irrational or hopeless desire is a modern European historical invention, we could also look to Melanesia and elsewhere to locate other constitutions of wanting. There is good evidence that notions of romantic love have differed historically and culturally. So might larger discourses of desire. Even if one accepts some limited number of biological needs—perhaps food, sleep, and sex (though even these supposed universals may be debatable)—modes of desiring these needs may differ across time and space. Popular cargo stories evoke the sort of persistent but unrequited desire that most of us experience and know, but this is certainly an inadequate description of Melanesian longing. It may be that Islanders indeed fixate on refrigerators, but their experience of this desire may differ from that of our own, as Robbins (1998a), Lattas (1998), and others have explored.

The structure of desire that dominates the present has a history. Cargo cult stories mirror a mode of desire that is perhaps only two centuries old. Colin Campbell (1987) located the origins of contemporary desire partly in the emergence, in the eighteenth century, of a "romantic ethic" and an attendant cult of sensibility. Puritans and other early moderns began seeking signs of God's grace within the inward experience of being born again, a state proved by the quality of a person's emotions. Campbell argued that this "emotionalist version of the Calvinist doctrine of signs develops first into the cults of benevolence and melancholy, and then into a fully fledged Sentimentalism" (1987: 137; see also Illouz 1997). Today's mode of unending desire traces to this cult of sensibility that, by the nineteenth century, had also generated practices of fashion, romantic love, taste, and the reading of novels. Longing became a permanent mode of feeling: "dissatisfaction with existence and the consequent readiness to seize whatever new pleasures are promised. ... characterize the modern attitude of longing" (Campbell 1987:90). Such restless wanting is distinctive, relative to earlier forms, in that we now actively seek out "opportunities to create desire, not merely to satisfy it" (Campbell 1987: 222).

Before the eighteenth century, people perhaps more easily satisfied their desires most of the time. We might here recall Marshall Sahlins's speculations on the limited wants of hunting and gathering peoples—a way of life he famously called the original affluent society. Sahlins proposed that most humans have desired in ways that were limited and satiable, that "it was not until culture neared the height of its material achievements that it erected a shrine to the Unattainable: *Infinite Needs*" (Sahlins 1972: 39; original emphasis). Or there are all those troublesome peasants and petty craftsmen, famous within comparative economic theory for being Uneconomic Man, for whom higher wages are a disincentive. The more one pays, the less they work. Marx's theories of alienation and commodity fetishism within capitalist production also help historicize desire (Otto 1999: 96). And then there is the Buddha. Fervid cargo cultists, wherever they are, might well contemplate the concept of nirvana (cf. Robbins 1998a).

Cargo cults make good stories because they remind us that modes of desire differ and have histories. Such stories do recommend we undertake a genealogy of desire. Why is the mode of longing that will take us into the third millennium one in which we desire desire, love love, yearn for yearning, long for longing? How did it come to be that we enjoy the pain of endless waiting on metaphoric beaches for cargo ships that do not come, or partake in incessant quests for love that never proves true?

Beyond 2000, cargo cults may evaporate in Melanesia as people's energies invest instead in different forms of organization. But cargo cult stories will continue to cast long shadows outside the Pacific. As long as insatiable desire is our normal mode of longing, we probably cannot stop talking about cargo cults.

Notes

1. R. Wagner (1975: 31). See also Dalton, Jebens, Otto, and Robbins (present volume).

2. Or at least they used to. Some Melanesians nowadays have adopted the term to frame their own tales of cargo cults. See Hermann, Jebens, and Leavitt (present volume).

3. See Dalton, Hermann, and Jebens (present volume).

4. "Destination Vanuatu" also records this object of desire.

5. In their conversation, Nampas uses a 1960s urban register of Bislama, and Attenborough uses a sort of pidgin Pidgin, the meaning of which I expect most readers can puzzle out.

6. This discussion borrows from Lindstrom (2000).

7. I hasten to add that this rich text is of course much more than this. Part of the argument draws on Lindstrom (1999).

8. Harris (1975: 151). Harris claimed he was a materialist, although not a Marxist.

9. And see also Christopher Wood's *Kago*, for an adult telling of the cargo tale: "That plane will come, but the cargo it brings is death" (Wood 1986, jacket).

quate, I propose that it be written *sous rature* (i.e., "under erasure").[3] To place something under erasure is a writing convention used by Jacques Derrida. According to Gayatri Chakravorty Spivak (1976: xiv–xviii), who translated Derrida's *De la Grammatologie* into English, this strategic writing convention of Derrida's apprises the reader that any word written in this manner is at once inaccurate and necessary (Spivak 1976: xiv). The word is first written and then crossed out because it is inaccurate. Then word and deletion are printed and so become legible, because the word is necessary after all.[4] Vincent Crapanzano (1981: 131) correctly pointed out that even this strategy of writing under erasure can founder if applied, in fullest consequentiality, to those countless concepts of Western thought whose limitations are such as to merit crossing out. Crapanzano, however, pointed out that, besides other writing strategies, our anthropological habit of using quotation marks is intended to perform the same function as under erasure. Writing a concept under erasure, as Crapanzano specified in our workshop discussions, is even more powerful than placing it within quotation marks—thus—and we agreed—its use is justified in the case of individual problematic concepts.[5] Accordingly, I shall use the "cargo cult" concept as follows: even when legible and placed within quotation marks, as it must be mentioned as the object of various discourses, it is to be understood as crossed out (figure 3.1)—this because it is inaccurate, or rather "inadequate," a characterization I have borrowed from Madan Sarup (1993: 32).

As another step in my quest for a critical reading of the Western constructions of Melanesian movements as "cargo cults," in this chapter my concrete concern shall be to study the thus-predicated colonial-popular, missionary, administrative, and early anthropological discourses in light of the constituting (which is implied therein) of a dichotomy between the Other and the Self. Although these discourses vary among themselves, they share a characteristic of attributing to the actors expectations of "cargo" and "cultic" activities. This depiction enables all these discourses to effect a social demarcation (Hermann 1995: 169). Inasmuch as each construction of the Other, in a complexly circular fashion, also

Figure 3.1 "Cargo cult" crossed out.

involves constructing the Self, as Crapanzano (1990b: 401) has emphasized,[6] I will be mindful of this implication.[7] My concern will be to show how the various "cargo cult" discourses relegate the indigenous actors to a social category radically other than those categories reserved for one's own respective communities with their European roots. In the case of the colonial discourses of the settlers, the administration and the mission, an Other was created—in close nexus with discourses constituting "race" in colonial Melanesia—which was definitively subordinated to the European Self. As to the early anthropological "cargo cult" discourse, here too arose an image of the followers of Melanesian social movements as the Other. Despite being viewed from the perspective of humanist ideals, they were still ranged against one's own Self as fundamentally Other. Thus, all these discursive formations relating to "cargo cult" were coopted into a process that Spivak (1985: 134) has aptly dubbed "othering."

Permit me now to set out on the "road belong cargo cult" and explore the dividing line therein between the Self and the Other; this I will do by first passing cursory review of early way stations of the "cargo cult" genealogy.

Historical Localization of "Cargo Cult"

As far as the exploration of the term "cargo cult" is concerned, it was not uncommon for early studies of the topic to dispense with all explanation of its origins. A number of scholars who must be excepted from this trend—namely, Bodrogi (1951: 266), Berndt (1952/1953: 47–48), Hogbin (1958: 208), and Jarvie (1964: 58–60, 1972: 134)—referred to Lucy Mair's *Australia in New Guinea* (1948) as containing the first anthropological mention of the term; however, Lucy Mair herself pointed out, significantly, that when she wrote her book "cargo cult" was already in common use (1948: 64).

In fact, the term had already found its way into the public media (e.g., into the pages of the magazine *Pacific Islands Monthly* [*PIM*]) in the immediate postwar era. Published in Sydney and widely read throughout the Pacific, *PIM* circulated news of colonial interest to Europeans living in Oceania. Because this magazine also provided a public forum for news about social movements among the Pacific Islanders, we find a dialogue being waged between *PIM* writers and their readership on the subject of "cargo cult," as documented in issues from the second half of the 1940s. Thus, in the *PIM* volume of November 1945, the term "cargo cult" is introduced by N. M. Bird, a settler in the Territory of New Guinea: "Stemming directly from religious teaching of equality, and its resulting sense of injustice, is what is generally known as 'Vailala Madness,' or 'Cargo Cult'" (Bird 1945: 69).

In subsequent years, further contributions were made to a growing debate on whether the mission societies active in the country or the Australian administration itself had played the greater role in abetting the rise of these movements.[8] The authors attempted to explain the phenomenon, reiterating the "cargo" myth and relating other events to the "cargo cult" context. In some of the *PIM* articles, the potential for aggression was conjured up as an integral part of these movements, ready at any time to vent itself in revolt against the resident whites. But for all their differences of opinion, the contributors concurred that the inhabitants of Papua and New Guinea—whom they did not omit to dismiss as "primitives"—had plunged into "madness" or had, at the least, succumbed to "confusion."

Though the early anthropological concept may well have drawn a less drastic picture than popular discourse, the feature of irrationality was held, by some at least, to be constitutive of these movements. Mair, for instance, explained "cargo cult" in terms of the Vailala Madness: "A notable feature of the reaction of the peoples of New Guinea to white rule is the occurrence at different times in almost every part of the Australian territories of a manifestation which used to be known as the 'Vailala madness,' but is now more commonly described as the 'cargo cult'" (Mair 1948: 64). She was referring to events that had occurred in 1919 on the Vailala River of Papuan Gulf Province—they had been reported by F. E. Williams, then the assistant government anthropologist, under the heading of "Vailala Madness" (1976a, 1976b). For Mair, as for Bird before her, the Vailala Madness represented the prototype of the "cargo cult." Summarizing the phenomena as reported to date, Mair, like her predecessors in *PIM*, stressed the importance of the movement's designs on "cargo": "The common characteristic is the insistence on the cargo of European goods to be sent by the ancestors, and the disappearance of the white man and his rule" (Mair 1948: 66).

This brief review attempts to highlight that the anthropological concept of "cargo cult" did indeed crystallize as a reaction to colonial notions as enshrined in popular, missionary and administrative discourse. A number of negative stereotypes that were part and parcel of the colonial image were not taken up into anthropological thinking.[9] One need only reflect on the chief characteristics of the diverse "cargo cult" discourses, however, to see the genealogical lines connecting popular, missionary, administrative, and anthropological notions.

Here it is already apparent that Western "cargo cult" discourses constructed the Melanesians involved in social movements as being radically Other. In popular discourse— as in its missionary and administrative counterpart—"cargo cultists" were blatantly accused of "madness," a label diametrically opposite to the "common sense" the European colonists were plainly bent on reserving for themselves. In anthropological discourse, indigenous "activists" were said to be in the grip of an irrationality far removed from a Western rationality capable of judgment. Besides the criterion of rationality, economy and know-how served as difference-creating traits. Thus, all the Western "cargo cult" discourses, each in its own specific way, opposed "cargo"-demanding Melanesians to "cargo"-possessing Europeans. Into the colonial discourses of settlers, missionaries, and administrative officers infiltrated other oppositional stereotypes, characterized by racism and by an evolutionary ideology. The popular colonial discourse sometimes described "cargo cult" by invoking the image of the "primitive savage" (Bird 1945: 70), which permitted the "civilized" to look down on him. Representatives of the colonial power saw themselves as confronting a "backward people," while the ambassadors of Christianity, for their part, condemned "cargo cultists" as "pagans." Common to all these discourses is the frontal opposition between the observing European and the "activist" Melanesian Other.

The Construction of Cargo Cult in the Rai Coast Region

Among written documents relating to the Rai Coast region in the southern part of Madang Province, the term "cargo cult" is first listed in a patrol report of June 20, 1946 (Prowse 1946). Ever since the end of the World War II, the Australian administration had cast around for some way to deploy a Rai Coast inhabitant, a certain Yali, in pursuit of its goals. Yali, who came from the village of Yasaburing,[10] had served during the war in the Australian army and proved his loyalty to the Australians.[11] In the 1946 patrol report, the officer recommended that Yali be taken back into Australian service, making the point that Yali would discourage "cargo cult" in his speeches. Perceiving Yali as trustworthy, the Australian administration appointed him "overseer" and commissioned him to run their rehabilitation scheme.

The following years, however, were filled with entanglements, in the center of which Yali emerged as an initiator of "cargo cults." During the years 1946–1948, in the course of monitoring Yali's activities, rumors citing Yali in connection with "cargo cults" came to the attention of the administration, which nevertheless remained convinced that Yali was not responsible for such occurrences. In the years after 1948, however, when the Lutheran mission began systematically to build up Yali as the instigator of "cargo cults," the administration fell into line.

The 1947 annual report of the Lutheran mission gives the following assessment of "cargo cult": "Outwardly the cargo-cult is a result of the war and its confusion caused in those primitives, who, a few generations ago, lived still in the 'stone age.' As for the inward reasons it is the result of the growing materialistic thinking which already had set in before the war, but now, seems to have seized their confused minds completely. Connected with it is, and was, a growing loosening from the gospel. The inward apostasy resulted in an open reversion into heathenism."[12] After 1948, though, the Lutherans were no longer content to simply complain about signs of alleged "cargo cults," which they assigned to Yali's agency: they also began to collect incriminating evidence against him. Later the Australian administration conducted an inquiry on Yali and, in July 1950, after proof of offenses was furnished, he was tried and sentenced to six and a half years imprisonment.[13]

Although Yali was formally convicted of legal violations other than "cargo cult" agitation, he was popularly condemned as the "cargo cult" ringleader. The allegation that Yali had initiated an outbreak of "cargo cults" was, however, a cultural fabrication based on rumors and suspicion: none of the missionaries and administration officers had ever witnessed a cargo cult. Even so, Yali had become the talk of the province: local employees referred to him when they refused orders from their colonial employers, and a number of Europeans cast him in the role of instigator of an anticolonial revolt.[14]

Administration documents show that, during the early 1950s, officers patrolling Yali's home region stereotypically perceived the local people as "cargo cultists," describing them in one instance, as "very backward, ridden with carge cult [*sic*] ideas and very lazy" (Reitano 1949/1950: 4).

Written statements of the administrative, missionary and popular discourse on cargo cult in the Rai Coast region altogether strike exactly the same tones as do the supraregional "cargo cult" discourses. Thus was routinized, with respect to parts of the regional population and individual persons like Yali, the opposition articulated in those discourses between the control-enabled European Self—superior in its rational actions, in its partaking of the one, true faith, in its mastery of economic production and development of "civilization"—and the Melanesian Other—"confused," "heathen," "lazy," "backward," "primitive"—in short, the quintessential Other.

Though the dichotomous construction of Self and Other in all these colonial "cargo cult" discourses might suggest that this process is best encapsulated in dyadic terminology, it should be noted, following Crapanzano, that what we have here, in fact, is a triadic relationship, for the constituting of Self contains also in this case a "Third" as the "guarantor of meaning" (Crapanzano 1990b: 403). This Third is a function that we may imagine as symbolized by such Western discourses as did, at the time, represent specific truths for members of European or American cultures. Chief among these discourses are formations of statements concerning rationality, the production of goods, civilization, and Christianity such as function—or did then function—in Western societies as received truths. Only by referring to the authoritative truth of such Western discourses was it possible for these representatives to constitute their Self and the Melanesian Other as significantly distant from each other.

The Reconstruction of "Cargo Cult" by the Local People

This image of "cargo cultists" crafted by the colonial institutions soon became a subject of debate for the inhabitants of Yasaburing, Yali's home village. Following the investigations by mission and administration in the late 1940s, the Yasaburing were regularly visited during the 1950s by Europeans who checked on perceived "cargo cult" activity for administrative, missionary, or journalistic interests. Retrospectively, the Yasaburing assign the "cargo cult" events to the mid-1950s—the time when they were increasingly reproached for engaging in them (Hermann 1992b). Only after the Europeans had confronted the local people with their "cargo cult" construction did they come themselves to perceive "cargo cults"—ascribing these to the activities of nonlocal Yali adherents in Yasaburing.

The inhabitants of Yasaburing reconstructed the meaning of the term "cargo cult" from its contexts of application in the colonial encounter. The term was taken up into Tok Pisin as *kago kalt* and, as such, woven into vernacular speech. The conceptual content of the term was determined by the colonial definitions of the Europeans. As a woman from Yali's family put it, *kago kalt* means, "People sit around doing nothing, hoping that money comes up or 'kago' comes up" (Mrs. Teti, interview, August 13, 1990).

Kago kalt, I was told repeatedly by the Yasaburing, signifies an attitude of passivity coupled with an expectation of cargo materializing out of nothing. *Kago kalt,* the Yasaburing stated as with one voice, represents a type of behavior that leads nowhere. This component of the indigenous definition of *kago kalt* clearly reflects some facets of the meaning of "cargo cult" as defined in the diverse colonial discourses, namely, that it is connected with inactivity and laziness and tantamount to "madness."

The Yasaburing categorically reject any assumption that they would ever have participated in such an absurdity. By thus rejecting the charge of "cargo cult," they are protesting, on the one hand, against the hegemonic "cargo cult" discourses of the missions and the administration and, on the other, against the anthropological account given in Lawrence's *Road Belong Cargo* (1964), which representatives of these institutions had told them about. From their perspective, it was Yali's adherents from distant regions of Madang Province who had staged "cultic" rites in Yasaburing, thereby giving rise to the "cargo cult" censure. Thus, they adamantly deny "cargo cult" in their own regard. In the context of the hegemonic conditions under which they were induced to consent to the "cargo cult" fabrication of Western hegemonic discourses—including the anthropological one—they in no way doubt the truth and existence of "cargo cult," but insist it should only be ascribed to nonlocal Others.

The villagers explain that *kago kalt* occurred when these outsiders sought out trees and rocks and supplicated under them their ancestors for *kago.* The majority of Yasaburing also classify the flower ritual as *kago kalt.* This was a ritual performed by Yali and his devotees, who placed vases of special flowers on tables in the expectation that a pile of money would materialize on the spot. In Yasaburing historiography, it was experiments such as these that led to their village being associated with "cargo cult," thus blackening its name and causing them to feel ashamed.

By pinning the *kago kalt* label on Yali's outside supporters, not only do the Yasaburing reproduce and recontextualize conceptual components of Western "cargo cult" discourses, but also, in their own specific way, make use of the strategic construction of Self and Other as implicated in these discourses. With all the negative connotations associated with "cargo cult," the Yasaburing have since the 1950s taken to a strategy of distancing their collective Self from such low-esteemed practices. Yali, for his part, was very concerned to distance himself from any and all association with "cargo" talk (cited in Morauta 1974: 170). His supporters in the more distant parts of Madang Province reacted similarly, as Louise Morauta (1974: 154) could document for the hinterland of Madang (and which I can myself confirm from my conversations with former members of the social movement in diverse villages on the Rai Coast, in the environs of Madang, in Trans-Gogol, on the North Coast, and on Manam Island). Moreover, the political and educated elites began to conduct discourses on "cargo cult"/*kago kalt,* the intention being to create an Other from which one could demonstratively distance oneself (Hermann 1992b: 68). "Cargo cult"—soon there could be no doubting it—had come to function as a demarcation line—those deemed to engage in "cargo cult" or *kago kalt* were always and invariably the Other,[15] whereas the Self could empower itself through its knowledge thereof.

In that the Yasaburing took the "cargo cult" and *kago kalt* charges directed against them and passed them on to their outside compatriots, reproaching them with aberrant conduct, they too—so much is clear—turned the Yali supporters concerned into the Other. Despite their still insisting on this cultural difference, it is nevertheless true that the Yasaburing's construction of Self and Other is not the same as those in Western discourses. Moreover, it is not predicated on the same dichotomy. For one, the indigenous distancing is not based on the same binary oppositions of civilized versus uncivilized, Christian versus heathen, or rational versus irrational, such as infused the Western-colonial construction of the Other in "cargo cult" discourses. For another, the Yasaburing in their efforts of self-differentiation from those compatriots they implicate in *kago kalt* are in a structurally different position from those from which Western discourses were (and are) conducted. Whereas the Western Self in popular, missionary and administrative discourses long spoke from the position of the colonial overlord (or speaks in the present from a corresponding neocolonial position), the Yasaburing argue from the position of the formerly colonized. The indigenous discourse is not, as is the case with the discursive practices of colonial institutions, interwoven with goals of conquering, missionizing, and "civilizing" others—goals that in the colonial era were permeated with racist thinking.

So revealed, the indigenous construction of Self and Other by means of *kago kalt* discourses is to be clearly distinguished from the dichotomous manifestations in Western "cargo cult" discourses. That said, it is important to note that indigenous distancing is only possible through reference to the Western discourses (even though this reference is not always explicit). The Yasaburing exonerate themselves from Western cargo cult accusations by accusing others of *kago kalt*. The thus-enacted indigenous construction of Self and Other is therefore triadic in a specific way (see Crapanzano 1990b). This triadic relationship harks back to complex power constellations and is qualitatively very different from those inherent in Western "cargo cult" discourses. When the indigenous Self exonerates itself from European "cargo cult" accusations and redirects *kago kalt* against their compatriots, in the process turning these into the Other, it is still able to feel subordinated to a third position of power from where these Western discourses are conducted. Yet the indigenous Self can also—this must be stressed—deploy its own power against this third instance. And it is possible, too, for an indigenous self-differentiation discourse to seize the chance to invoke the power of Western "cargo cult" statements the better to empower oneself against an indigenous Other.

The Yasaburing's attribution of *kago kalt* to others is primarily channeled through the shared counterhegemonic discourse all the villagers conduct against nonlocal Yali followers. In some rare cases, however, it is also mobilized within the village itself, for purposes of reprimanding a person or group of persons (see, e.g., Hermann 1995: chap. 7.2). The message mediated by *kago kalt* allegations of this kind is clear: it is not only to censure those so singled out, but also to do this by invoking the power of the extraneous Western "cargo cult" stigmatization to render more efficient one's influence over the Other.

In the course of cleansing their collective identity of the "cargo cult" stigma, the Yasaburing have developed a set of counterconcepts to "cargo cult." Among them the concept of traditional culture *(kastom)* is invoked to refute any "cargo cult" suspicions (Hermann 1997). Thus, the villagers argue that their own religion, based on invocation of their male and female ancestors, embodies pure *kastom* and must therefore never be associated with "cargo cult," as some outsiders have done (cf. Kempf 1994: 115; 1996: 103). While underlining their integrity in matters of traditional religion, they simultaneously accentuate their actual practice of Catholicism, a fact that in their eyes overturns the "cargo cult" surmise.

Further counterconcepts concern the fields of work (in Tok Pisin, *wok*), business (*bisnis*), and development (*developmen*). Thus, the women and men from Yasaburing point out that, as subsistence horticulturists, they have never sunk into inactivity and idleness. All their lives they have engaged in hard work. They stress, too, that they never followed Yali in any of the ambiguous activities he engaged in under the influence of his nonlocal followers—only in *bisnis* activities propagated by him. As proof, they point to the copra, coffee, and cacao cash crops produced on their small plantations. Finally, further pursuing the same line of reasoning, they insist that they were never interested in *kago kalt*—only in *developmen*—in striving to build better houses and roads in order to contribute to the country's future.[16]

Reverberations of Cargo Discourses

The local people's emphasis on *wok*, *bisnis*, and *developmen* resulted from their dealings with Europeans. Exposed for decades to the white men's imperatives of work, business, and development, they have learned to subscribe to them. Catholic missionaries of the Societas Verbi Divini (S.V.D.), who were active in the region from the early 1930s, preached salvation together with an immediate improvement of living conditions through hard labor. European settlers, the successors to those who had settled at the onset of colonization in 1885, employed the local people in business projects, urging them all the while to work hard. And Australian administration officers, particularly after the end of World War II, enjoined them to plant cash crops in order to participate in the development programs.

All this could not but leave deep traces in the local people's consciousness, even as it familiarized them with the foreigners' fixation on capital, cargo, and business activities. Moreover, the local people picked up from the colonizers' discourses that Europeans based their claim to superiority, their legitimization to rule over Papua New Guineans, on their mastery of technology and their control over industrial products (cf. Mortimer 1979: 168). As the Yasaburing see it, this capacity represented a power that condemned them to relative powerlessness and dependence. Motivated by a desire to escape from this state, they seized the opportunity to participate in the Europeans' work programs with a view to acquiring knowledge of Western production methods.

Yali was not the first person from the region to enter the European's service, but he was certainly the most prominent one to work with and learn from them. The Yasaburing place great emphasis on the fact that, during and shortly after the war, Yali had even been to Australia, where he was able to gain knowledge of Western industrial culture. They stress

Yasaburing, her actual words in Tok Pisin were: "Orait mi tok: 'Mipela olgeta bilong kago kalt tasol!'" As she was addressing me, she used the personal pronoun "mipela" (we) to express that she included the Yasaburing in the allegations made against her.[19] She did not use the personal pronoun "yumi," which would have indicated that she wanted explicitly to include me, together with other Europeans, in what she was saying. As the quotation of her defense at the trial in the 1950s makes clear, however, she frequently alluded to Europeans as the true inspirers of those activities later dubbed "cargo cult." Therefore, I felt it worth reflecting on her statement a little, thinking she might have included us in the indictment as well.

As I see it, Bikmeri has provided a powerful analysis in her own terms by referring to Western responsibility for the "cargo cult" complex. In the course of colonization and missionization, Germans, British, and Australians successively overran with their capitalist interests the erstwhile territories of Papua and New Guinea (Amarshi, Good, and Mortimer 1979). In the process, the colonizers not only imported large quantities of cargo, but also launched cargo discourses by arousing the indigenous peoples' interest in Western consumer goods. In a context of colonial power relationships, Westerners have in fact involved Papua New Guineans in a cargo discourse of their own, emphasizing the need to work first in European-owned enterprises and afterward in their own businesses so as to earn money to buy cargo products (cf. Pem Buck 1988). It is also a fact, as the women and men from Yasaburing assured me, that the Europeans instructed the locals to copy European methods and practices, whether in the linear layout of village houses or in table decorations with vases of flowers.[20] It was therefore at European instigation that Yali's adherents had taken to making their flower decorations, just as Bikmeri said. Thus, within this context, the indigenous activities so promptly dismissed as "cargo cult" appear rather as reverberations of Western cargo discourses and various Western cultural practices.

Conclusion: Dissolving the Self-Other Dichotomy

In conclusion, I would like to take up Bikmeri's statement again. I would suggest that, in a sense, "all of us actually belong to 'cargo cult,'" (i.e., by virtue of a genealogical relationship). This relationship was created by Westerners from various professional fields in general and by anthropologists in particular, both contributing to the construction and routinization of the concept, whether in its popular, missionary, administrative, or analytic incarnations. Following the initial construction of "cargo cult" as a concept, we have gone on to construct "cargo cults" as social events in line with certain conceptual criteria.[21] Moreover, with this construction we have created "cargo cultists" as the Other, while remaining unaware of our own contribution to this Other.

The Yali movement was for so long (from the late 1940s on) treated by colonial discourses and practices as "cargo cult" that it became true for European and indigenous outsiders alike. Even with the people from Yali's home village, the hegemonic articulations finally commanded assent, for all that the Yasaburing categorically excepted their own participation in the "cult" for "cargo."

This process of truth production has been appositely described by Martha Kaplan for "cult," with respect to the movement that grew up around Navosavakadua in colonial Fiji: "Reconsidering cults as a colonial category, we may find that they were first imagined, and then became real, at least in colonial perception and record, and, sometimes but not always, real as well in indigenous practice and self-definition, through the influence of powerful colonial projects of inquiry and regulation" (Kaplan 1990b: 5). In constituting the Yali movement as "cargo cult"—and this is no different from the case of the so-called Tuka movement to which Kaplan refers, nor to be sure from other, similar indigenous undertakings—an aspect of truth production may be discerned that I wish at this point to again highlight—namely, that of constructing its members as "cultic" Others.

In my portrayal of the Yali movement, I have in this chapter focused mainly on colonial popular depictions, in the belief that they reveal most clearly the upshot of construction. By contrast, Lawrence (1954, 1955, 1964) provided a particularly differentiated representation of the Yali movement. While addressing itself to colonial institutions in order to remove popular prejudices linked to these, however, his account also furnished the same institutions with legitimizing arguments for combating the movement, thus reinforcing the construction of the movement's followers as Others who have yet to be civilized. Moreover, Lawrence's account was relayed numerous times by different authors, nonacademic and academic alike, some of whom distorted his differentiated picture to the point of reestablishing the negatively charged "cargo cult" vision of the movement as an "aggressive" and "dangerous" Other (see, e.g., Uplegger and Mühlmann 1961: 180).

As to the anthropological concept of "cargo cult," it is right to point out that it differs markedly from the one enunciated in the popular, missionary, and administrative discourses. Some of the more pejorative stereotypes built into the colonial image were omitted in the analytic notion. On the other hand, it must be noted that other criteria indicated by early popular reports of the movements did find their way into the anthropological conceptualizations. Thus, the trait of irrationality has survived in some descriptions (e.g., Burton-Bradley 1981). Another feature held to be essential to the social movements in question—namely, the call for "cargo"—was constitutive for the anthropological concept. Although a number of scholars have pointed out that a craving for "cargo" is frequently secondary to a desire for equality with Europeans (Burridge 1960) or for access to their knowledge (Lindstrom 1984: 303–304)—or is even, to take the extreme case, altogether absent from a movement's agenda (Walter 1981: 83)—the cargo component still figures prominently in the analytic definitions. Perhaps, as Hau'ofa has suggested, it is the Westerner's tendency to construct the Melanesian as a caricature of the Western capitalist that has been instrumental in moving scholars to concede priority to the "cargo" notion (Hau'ofa 1975: 285).

Through the ascription of these semantic aspects of irrationality and "cargo" striving, all the Western discourses contributed, each in its specific fashion, to a process of "othering." In the diverse colonial "cargo cult" discourses, othering often went hand in hand with pathologizing and racializing (Clark 1992; Lattas 1992b) as also with criminalizing (Kaplan 1990b; Hermann 1995: 301). As variations of colonial discursive formations, popular, missionary, and administrative "cargo cult" discourses doubtless played a leading role in constructing Melanesian "activists" as the radical Other in opposition to the European Self. Although the anthropological discourse on "cargo cult" differed from these discourses in respect of this dichotomous opposition, it was not uninfluenced by the same structuring principle. What I would deem important to note in this context is that the more subtle dichotomizing of Self and Other, as expressed in the anthropological discursive formations, must have had similar effects on the indigenous people as the radical opposition found in popular, missionary, and administrative discourse. By constructing "cargo cultists" as "irrational" and "economically unmotivated" figures, anthropological discourses also produced knowledge conducive to ruling over and colonizing those others so characterized.

These reflections on both the Western "cargo cult" discourses and the indigenous *kago kalt* discourse, such as I have described here,[22] will (I hope) have shown that the Western Self can in no sense be divorced from the indigenous Other. For, with the constituting of the Other enacted through Western discourses and practices, the Self already leaves traces in the Other. The Self cannot therefore be seen as completely disconnected from the Other, even when Western "cargo cult" discourses assert a dichotomy. Precisely the indigenous discourse, I would contend, is proof positive of this, with its reverse reference to the Western discourses. In their reception of the diverse Western "cargo cult" discourses the Yasaburing signal clearly, in their counterdiscourses, that they do not accept being declared the Other. Especially Bikmeri, in the speech she reproduced for my benefit against the administrative officer, explicitly stated that she would not allow herself to be dismissed as a "cargo cultist," because she had—along with Yali and the other members of the movement—only done what the Europeans had advised them to do. Thus, she too alluded to the indissoluble link between the indigenous Self and the Western actors. A closer look at the references, contained alike in the indigenous discourse and in the genealogy of Western discourses, to reciprocal linkages, shows that the Self-Other dichotomy dissolves in enmeshments evolved in the midst of complex power relationships.

That the construction of the Other in Western "cargo cult" discourses is closely enmeshed with the constituting of the Self has been discussed already by several authors. Pem Buck (1988: 158), Kaplan (1990b: 4), Lindstrom (1990a: 241), and Michele Stephen (1997: 335), citing Edward Said's analysis (1978) of "Orientalism" as an analogous discourse, have all discussed the "cargo cult" fabrication that constructs the Other in order to empower itself. Thus, Stephen puts it cogently: Cargo cults are among the most exotic forms of exotic beliefs—"the most other" (1997: 335). That the hegemonic construction of the Other also feeds back on how the Self is constructed has been stressed, in each case with a specific accentuation, by Pem Buck (1988: 158), Lindstrom (1990a: 241), Lattas (1992b: 1), Stephen (1997: 336), and Jebens and Kohl (1999). And not least, I would like to refer to the valuable comment by Nancy McDowell (2000), in which she criticizes the fact that most cargo cult studies postulate a dichotomy between "them," the so-called cultists, and "us." Thus, they are led to focus on a negatively connoted "otherness" rather than on the similarities between them and us. With their analytic insights, all these studies have contributed much to the critique of the binary Self-Other construction in Western "cargo cult" discourses.

The Self-Other dichotomy is just one of a gamut of aspects alerting us to the problematic anthropological concept of "cargo cult." Though the "cargo cult" of earlier colonial discourses has continued to make headway in a contemporary global universe of discourse (see Lindstrom 1993)—a terrain where anthropology doubtlessly exercises little influence—within anthropology itself (and several related fields) a process of critical scrutiny has begun. A glance at recent studies of "cargo cult" discourses suffices to reveal that, for some time now, a plethora of voices has been mounting a deconstructive effort, which may indeed point to the necessity of writing "cargo cult" *sous rature*.

Meanwhile, different researchers, noticing the absence of the "cargo" motif, have rehabilitated a number of social movements of the Pacific hitherto classified as "cargo cults." John Waiko (1973: 420) has done this for the "Taro cult" and the "Baigona cult" of the Northern Province of Papua New Guinea. Willington Opeba (1981: 128) has also reached the same conclusion. Roger Keesing (1978: 243, 270) has ruled out any "cargo cult" classification of the Maasina Rule movement of the Solomon Islands. Kaplan (1990b: 3, 4) has criticized the "cargo cult" construct in connection with the "Tuka" movement of Fiji. Lindstrom (1990a:240, 241; 1993) has mounted a critique of the "cargo cult" theory in his investigation of the John Frum movement of Tanna, Vanuatu. And Wolfgang Kempf (1992), too, in his study of indigenous ideas of change, has deconstructed the "cargo cult" classification of an early millenarian movement among the Ngaing of Papua New Guinea.

Aware of the pejorative overtones of "cargo cult," some scholars have adjudged it a label disparaging the movements concerned.[23] Others have pointed out just how constructed the "cargo cult" concept is. Among these authors, McDowell (1988: 21) has clearly deconstructed this analytic category by questioning a working strategy that elevates a skein of cultural features into an institution by taking them out of context. Pem Buck (1988: 158) pointed out that "cargo cults" as objects of analysis exclusively result from Europeans imagining "cargo" elements. Focusing on the historical agency of members of the Tuka movement in Fiji, Kaplan has analyzed "cargo cult" as a Western reification applied in colonial practice.[24] In the introduction to a volume of essays carrying the highly revealing title *Imagining Cargo Cults*, Ton Otto (1992a: 1) has expressed serious doubts about the analytic value of the same concept. Critically resisting the interpretation of Melanesian religion in terms of "cargo cult," Joel Robbins (1998a) has suggested in its place an examination of the indigenous model of the role played by desire. Reviewing the genealogy of the term "cargo cult" and its colonial ballast, I pleaded for its serious revision (1992a, 1992b, 1995). In the context of this growing critique, Kempf (1992: 84) spoke of the cargo cult concept as already an historical "monument in the landscape of anthropological enquiry and discourse." Consequently, Lindstrom (1993: 40) and Sjoerd Jaarsma (1997: 85) have suggested that academic "cargo cult" discourse might fairly dissolve on the strength of its own critique of the concept.

These anthropological reflections indicate that a deconstruction of "cargo cult" is now under way. In a remarkable parallel, the indigenous reflections cited above may also be read as implying deconstruction of the very notion of "cargo cult," indicating that the concept's roots should be sought rather in the Europeans' own culture than in indigenous traditions.

"Cargo cult" should be written under erasure for the good reason that it is an inadequate concept. It is definitively untenable in respect of those persons and groups that associate "cargo cult" with hegemonic disdain and feel stigmatized when thus labeled. Yet when written under erasure, the concept is necessary to designate diverse Western "cargo cult" discourses as the object of our critical attentions. And it is no less necessary for the indigenous discourses, in light of the fact that it furnishes the reference point for such counterdiscourses as are then mounted. The matching indigenous concept that I decided—reflecting the substantive differences therein contained—to write as *kago kalt* plays an important role here in exercising indigenous counterhegemony and as an authentic concept laden with a critique of its own is not contested in the present debate.

In their various discourses, the Yasaburing have tendered powerful analyses of the subtle mechanisms inherent in Western "cargo cult" discourses. Here they were able to communicate to me their view that "cargo cult" is constructed as a term of exclusion (cf. Lindstrom 1990a). Through prefixing, as a thesis, this chapter with Bikmeri's statement that "All of us actually belong to 'cargo cult,'" I was attempting to put in place a further construction: one favoring inclusion. For thinking in terms of inclusion can help us deconstruct the discursively constituted dichotomy between Self and Other, the better to create a pivotal requirement for interlocutionary anthropological projects.

22. Depending upon the specific history of confrontation with Western "cargo cult" allegations, it was doubtless the case that various locally specific *kago kalt* discourses arose in Papua New Guinean societies and interest groups. See, e.g., Morauta (1974: 154), and Jebens (present volume).

23. See Hau'ofa (1975: 286), Hempenstall and Rutherford (1984: 120), Hermann (1987), and Rimoldi and Rimoldi (1992) and, with reference to the concept of "cult," McDowell (2000).

24. See Kaplan (1990b: 5; 1995a, 1995b) and her contribution to the present volume.

CHAPTER 4 Neither Traditional nor Foreign
Dialogics of Power and Agency in Fijian History

Martha Kaplan

Two Ethnographic Vignettes and the Theoretical Agenda

PLAYING OFF of a contrast between Peter Worsley's cargo cults as protonationalism and Henry Rutz's recent argument concerning the use of "tradition" in rhetorical strategies in Fijian national politics, this chapter considers some aspects of political agency in Fiji's colonial and postcolonial history. Particular attention is paid to the vicissitudes of Navosavakadua and the Vatukaloko people (of the famous "Tuka movement"), very much, however, in the context of wider and contrasting possibilities for imagining selves and others and making power real in Fiji's history. In the case of Fiji, at least, an analytic framework using "cargo cult" can fruitfully be replaced by a dialogical account of a colonial and postcolonial history. A pair of ethnographic vignettes, to which we will return, illustrates this narrative account.

First, *hunger strikes*. During my first visit to Fiji, in 1981, I witnessed a protest by students at the University of the South Pacific who, on finishing their degrees in teaching, were required to pay back scholarship aid to government. Unable to obtain teaching jobs, the protestors—who were for the most part Indo-Fijians—staged a hunger strike in a public place in the capital city of Suva, engaging press, photographers, and passersby. Three years later, during fieldwork in Drauniivi village,[1] I accompanied a busload of ladies bringing their donation (massive quantities of tea and sugar) to the annual Fiji Methodist Church conference. The ladies told me[2] that the conference delegates[3] were fasting and praying. The ladies were neither awed nor impressed by the fasting; rather they were embarrassed and mystified. "Poor things," they clucked, "It's pitiful [*vakaloloma*]."

Hunger strikes were a major and effective tactic in Gandhi's Indian nationalist movement and in the Indo-Fijian efforts to win rights in British colonial Fiji early in this century. With the exception of Prime Minister Timothy Bavadra (of the Fiji Labour Party) and his ministers' brief hunger strike following the coup of 1987, it has never been used by ethnic Fijians as a political strategy. Quite the contrary, lavish prestations, demonstration of wealth and plenitude of people, goods and valuables mark most Fijian claims to power, both by those who hold power already and by challengers to them.

Many tales of Navosavakadua involve his ability to bring forth food from barren land, and (as a chief would) create a state of *sautu na vanua* (peace, fecundity, and abundance in the land). His miracles are often compared to—and even identified with—Jesus' miracle of the loaves and fishes. Tales of Navosavakadua's white pig (to be eaten as a surrogate for white colonizers and missionaries?) continue to intrigue us all. I puzzle over the whiteness—did fearful colonizers perhaps make up that aspect of the tale?—but am quite confident that Navosa[4] intended to feed the people as any powerful Fijian leader must.

Second, *representations of Navosavakadua in the late twentieth century*. In the 1980s, during years of field and archival research in Fiji, I came to understand how, in the 1880s, Navosavakadua's so-called Tuka movement mobilized the Fijian principle of the power of people of the land to create a new kind of polity, in opposition to Christian-colonial Eastern coastal chiefs and British rulers in 1881. Navosavakadua's polity was antichiefly, anti-Christian, and anticolonial, though at the same time, it mobilized practices and elements from chiefly, Christian, and colonial discourses. The narrative of Fiji's history, told at the Fiji Museum in Fiji's capital, had no place for this interloper and challenger. In 1991, however, three years after Fiji's first traumatic military coup,[5] I was fascinated to find a version of Navosavakadua's story alongside those of chiefs who sought to contain and deport him, the high chiefs of the eastern coastal kingdoms of Bau and Rewa. The story was on a poster display at the Ka Levu Center, a cultural center and locally produced tourist attraction on the main road in a region that is politically less central, but is much traveled by visitors because of its closeness to many tourist hotels. How did Navosa come to be, in some eyes at least, one in a crowd of past, exemplary leaders, one of the archetypes of embodied *mana* (truth, or effective power)?

"The first stirrings of nationalism," wrote Peter Worsley of cargo cults, in 1957. He continued:

> We are, in fact, witnessing the early stages of formation of national groupings in Melanesia. ... Some tribes are breaking up, others are coalescing to

> form higher social formations. The process is obviously one, however, which will not be controlled by the limits of arbitrary existing political boundaries, though these will affect the result. The new pressures shaping the future of the region will cut across these units as they cut across village, tribe, and clan. As in India and now in West Africa, ancient cultural ties may become factors of revived importance in shaping the ultimate political units of the region. If one can discern only the most tentative regional groupings, then, this is because the region is only giving birth to what I have called "protonational" formations of a transitional kind. M. Jean Guiart was therefore correct in referring to these movements as only "forerunners to Melanesian nationalism." (1968: 254)

In 1957, Worsley concluded, with great political confidence, that cargo cults were protonationalist movements. Their religious aspects would diminish, and the class consciousness established by such movements, crossing previous boundaries of clan, territory, and so on would enable the growth of proper political and economic vehicles of social change: unions, parties, nationalist movements, indeed nations.[6] In Worsley's late 1950s vision, the trajectory for change was quite clear, from a local tradition—not to be despised but fated to be replaced—to a "modernity" whose range of characteristics might be influenced by "ancient cultural ties," but the form of which—the nation—was already known in the West and was spreading throughout the world. I have great respect for Worsley's work, in particular his careful if brief study of colonial archives concerning the Fijian "Tuka" movement. Nevertheless, of all that is wrong with past theories of the cargo cult, the assumption that somehow they are transitional, a moment in a trajectory from traditional to modern is perhaps the worst, implicated as such a trajectory is in the assumptions of social evolutionary theory. And, of course, the assumptions of modernization theory, and of Marxist theorists, too, about this trajectory have been criticized quite thoroughly (e.g., Pletsch 1981). In this chapter, however, I will focus on a recent argument that has redefined and newly problematized the categories of tradition and nation and their relationship in Fiji.

Writing in the early 1990s, Rutz surveyed the postcoup Fijian political scene, and argues that the nation, in Fijian politics, was being shaped via a debate concerning tradition. He wrote:

> In brief, the Fijian narrative of nation, like so many others in Melanesia, is a contest about "tradition." Tradition, in the first instance, has been deployed as a rhetorical device to legitimate claims of a single "racial" com-

> munity—Fijians—against those of an "alien" community—Indians—to govern the sovereign state of Fiji. But in the light of recent military coups that settled the question of legitimacy by force, at least for the time being, "tradition" has become a rhetorical battleground for a contest of nation making within the Fijian community. ... A Fijian image of "the nation" is assured for all the citizens of Fiji, but which one? To establish this level of analysis within a larger field of political ideology and action, I use the phrase *rhetorical strategy*, by which I mean a tactic that captures "tradition" in a way that is persuasive and compelling to a constituency predisposed on other grounds to contend the legitimacy of the nation.
>
> The idea I have in mind [Rutz continues] is captured by the political philosopher J. G. A. Pocock (1971: 247–248) in a conclusive comment on the practice of dynastic politics in ancient China. [Here is Rutz quoting Pocock]: "But Mo Tzu was in the strict sense a radical: that is, he was adopting the posture appropriate to a rebel in a traditional society [*sic*], which is that of a reactionary. The appropriate location for his image of antiquity was the remotest accessible past, since there the presumption of continuity with the *traditional present* would be hardest to apply and, once he had occupied the headwaters of tradition, he would be in a position to maintain that the stream had been diverted from its proper course. Instances of this radical strategy the advocacy of return to the roots or sources abound in the history of argument within systems of authority."
>
> Like that of Mo Tzu, the rhetorical strategies of Fijians constitute so many attempts to occupy the headwaters of tradition—a return to roots or sources as a form of advocacy of a particular system of authority. And the notion of the "traditional present" captures the point succinctly, that whatever contests are waged, however much the headwaters are diverted, the result is a victory for tradition. (Rutz 1995: 72–73; his emphasis)

Rutz is interested in how "tradition" is a powerful political object, to be made and remade, claimed, revised, contested.[7] In this marvelous article, we see how, in the 1980s and 1990s, the concepts of tradition and nation come into play not as fixed stops along a timeline where tradition represents an ancient and other cultural past and nation the known, Westernized, and desirable modern. Instead, our scholarly move has been to use the concepts in a new relationship, to see tradition as an essential component of the making of nations.

As readers no doubt have gathered, this chapter is not going to be an attempt to refine a new definition of the cargo cult.[8] Nor will it be an inquiry into the twentieth-century desires that have led past anthropologists to long for such a definition.[9] Rather, I will consider the life and project of Navosavakadua and the Tuka movement, flagship example of cargo cult for Worsley (1968) and of millenarian movement for Kenelm Burridge (1969a), but only within a wider context of the history of political agency in Fiji. In the past two decades, that context has been one in which the establishment and imagination of the Fijian nation has been a paramount concern for the people of Fiji. I also definitely do not intend to try to establish a reified and single definition of "the nation" in some sort of parallel to "the cargo cult." Nor do I want us all to turn our attention from cargo cults to rhetorical strategies and uses of tradition in postcolonial politics. I do not argue that all political projects (including nations) must use tradition as a ground to authorize themselves.[10] Instead, I have found this contrast between Worsley and Rutz to be one fruitful way in which to tell some of the events of Navosavakadua's life, in a different context from that in which they occur when considered as cargo cult (by, e.g., Worsley and Burridge) and in a different way from my previous writings as well (Kaplan 1995b). Choosing to see how much can be learned by analyzing these events without using "cargo cult" as a framework, here I consider them moments in an ongoing dialogue between Melanesian selves and others. I hope to continue the project of moving beyond definitions and reifications, to the study of real histories, imaginations of selves and others, power made real in colonial and postcolonial societies such as Fiji.

In what follows I will first provide a brief reiteration of the problem with the concept of cargo cult and then turn to the central issue at hand, the problem of seizing the headwaters of tradition in Fijian political discourse. In doing so I will consider three historical moments: the recent debates over the nation;[11] Navosavakadua and the Tuka movement, as an example of seizing the headwaters of tradition in order to authorize a polity; and the most recent debates over the nature of selves and others in a global, United Nations–shaped world, resulting in Fiji's current constitution. I conclude with further reflection on reification, the use and abuse of trajectories, and the possibilities for comparison in anthropology.

As We All Know ... Some of the Problems with "Cargo Cults"[12]

Theorists of "cargo cults" or "millenarian movements" were among the first scholars to have acknowledged and politically engaged the issue of the agency of "others" in cultural change in colonial contexts. Whereas

Capturing the Headwaters of Tradition in Independent Fiji, 1970–1999

In Fiji from independence in 1970 on, the postcolonial constitution effectively disenfranchised Indo-Fijian citizens (one half the population of the nation) by way of a skewed and disproportionate system of representation.[15] What is more, Fijian politicians, like the British before them, insisted on opposing Fijian "selves" to Indo-Fijian "others." A potential narrative of Fiji as "three-legged stool" popularized briefly during the 1970 independence era and dramatized in the independence rituals (Kaplan 1995a) failed utterly to "occupy the Headwaters of Tradition"[16] and did not solidify into a multiracial narrative of the nation. When Indo-Fijians, in coalition with the ethnic Fijian Labour Party, briefly elected a "multiracial" national government the 1987 national elections, an ethnic Fijian–led, and –supported, military coup replaced that government, installing a new constitution and a succession of Fijian-led governments.[17] Many Indo-Fijians retreated from the national political arena, "aspiring to minority" (J. Kelly 1998). Thus, from 1970 until the new constitution of 1997 and election of 1999, it is accurate to say that, continuous with the colonial era in Fiji, ethnic Fijian political leaders, and ongoing contests among Fijians, shaped the nation as a whole.

As Rutz (1995) has shown, for two decades Fijian political leaders vied to establish their own political power via three contesting narratives that focused on "tradition" and the origins of the Fijian nation: the "royalist strategy," "the betrayal of the land," and the "strategy of divine intervention." All three narratives find "Fijian tradition" to be a compelling source for the legitimacy of their own leadership and of the nation as a whole. All three are concerned to explain how *turaga* (chiefs), *itaukei* (prior, original people, landowners, indigenes), and *lotu* (Christianity) are related.[18] The royalist strategy, employed by high chief Ratu Sir Kamisese Mara, prime minister of Fiji from independence in 1970 until 1987, continued colonial themes, arguing that chiefly leadership was necessary for Fijians to protect themselves from capitalist markets and political democracy. Its narrative located chiefly authority in the cession of Fiji to Queen Victoria by high chiefs in 1874 and the queen's (and colonial governments) subsequent and ongoing reauthorization of Fiji's high chiefs, up to and including the crown's "gift" to Fiji of independence and the constitution of 1970.[19] Regionally in Fiji, this strategy found favor with chiefs and people of the eastern coastal kingdoms, such chiefs having formed the backbone of the colonial "Native Administration" and (like Ratu Mara) dominated national government from independence until 1987. As Rutz points out, the royalist tradition put itself at risk when sacred kings engaged in electoral politics. In 1987 Ratu Mara and his party would lose the national election to a coalition of the opposition Indo-Fijian party and the nascent multiracial Fiji Labour Party, which espoused a rhetorical strategy of democracy and mildly leftist economic policies[20] and, most crucially, equal citizenship for all residents of Fiji.[21] This government, led by Fijian commoner Dr. Timothy Bavadra, would be ousted by a military coup in 1987.

As Rutz recounts, two other rhetorical strategies were important in Fiji during the period from the 1970s through the 1990s. The "betrayal of the land," has been a strategy of "disgruntled and discontented commoners," both antichiefly and anti-Indo-Fijian, whose spokesman was Sakeasi Butadroka, founder and leader of the Fijian Nationalist Party (see Premdas 1980). Typical of Butadroka's rhetoric is the utterance, "Fijians have nothing in their own land."[22] Butadroka has had considerable support in the areas of Ra, where I did my field research. Of note, some of his support overlapped with that of the Labour Party, a key sticking point being whether Fijians were more anti-Indian or antichiefly. The betrayal-of-the-land argument is that the chiefs betrayed the Fijian people when they ceded the island to Queen Victoria in 1874. Because Fiji was not theirs to give—chiefs have the *lewa,* but not the ownership, of the land—Queen Elizabeth II should have given Fiji back to the Fijians at independence in 1970. Instead, Fiji was given to "Fiji Citizens," including Indo-Fijians. To Butadroka, this was a second act of betrayal.[23] As Rutz notes, "Here the real headwater of tradition in the strategy of betrayal is the idea of 'original settlers' that excludes immigrants from political power" (1995: 84). Immigrants so excluded can include exploitative chiefs and colonizers, Indo-Fijians, and importers of putatively "Western" concepts of democracy and human rights.

The "strategy of divine intervention" emerged in 1987. Promulgated by coup leader Colonel Sitiveni Rabuka, who overthrew the multiracial Labour Party coalition that won the 1987 election, it seized the headwaters of tradition by claiming that the Christian God has authorized both chiefs and people. Cession was reinterpreted as a point where chiefs sought to increase Christianity in the islands; thus, chiefly leadership and wisdom was authorized because they are a conduit for Christianity and tradition. This version thereby incorporated aspects of the royalist strategy.

It also incorporated the betrayal strategy, arguing that the queen erred in returning sovereignty to all the people of Fiji in 1970. More appropriate, goes the argument, would have been to restore sovereignty to the chiefs, the conduits of religion and tradition. Rabuka sought to legitimate his 1987 coup as the correction to the errors of the past, the establishment of a Christian Fijian polity with little to no place for Hindu and Muslim Indo-Fijians (Rutz 1995; see also Kaplan 1990a). Militarily and rhetorically, Rabuka had quite a run, eventually being elected prime minister, as God's instrument in the transformation of Fiji.

As this very briefest consideration of Rutz's wonderful analysis shows, to understand the Fijian nation, we need to use an analytic framework that shows how a discourse of tradition has been central to authorizing colonial Fiji and to constituting the independent nation. If we reject an analytic framework that sees a static traditional past superseded by national modernity, instead understanding tradition and modernity and the nation as discourses, then we also remove the framework of trajectory within which Worsley, for example, established the cargo cult as a transitional, protonationalist, phenomenon.[24] How might we shift our sense of units and history in Fiji if we now returned to Navosavakadua and Tuka and inquired into them as attempts to seize the headwaters of tradition?

Capturing the Headwaters of Tradition in Fiji, c. 1870–1890; or, Rhetorics of Power and Authority in the Making of Colonial Fiji

Let us imagine the rhetorical strategy of Navosavakadua of the Vatukaloko people, in the northern and hill areas of Viti Levu island, in the 1870s. Let us consider his project to be the definition and defense and indeed innovation of a land-centered ritual polity.[25] Navosavakadua, like Ratu Mara, or Sakeasi Butadroka, or Sitiveni Rabuka[26] wanted political power, to organize people and territories, to define entities, to conduct, to control past present and future events. As Worsley saw, quite accurately, Navosa, as an oracle priest, was in tension with the claims of chiefs and Christians. As I have shown, his people, the Vatukaloko, had a long history of resistance to military and economic encroachment in their area by Bau and its vassals and they had different resources than many others in Fiji, because of their physical and ritual proximity to the Kauvadra mountain range, site of Fijian indigenous ancestral deities. The Vatukaloko, and oracle priests like Navosavakadua, were preeminent, powerful *itaukei* (people of the land).

Now, let us turn to a history of three rhetorical strategies of the 1870s–1890s, in the making of colonial Fiji:

Cakobau's "*lewa* strategy" was based on chiefly *mana*—and the *mana* of the kingdom of Bau in particular—and intends an extension and consolidation of that rule. In Cakobau's narrative and ritual-political practice, chiefs have come, married people of the land, and produced their chiefly lines. These chiefly descendents are then supported, installed, and worshipped by the prior, indigenous people of the land (Sahlins 1985). Chiefs (*turaga*) hold the *lewa* and the right to levy from the people, and Bau's territorial rights stretch throughout the islands. He claims the right to cede Fiji to Queen Victoria. He does so, on behalf of the people of Fiji, now becoming inundated by increasing numbers of white settlers, and on behalf of chiefs such as himself—in debt to various foreign governments—who will now receive payment and protection from the British.[27] His position is that chiefly *mana* (his, and Bauan supremacy overall, in particular) is the headwater of tradition. He may be right; when he converted to Christianity in 1854, so did most of Fiji. It is ironic that, in exercising his *lewa,* he positioned himself as the representative of the *itaukei* who give the rule to chiefs,[28] but there is a strong tradition in Fiji of *bati,* vassal lords who hold honorable, never subservient positions to overlords. And he—or other chiefs of Fiji—would get the chance to be new kinds of rulers through the Native Administration, though I do not know whether Cakobau envisioned it.

Sir Arthur Gordon, son of the Earl of Aberdeen, protégé of Gladstone, past governor of Mauritius and Trinidad, advances a "nativist or paternal native management strategy." In doing so, he argues, "It is of the utmost importance to seize, if possible, the spirit in which native institutions have been framed and endeavour so to work to develop to the utmost possible the latent capacities for the people for the management of their own affairs without exciting their suspicions or destroying their self respect."[29]

A reader of J. W. B. Money's book on Java and native management (Money 1861; see also J. Kelly, 2003), he seeks a stable colony that does not allow competition between white settlers and "natives." It is interesting, however, that he will create that stability by dealing out the white settlers and concentrating on a Fijian polity within the polity. He assumes that "native" commoners will want security and that "native" chiefs will want power and prestige. A reader also of such social evolutionary anthropologists as Sir Henry Maine, Gordon rejects establishing a colonial polity as a supplanting, transforming break with tradition. For, although he never doubts his own Christian civility, Gordon longs for a past he imagines as part of his own Scottish tradition. His rhetorical strategy fits well with Cakobau's: he finds the Fijians at a social evolutionary stage similar to that of the Scottish highland clans hundreds of years earlier, whose social order depended on clan chiefs. Fijian chiefs and their Christianity are good signs. Disliking low-class white settlers, he wants to create a colony that will preserve the natives from the too-advanced rough-and-tumble of the market.

Rather, he wants to rule them through their own chiefly leaders and customs. He will set in motion the Native Administration, with its hierarchy of Fijian governors, district officials, and village headmen and its native stipendiary magistrates. Quite often he and his subordinates will follow Bauan boundaries, practices, and personnel. He will authorize the Native Lands Commission, which will eventually reserve 83 percent of Fiji's land for Fijian kin groups, indivisible and inalienable. His narrative gives God and the queen, (Christianity and the pinnacle of social evolutionary possibility) the right to reorganize Fiji, but also the duty to do so according to the most advanced principles, and those principles require an understanding of who the colonized are. And they are found to be at a certain social evolutionary stage, still deeply dependent on tradition for their social order. It thus becomes Gordon's duty to codify it for them, to give them their tradition as law in the new colonial polity. Next, he will make the colony pay by establishing the separate sphere of the market, of the sugar cane industry (with a special privilege for the Australian Colonial Sugar Refinery as local monopsony) and the Indian workers who will make it possible.

Navosavakadua and the Vatukaloko will attempt to put into place a different polity. Navosa's "landcentric" rhetorical strategy asserts the origins of power in "the people of the land," insisting on their ritual and political priority and autonomy. His rhetorical strategy is to encompass eastern coastal chiefs, colonial whites, and Christian gods in a narrative of the ritual-political powers of the *itaukei*. He needs to encompass Cakobau's consolidation of Fiji, British royal, legal, and divine power and to unmask the hierarchical implications of Gordon's native management plan. He will put the headwater of tradition, the source of all power and legitimacy in Fiji, right at the heart of the powers of the people of the land: the Kauvadra mountain range, home of Fijian ancestors, where the Vatukaloko people have their lands, where his followers will build his pilgrimage center. Navosavakadua prophesied the return of Nacirikaumoli and Nakausabaria, Fijian ancestor gods who were also Jesus and Jehovah. They were coming to tread the land and reestablish a polity in which

Navosa, and people of the land would rule, expelling eastern coastal foreigners and whites. Here again the Kauvadra range, ritual center of Fijian gods and Fijian power is the wellspring of power. If Jesus and Jehovah are powerful, it is because they are actually indigenous, Fijian gods. The Bible's story of Exodus is Navosa's story.[30] Echoing claims made by Vatukaloko people for several generations, Navosavakadua rejected Bauan power over himself or his people. They were bati, they claimed, noble allies, not ruled subjects. Sometimes Navosavakadua's claims to power sound like Cakobau's source of power, the *mana* of a chief. Especially by the 1980s, his descendants often call him *Ratu*—Sir, a chief's honorific.[31] Navosavakadua's headwaters of tradition, his fount of power, were the literal springs of the Kauvadra range, whose water he distributed as *wai ni tuka* (water of health and immortality) to those who became part of his polity.

Here we have recontextualized a story, once told as cargo cult, amid a field of contest to capture the headwaters of tradition, of power, in making Fiji in the 1880s and a century later. When the story of Cakobau, Arthur Gordon, and Navosa follows that of Ratu Mara, Sakeasi Butadroka, and Sitiveni Rabuka, suddenly no one seems worth singling out as transitional, or in need of special explanation. Having shown how we can, fruitfully, submerge Navosa in this wider political history of selves and others, let us pull the story into the present.

Capturing the Headwaters of Tradition in 1990s Fiji

In 1990, Fiji got its first, postcoup new constitution as a republic. Written under the influence of Sitiveni Rabuka, authorized by the Great Council of Chiefs, it insisted on a Fijian, Christian nation. This document institutionalized much of Rabuka's "divine intervention" narrative. Although Rabuka (a commoner) became prime minister, the role of chiefs as conduits of order and Christianity was also crucial. Everything happened as if, in effect, the chiefs had simply taken back their gift of sovereignty. The new constitution mandated a seventy-seat house of representatives (thirty-seven Fijians, twenty-seven Indians, five general electors, and one Rotuman) and a thirty-four-seat senate (twenty-four Fijians, nine others, one Rotuman). Fijians held all the cards, and the constitutions they debated and the one they promulgated reflected that sensibility. Not only were the races out of balance and demographically disproportionate, but major offices were reserved for Fijians.

It would not be long, however, before political infighting among

rhetoric of compliance with international human rights requirements seems to invoke a future, perhaps a call to "modernize," perhaps simply a call to join a growing consensus, rather than invoking past, traditional rights, and obligations. Rather than the past, and tradition, the position at the headwaters or origin, outside examples and the moral community of international audiences are invoked. The title of the Report of the 1996 Constitution Review Commission, "Fiji: Toward A United Future," illustrates this point. But how "new" are such invocations, such bridges to the horizon?

First, not all nations have invoked tradition as the wellspring of their national narrative, and not all politicians seek to occupy the headwaters of tradition in order to gain national power. In the United States, there is a strong narrative that chronicles the rejection of tradition by the polity; the narratives of modernity, progress, technology, and innovation are extremely powerful political strategies. In social evolutionary, British colonial discourse, colonizers placed themselves at the pinnacle of social evolution. Though charmed and compelled by "tradition," they saw their ultimate power and right to authorize it to be rooted in having passed through all previous stages to that of civilization. Even for Navosavakadua, one could say that though his polity was to be land centered, authorized by the special power of the *itaukei,* those Fijians who were there first, ever before the chiefs came, still his sense of the necessity of insisting on this rootedness came from his knowledge of the claims of outsiders to be more powerful. Faced with an obvious globe of difference (Jehovah and Jesus, white settlers, missionaries, and colonizers) Navosavakadua—who is said to have worked on plantations outside of the Ra area and who, through punitive deportation, came to know diverse areas of Fiji—placed the ancestors of all powerful others in Fiji. In his stories, they do not then remain in Fiji, but go out, to populate the world, eventually returning to their originating land.

Using the gaze of others as the gauge of moral position is no recent phenomenon either. And here we return to the ethnographic vignette of the hunger strikers in my introduction. Though not an ethnic Fijian tactic, there has been a deep Indo-Fijian history of hunger striking, of awareness of the outside gaze, and of moral appeal to rally support and to touch the conscience of the outside power in Fiji. The past master of this tactic was Mahatma Gandhi and the hunger strikers and nonviolent resisters of the Indian Nationalist movement. Of course, Gandhi also strategized a nation built on indigenous rights, Swaraj (self-rule). But Indo-Fijians, while following many of Gandhi's leads tactically, have also diasporically, for a century, built their claims with reference to a world of people in motion, whose sources of moral authority include the bridges they have made to and from other members of a wider world than Fiji.[39] Even Navosavakadua found an audience, and he has even found a moral authority in an overseas audience (though not the latter in his lifetime). After all, colonial officials around the world swapped memoranda on local forms of disorder creating a global juxtaposition of freemasonry, Indian Mutiny, Maori HauHau, Fijian Tuka, Sudanese Mahdi, and so on that initiated the concretization of the category. And as we gathered at a workshop on the legacy of cargo cults, we should note that it was another sector of the global audience, anthropologists such as Peter Worsley and Kenelm Burridge, across the world from Fiji, who in the 1960s reevaluated the colonial criminalization of Navosavakadua, Tuka, and the "movements" they saw as similar, finding in them heroic resistance to colonial domination, racism, and exploitation.

Looking comparatively at formations and contestations of political power and right, and thinking critically about dialogical processes, we might be better served to expect the most dynamic movements, and moments, to be neither "traditional" nor "foreign"; like Navosa's or Cakobau's or Rabuka's or the Constitutional Commission's efforts, to have aspects out to capture headwaters of tradition and aspects out to build or seize bridges over horizons.[40] No doubt the proportions and dimensions of continuity or borrowing will be worth noting as analysis proceeds,[41] but it will be better to expect both dimensions, looking back and looking out beyond, everywhere and every time, rather than accept evolutionary narratives of a traditional versus a modern. After all, traditions and foreign things (things from beyond) are both always available for alliance, use, and connection. They are always being made use of, never what simply is. If tradition was present, it would not be tradition; it has to be addressed as the past to be traditional, just as the foreign, the beyond, is not beyond if it is here, if we are it. Arjun Appadurai once wrote of "the past as a scarce resource." So, too, are foreigners; the future is more open but in all cases what really shapes the political moment is not merely one's own sense of primacy, past versus foreign versus future, but rather one's confrontation with the actions and assertions of others (i.e., not "the Other" but active political others of one's own place and time).[42] Thus, issues concerning tradition and that which is beyond are framed in actual political dialogues, not scholarly reifications.

Notes

I thank the government of Fiji for permission to pursue research in Fiji in 1984–85, 1986, 1991, and 2002. I warmly thank many colleagues and friends in Fiji. I also thank the organizers and participants of the "Cargo, Cult, and Culture Critique" workshop for a most stimulating setting in which to reengage this topic. Funding from the National Science Foundation, Fulbright-Hays, the Institute for Intercultural Studies, Wenner Gren, and Vassar College supported the research in Fiji over the years. Responsibility for the opinions, analysis, and conclusions in this chapter is mine.

1. This is the home of the Vatukaloko people, relatives and descendants of Navosavakadua, famed leader of the 1880s "Tuka movement."

2. They were puzzled, uncomfortable, simultaneously asking me for explanation.

3. "Ethnic Fijians [*itaukei*] also!" they said, amazed.

4. Navosavakadua is frequently referred to as Navosa, a shortened version of his name.

5. Fiji's political crisis of 2000, in which a failed businessman and ethnonationalist ethnic Fijian, George Speight, with varied supporters, overthrew the democratically elected, multiethnic Labour Party–led coalition government of Prime Minister Mahendra Chaudhury, took place after the research on which this chapter is based, but see Lal (2000), Kaplan (2003), and Kelly and Kaplan (2001).

6. We might pause to note that the most successful of all anticolonial movements, Gandhi's Swaraj Indian nationalism proceeded via a method, *satyagraha,* that insisted on the interpenetration of god and society, but that is not really our topic here.

7. Rutz argues along with Pocock, but also very much in the spirit of Hobsbawm and Ranger (1983), Keesing (1989), and B. Cohn (1987, 1996).

8. Though I would insist (with Marshall Sahlins, for example) that there are Fijian cultural ways of organizing a politics that require our study, I am not looking for a general theory of cults and movements, nor even of "Melanesian" movements.

9. Although I do think that the nineteenth century colonial imagination and colonial fears as well as desires had a lot to do with the beginnings of the making of "Tuka."

10. Indeed, the United States, for example, made itself quite a narrative as a place that broke from the past in myriad ways (e.g., from monarchy, from European domination). See Benedict (1946: 98).

11. This draws on Rutz (1995) and on my own and John Kelly's work (e.g., Kaplan 1995b; Kelly and Kaplan 2001).

12. This section reiterates, with some compressions and other amplifications, arguments I have made previously (Kaplan 1990b, 1995b). See also Kaplan and Kelly (1999) and Kelly and Kaplan (1990).

13. Indeed, Sahlins (1985) studied this conversion as part of a ritual-political kingship politics without finding any need to refer to "cults."

14. Whereas McDowell is most interested in establishing a Melanesian view of historical change, my sense of the history at issue will be more dialogical. For a finely detailed account of Pacific informants' opinions of the term cargo cult, and its existence and value as an analytic category, see also Hermann (present volume).

15. See Lal (1988, 1992), Howard (1991), Kaplan (1988; 2003), J. Kelly (1988), and Kelly and Kaplan (2001). I will assume that my readers have some familiarity with Fiji's complex history and peopling. The islands, consisting of chiefly led kingdoms, and numerous smaller polities as well, largely converted to Wesleyan Methodism by 1854, were colonized by ("ceded to")

Britain in 1874. The British ruled Fijians paternalistically, using nineteenth century social evolutionary and racial theories to codify Fijian practices: they reserved 83 percent of lands for Fijians, held inalienably and communally ostensibly following Fijian land tenure traditions; administratively they established the "Native Administration," a Fijian polity within the colonial polity that colonial officials and Fijians alike authorized as based in Fijian traditional practices. Ongoing and new Fijian projects intersected with the colonial project, from the Christian-colonial high chiefs who became officials in the Native Administration to the leaders like Navosavakadua who challenged it. South Asian Indians came to work on Fiji's sugar plantations in the 1870s and many remained. For the standard history of Indo-Fijians see Gillion (1962, 1977), and Lal (1992). In the twentieth century, south Asian Indians became, for a time, Fiji's majority population. Since the colonial era, the term "races" had been used locally to describe kinds of people, the three "races" of Fiji being "Fijians," "Indians," and "Europeans." I will take this opportunity to note that my own political sympathies lie with the antichiefly and anticolonial movements, such as that of Navosavakadua and his descendants, and even more strongly with Indo-Fijian anticolonial struggle and with the Fiji Labour Party.

16. As above, I borrow this phrase and much of the analysis from Rutz (1995).

17. This tragic scenario was repeated in 2000, when a coup again toppled a multiethnic Labour Party government (see note 5).

18. Again, I want to reiterate that not all nations use "tradition" as the basis of their narratives, and those that do use it do not all do so in the same way. One of the reasons that tradition is such a powerful authorizing term in Fiji is because the colonial British used it so powerfully in establishing governmental and land-owning institutions and rights. Another reason is the intersection of these colonial usages with a malleable nineteenth-century Fijian understanding of the relationship of *itaukei* and *turaga* (chiefs, rulers who rule but do not own the land). See Sahlins (1985). For an extended discussion of different Fijians mobilizations of the differing authorities of *taukei* and *turaga,* and indeed of the malleability of this relationship, see Kaplan (1995b).

19. Rutz (1995: 79–81), see also Kaplan (1988, 1990a).

20. This included support for workers and unions, reduction or abolition of school fees, lower mortgage rates as well as free bus fare for school children and old-age pensioners.

21. They proposed using the term "Fijian" to apply to all Fiji citizens regardless of heritage.

22. I paraphrase from my recollections of newspaper accounts of his many public pronouncements over the past two decades.

23. Rutz (1995: 82–83), drawing on Premdas (1980).

24. As above, I note that I have used Worsley as a straw man here, that few of my colleagues, if any, would hold a brief for Worsley's old argument.

25. I have always done that. See Kaplan (1995b).

26. Or like his 1870s contemporaries, "King" Cakobau of Bau, instigator of Cession, paradigmatic Christian, eastern coastal chief, leader of the dominant polity in the islands, or Sir Arthur Gordon, new colonial governor.

27. So, his "Lewa" and consolidation strategy includes debt consolidation as well!

28. That is, he is now taukei to Queen Victoria's turaga.

29. See, for example, Gordon (1879a: 11; 1879b).

30. He was widely known as Mosese Dukumoi.

31. And by the 1980s, chiefs, like Jesus, all performed miracles of producing plenitude (loaves and fishes), though chiefs relied more on redistributing foreign aid.

32. This indeed was the context in which the exhibit at the Ka Levu Center described at the beginning of this article was developed.

33. Its three members were New Zealand jurist Sir Paul Reeves (a Maori), Fiji historian and Australian National University professor Brij V. Lal (an Indo-Fijian), and Fijian longtime parliamentarian Tomasi Vakatora (an ethnic Fijian).

34. See Kelly and Kaplan (2001). While it continues the 1990 constitution's variety of concessions to Fijian custom and chiefly power (the Great Council of Chiefs will appoint the president and vice president, the largely ceremonial head of state), it alters the "racial" composition of representation in important ways. The house of representatives consists of seventy-one members, to be elected from five electoral rolls (twenty-three by Fijians, nineteen by Indians, one by Rotumans, three by others, and twenty-five by all voters on an "open roll"). The prime minister must invite into his (or her) cabinet members from other parties that obtain 10 percent of the seats or more in the house of representatives, in numbers proportionate to the total percentage of members in the House. Thus, when this constitution was set in place, a vast change had taken place. Unfortunately, it was soon to meet a hostile backlash.

35. For example, the ILO Convention 169 on Indigenous and Tribal Peoples, and the draft Declaration on the Rights of Indigenous Peoples.

36. It derived from such documents as the Universal Declaration of Human Rights, the International Covenant on Civil and Political Rights, and the Convention on the Elimination of All Forms of Racial Discrimination.

37. For example, it did not grant cabinet portfolios to the Labour Party, even though Labour had far more than the requisite 10 percent of seats.

38. Because I am deeply opposed to social evolutionary stage theories, I am viscerally averse to assuming that there must be differences between eras of Fijian kingdoms, colony, nation, nation in globalization, but let us at least consider the possibility.

39. These include those opened by Gandhi to and from Christian protest traditions, including such protest tactics as boycotts and fasting.

40. Indeed, insofar as Pocock distinguishes the "traditional society" from other types, there is a real distance and difference between his analysis and mine. In fact, rather than associating a particular rhetorical strategy with a particular kind of society or polity, in all cases I would expect to find *both* efforts to capture headwaters of tradition and bridges over horizons (whether to imagined futures, or to spatial others, divinities, etc.). My goal is to follow Tambiah (1985) in his critique of Maurice Bloch on ritual. Bloch argued that ritual is a vehicle identified with Weber's "traditional authority." Tambiah argued that one cannot predict the turn ritual will take, it may be used to maintain those in power, or to overthrow them, to enable traditional or charismatic authority, to turn to the right, or the left. Like Tambiah, I would reject the association of a particular technique or strategy with any particular "kind" of society or authority.

41. Thus, for example, Rabuka's strategy of divine intervention depends heavily on an articulation of Christianity with Fijian-ness, while the Constitutional Commission's strategy is more heavily future- and foreign-directed.

42. For example, Navosavakadua responds to Cakobau and Gordon, Gordon responds to Cakobau and Navosa, the Constitution Committee to Rabuka, and so on.

PART II

EXPANDING THE FRAMEWORK

CHAPTER 5 Mutual Hopes

German Money and the Tree of Wealth in East Flores

Karl-Heinz Kohl

ALTHOUGH there are many historical, linguistic, and cultural ties linking the Eastern Lesser Sundae Islands—now the Province Nusa Tenggara Timor of the Indonesian Republic—to the island world of Melanesia, and although we find many similarities in social organization and cultural orientations between the two regions, the Solor-Alor Archipelago is not regarded as a classical area of so-called cargoism. There are some reports on anticolonial messianic movements on the island of Flores and the adjacent islands (e.g., Dietrich 1985), but as far as I know, no article or book was ever published on the social phenomena that in anthropological literature were labeled as "cargo cults." This may be related to the fact that the chain of small islands reaching from Flores in the west over Adonara, Solor, Lembata, and Pantar to Alor in the East has been neglected by professional anthropologists (figure 5.1).

For a long time, it was a kind of anthropological terra incognita. Although there exists a number of ethnographic monographs and articles published by Catholic missionaries of the Society of the Divine Word from the beginning of the twentieth century, systematic research by university-educated anthropologists only began in the 1970s. By this time, the Dutch colonists had been gone from the scene for more than two decades, and, if there were any cargoist or politically motivated movements in this remote and economically backward area, the new political authorities of independent Indonesia would have been embarrassed to reveal them to the public. In addition, the professional interest in cargo movements had already begun to decline when, in the late 1970s and early 1980s, American, Australian, British, German, and Japanese was embossed with could be regarded as material proof of the truth of a story owned by his own clan, but also known to the village's ritual authorities. The story went as follows:

> Once there lived a young girl in the village with the name of Ossi Tobi Lolon. Her mother had died. Her father did not like to work; he was a drunkard and he neglected his duties. Hence the children lived in poverty and often suffered from hunger. Ossi Tobo Lolon, who was the eldest, had to take care of her younger sisters. Every day she tried to find some food to feed her hungry sisters. One day, out on the village's coral reef, she caught a small, silvery fish, but the fish was not big enough to fill up all four of them. So she put it aside. The following night, she had a dream, sent to her by the heaven god Rera Wulan. The master of heaven told her to bury the fish in her hamlet's courtyard. Ossi Tobo Lolon did what she was told. Four days later, a tall tamarind tree stood where she had planted the fish. It began to blossom, and after another four days, the tree was full of fruits. But the tree's fruits were no ordinary tamarind fruits but golden earrings, elephant tusks, pearls bracelets, and precious silk clothes from India, together with rice and maize. Ossi Tobi Lolon and her sisters satisfied their hunger with the tree's fruits and left their house to go to a feast in a neighboring village. Meanwhile, the tree of wealth shone like a star. It could be seen miles away from the spot near the coast where she had planted it. The same night, some sailors of Sinajava [the collective term for all countries lying in the far west of Flores] came with their ship and saw the shining tree. They went ashore and tried to fell it with their axes. But the tree resisted. They tried it again and again till their axes became blunt. When Ossi Tobo Lolon came home and saw what the sailors were doing, she offered them her help. "I will give you the tree," she said, "if you promise to take us with you." The sailors agreed with pleasure. So she took the tree with both hands and, in one go, pulled it out of the earth. Together with her three younger sisters, she then boarded the foreigners' ship. Her father saw this from afar and tried to persuade his children to come back. But the ship with the four sisters and the tree of wealth disappeared forever over the horizon. Distressed about his own failure and his feelings of remorse, Ossi Tobo Lolon's father finally killed himself.

Since that time, so commented the village's ritual authorities after telling me this myth, the East has been poor and the West has been rich. Although the story was no ordinary fairy tale but part of the sacred knowledge of one on the village's clans, there were some doubts that everything really had happened that way. According to some more recent tradition, the foreign sailors had come from Japan. The Japanese were well known on Flores, where they had fought during World War II. And people also knew that Japanese and Germans were allies at the time. Furthermore, *orang Jepang* (Japanese) and *orang Jerman* (Germans) sounds very similar in Bahasa Indonesia. So it was clear that the tree of wealth had been brought to Germany. We ourselves had produced the proof. We had proved the truth of the story by our luxurious way of living, and we had proved it by this piece of German money that showed Ossi Tobo Lolon pulling the tree of wealth from the earth. Pleased by having found, or rather evoked an original cargo-type myth, I began to ask. "What happened to Ossi Tobo Lolon? Will she or some of her descendants ever come back to East Flores? Will they bring back the tree and all the wealth and items stolen by Japanese or German sailors?" People wondered about my naive questioning. Of course the tree of wealth had gone forever. What's past is past.

Without a doubt, the myth of the tree of wealth contains some cargoist elements.[1] But there was no hope that the stolen wealth would ever come back to its original owners, there were no prophecy or rituals connected to this myth. The story of Ossi Tobo Lolon was no more than an etiological explanation for why the West is so rich and why the East is so poor. It answered to the question of the origin of the most remarkable difference between the two cultures. If we define anthropology, in a very general way, as an attempt to explain the differences in human cultures, then the myth of Ossi Tobo Lolon can be regarded as an integral part of East Florinese indigenous anthropology.[2]

I

Although often criticized during the last two decades, the process of anthropological "othering" can also have some advantages for the one who has been othered.[3] The more or less distorted view of a culture the foreign observer produces can enable the so-called subjects of ethnographic research to see their own customs and behavior in a new light. This is also the reason why fictive ethnographies of European culture like Montesquieu's *Persian Letters* (1993) or Erich Scheurmann's *Tuiavii's Way* (1997) have always been so popular. Even in this fictive form, they show us our own culture from a new, alienating angle. What is a matter of fact in daily life and never noticed consciously becomes obvious. The foreign observer's misunderstandings especially can be very fruitful in understanding one's own culture in a better way. If we take the inhabitants of East Flores seriously as anthropologist colleagues, we also must ask for the hidden truth that lies behind their statements. To be sure, we do not believe in the overt content of the myth of Ossi Tobo Lolon. But if we take the theft of the tree of wealth as a metaphorical statement, we have to confess that the wealth of the West is based on the exploitation of the natural resources and of the labor of former European colonies. Of course, we also would reject the idea that the symbolic design embossed on a German fifty-pfennig coin represents an East Florinese young girl. Such an interpretation seems to be a classical anthropological misunderstanding, comparable to many similar statements Western anthropologists made about alleged religious symbols and beliefs. But what can we learn from such an obvious misinterpretation? Have we ever asked ourselves why we are putting symbols on our own coins and notes? And what is the meaning of these symbols? Is it not true that they also have some religious content and that they are related to certain myths of our own culture?

According to German historian Bernhard Laum's classic study *Heiliges Geld* (1924), money has a sacred origin in Western culture. For many thousand years, coins were made out of precious metals like gold and silver because they are rare and difficult to get, although their pragmatic use value is rather low. To be generally accepted as a universal equivalent in trade, it was necessary to attach a kind of imaginary value to them. Almost everywhere in the ancient world, in Babylon as well as in Greece and Rome, linking money to supernatural agencies was a means for providing this goal. In Rome, the goddess Juno, protector of hearth and family, was also regarded as a guardian of the money. Etymologically, the word money itself is a derivation of Juno's epithet "moneta," the name Romans gave to the bronze, silver, and gold bars produced in her temple. It was the deities themselves who had to watch for the value accorded to the new equivalent by social convention. Consequently, the oldest coins carried pictures of the gods, a custom that has survived until today. On each American dollar note, the only currency that is accepted all over the world, we still can read, "In God we trust" (Godelier 1996). So it is surely not wrong to link money symbols to hidden and today almost forgotten sacred traditions.

But what about the picture of that slim and barefoot working maid on the German fifty-pfennig coin? The first edition of this coin dates from 1948, when in postwar Germany a new currency was introduced. At a time when German cities lay in ruins, the tree-planting maid was obviously put on the coin as a symbol of hope in reconstruction and economic recovery. Similar symbols could also be found on almost all other coins of the new money. On the obverse of the one-, the two-, and the ten-pfennig coins, appeared a young oak tree, the holy tree of pre-Christian, pagan Germans, and oak leaves also figured on the reverse of the one- and two-mark coins. After the Reichsmark of the Second German Empire and the Rentenmark of the Weimar Republic had lost their value through inflation, following the two world wars, people hoped that the new currency would guarantee economic stability and prosperity. In the three years following the capitulation of the Nazi Wehrmacht in 1945, the German economy was at the lowest level it probably ever had been. The old mark had not only lost its former market value, it also had become almost useless. On the official market, food and commodities could only be bought on ration coupons issued by the Allied forces, while on the prospering black market, American cigarettes had become a kind of new standard currency. According to popular German folk mythology, on June 21, 1948, the legendary day the Deutsche mark was introduced in West Germany, the hunger and scarcity everyone had suffered from was immediately ended. Over night, the shops were filled again with all the food and goods one had so keenly missed during the previous three years. And all these commodities could be bought with the new currency. After the atrocious crimes of the Nazi regime and the political, economic, and moral breakdown of a whole nation, the currency reform marked a new beginning. On the level of symbolic representation, however, there was an amazing continuity. During World War II, oak leaves were an attribute of the highest military decoration the Nazi rulers gave to their obedient officers and executioners, the *Ritterkreuz mit Eichenlaub, Schwertern und Diamanten*. Transformed into a symbol of fertility and economic growth, oak leaves now decorated the new mark coins. Like this symbolic transposition, the almost unbelievable energy postwar Germany put into the task of economic recovery can be interpreted as a kind of collective repression of the darkest period of German history. War was replaced by work. The legendary German economic miracle began, which in popular consciousness was strongly tied to the Deutsche mark and its symbolic meaning. At least in the eyes of some of Germany's former enemies and new allies, by means of economic power and the Deutsche mark, the country seemed to realize what Hitler had failed to do by pure military power, namely, dominate the rest of Europe.

Gaining goods and wealth and thus regaining a state of equality that had been lost because of the crimes of Nazism, was without any doubt one of the major goals of postwar Germany's forced economic activities. If a similar endeavor had taken place not in Germany, but in an economically less developed country, anthropologists surely would have labeled it a cargo cult movement. Yet apart from the unusual success of these "cargo-ist" activities, there remains a difference that makes it difficult to apply the term. This difference consists in the role money plays in capitalist society. Cargo cults in the strict sense of the term can never occur in this type of society because, in capitalist economy, goods always appear in the form of commodities.

In capitalist society, there are no restricted spheres of exchange as in a multicentered economy such as that of the Tiv in Nigeria. Ideally, at least, everything can be exchanged against everything, although there are always certain "things that are publicly excluded from being commoditized" (Kopytoff 1986: 73). Money is the general equivalent that mediates between the goods exchanged. Because in capitalist society all trade goods are commodities measured by their abstract exchange or money value, money also incorporates, on a symbolic level, all other values as utility, prestige, or renown that are, according to social convention, attached to certain categories of objects. As a result of commoditization, all goods can transfer their social meaning and value to money. Especially when older social hierarchies have begun to disappear in the process of democratization, accumulating money in the form of capital becomes the preferred means for increasing social prestige. But this is not all. Because everything can be bought by money, money also incorporates the promise to satisfy each sort of desire. Maybe it is the *mean*—the ideal, typical construction of a stingy or miserly person—that represents the psychological results of commoditization better than anyone else. The mean refrain from satisfying their immediate needs and desires by spending their money. Instead, they save their money because the imagination is much more important for them, that one day, it will help fulfilling all their potential wishes. Accumulating money means accumulating the potential of satisfying every future desire. We are all familiar with the example of the multimillionaire dressed in rags and living from the scraps he finds in his neighbor's garbage. On the other side, we also know about the immense prestige value attached to the most expensive big label textiles or watches. They are bought and worn only for showing publicly how wealthy their owner is, even though their utility and their aesthetic value do not differ from much less expensive items. In a famous chapter of his *Capital*, Karl Marx analyzed how, in capitalist society, commodities, which originally were nothing more than "products of men's hands," were transformed into independent living beings, "entering into social relations both with one another and the human race" and, in a remarkable reversion of reality, becoming endowed with the capacity to create value (Marx 1970: 77). But Marx failed to highlight the fact that the same mystic quality that he called "commodity fetishism" is also attached to the general equivalent in which each commodity can measure its value. If there are social and pseudoreligious movements in capitalist societies that can be compared to Melanesian cargo cults, the object of desire must not be sought on a pure material level. According to the dominant role money plays in this type of society, it is not concrete goods that are the most desirable things, but the general equivalent in exchange for which each concrete good can be purchased. Therefore, money itself becomes the most important object of desire, because it not only mediates between all other kinds of goods but also confers high standing and social prestige.

The further history of the German Deutsche mark is a good example for the development of such a "money-cult" issuing from the very heart of a modern capitalist society. The introduction of the new currency in the Western part of the former Reich, then controlled by American, British, and French military commissioners, was the first step toward the political division of Germany. The currency reform of 1948 was a unilateral measure of Allied military governors that the Soviet government of occupied East Germany was not willing to accept. What in 1948 were only two different currency blocs became, one year later, the cores of the two postwar German states. Whereas in the German Federal Republic the capitalist free market system was restored, the purchasing power of East German money was restricted by the socialist character of the East German state. In the German Democratic Republic (GDR) the new state authorities controlled which kind of goods could be imported and which kind of goods could be sold and bought on the market. While West Germans were proud of their prospering economy and the proved stability of their new currency, East Germans suffered not only from the authoritarian measures of their former Stalinist regime, but also and maybe even more from the reduced value of money that had actually ceased being a general equivalent. Year by year, hundreds of thousands of East Germans left their country to settle in the obviously much richer and more prosperous "Golden West." To prevent one the of biggest demographic movements in recent European history, the government of the GDR decided to close the borders and built the Berlin wall. By transforming their so-called socialist state into an enormous prison, the communist rulers only increased the desire of their subjects to live a life of affluence. Reinforced by the advertisements in West German TV channels that could be received almost everywhere in the GDR, the Deutsche mark became a kind of mythical symbol. Was it not the Deutsche mark that enabled their brothers and sisters beyond the border to fulfill every wish? The peaceful revolution stimulated in East Germany in 1989 after the political constellations of the Warsaw Pact countries had changed radically was not motivated by nationalist feelings. Nationalism had almost faded away in both German states during the four decades following the defeat of the Hitler regime. When people shouted "*Wir sind ein Volk*" in the streets of Leipzig or East Berlin, national reunification meant for them integration into the prospering market economy of the West. When finally on November 9, 1989, the Berlin wall tumbled down and East German citizen were free to cross the border, a strange ritual took place. In West Berlin, many small Government offices were opened in which each GDR citizen was welcomed by a 100–Deutsche mark note, his so-called *Begrüßungsgeld* (greeting money), while on the streets, West German citizens offered gifts of bananas and other tropical fruits not available in the former GDR to their compatriots.

In classic Melanesian cargo cults, collective rituals were performed to accelerate the arrival of the desired goods, and "false" rituals were often made responsible when the ancestors and their cargo-laden ships did not come. In the months following the official reunification of East and West Germany, a very similar process could be observed. Disappointed in their hope of immediate wealth and prosperity, in Leipzig and other East German towns people began to take up again the traditional Monday demonstrations that in 1989 had been so useful in overthrowing the communist government. But this time it was the economic policy of the new government and their own desolate economic situation people were protesting against.

II

Describing German postwar history in terms and categories coined by anthropologists who studied Melanesian cargo cults may look strange, but besides its alienating effect, it also may give us some hints about the double origin of the concept of cargo cult itself. The economic growth and prosperity of the three postwar decades was not restricted to Germany alone. In this period, almost all Western industrial societies developed in the same direction. In his book *Age of Extremes*, British historian Eric Hobsbawm (1996: 257–286) called the years between 1945 and 1973 the "Golden Age" of the twentieth century, where everywhere in the so-called first world economy and industrial production seemed to prosper. The history of anthropology shows us very clearly how the anthropologist's view of other cultures is guided by personal experiences as well as by the political, economic, and ideological changes that are taking place in his or her own society. Criticizing Émile Durkheim's theory on totemism, Claude Lévi-Strauss once remarked, "Quand une coutume exotique nous captive en dépit (ou à cause) de son apparente singularité, c'est généralement qu'elle nous présente, comme un miroir déformant, une image familière et que nous reconnaissons confusément comme telle, sans réussir encore à l'identifier" (1962: 318).

According to Lamont Lindstrom (1993: 30), the term "cargo cult" did not appear in print before 1945. Its amazing career in anthropological writings began after Peter Worsley's *The Trumpet Shall Sound* was published, in 1957, followed soon thereafter by Kenelm Burridge's *Mambu*, in 1960, and Peter Lawrence's *Road Belong Cargo*, in 1964. In Germany, it was Wilhelm E. Mühlmann who made the term popular in anthropology by including a chapter on cargo cults in his influential book *Chiliasmus und Nativismus*, published in 1961 (Uplegger and Mühlmann 1961). Mühlmann, who was one of the leading anthropologists in postwar Germany and exerted a strong influence on the younger student generation, had been deeply involved in Nazi politics during the Third Reich, something none of his students had known until it was made public by a German magazine. The hidden topic of his worldwide comparative study on the psychology and sociology of nativism was the rise of the Nazi movement in Germany, which in 1933, "from the perspective of participant," he himself had called a "chiliastic millenarism."[4] He used cargo cults and other subversive nativistic movements such as the Mau-Mau upheaval in Kenya or the North American Ghost Dance religion as a kind of personal apology to relativize what had happened in Germany between 1933 and 1945. In a very similar way, but with a significant reversal in its political meaning, the student movement of the late sixties and the early seventies was fascinated by Melanesian cargo cults as well, now, however, regarding them as a critique of the irrationality of capitalist society (Kohl 1975).

Cargo cults seemed to be one of the many liberation movements of the so-called Third World, in which leftist students put their hope that they would help to defeat capitalism in the first world as well. After having rediscovered Worsley's thesis of the necessary transformation of the irrational religious cargo cults into political self-liberation movements—the revised new edition of *The Trumpet Shall Sound* was published in 1968—leftists believed they had found a new ally in their critique of the capitalist consumer society with its fetishist commodity cult. All of this happened during a period that was characterized by a steady growth of capitalist economies. When salaries did not stop rising and the shops were full of every kind of goods available for reasonable prices, people could afford to protest against consumerism and the dehumanizing effects of capitalism.

In 1973, however, the oil crisis came. The first serious economic depression of the developed market societies took place over the following two years, and industrial production declined by almost 10 percent, provoking deep doubts about the future of the Western affluence. In many industrialized countries, public welfare programs were stopped, and the unemployment rate began to rise. Although the economy recovered very quickly, the optimism of the fifties and sixties was replaced by a sense of crisis, increased still further by the new insights into the ecological by-products of modern industrial production. At the same time, the materialist orientation of the postwar decades with its cult of money, wealth, and consumer goods gave way to a more idealist, but also pessimist world view that had grown out of the culture revolution movements of the 1960s. And as the golden age of the twentieth century came to an end, in anthropology the interest in cargo cults began to decline. Other topics seemed to be more important now, such as the culture materialist school's consideration of the input-output ratio in different cultures and on the ecological frontiers of economic growth (cf. Harris 1975; Sahlins 1972).

III

The bizarre and exotic Melanesian cargo cults so many anthropologists of the prospering postwar period were fascinated by are indeed a "distorting mirror" in which we can recognize a familiar image of contemporary Western society, of its hopes, desires, and fears projected on to foreign cultures. Although we are reluctant to identify with this image, cargoism was a kind of behavior dominating Western societies in the first postwar decades. Viewed from a certain historical distance, the pursuit of wealth and money and the cult of prestigious consumer goods were characteristic features of this period. In Germany, the almost neurotic obsession by such material goals proved to be a means for suppressing the nation's criminal national-socialist past and for regaining the lost state of equality among its neighbors. If East Florinese anthropologists identify the symbols of postwar German coins as cargoist, they are not far away from reality. The proof of this interpretation was given by the events of 1989. And when in 2002, almost thirteen years later, the Deutsche mark was abolished and replaced by the Euro as a common European currency, a kind of apocalyptic feeling obsessed many Germans, an anxiety that the period of prosperity had come to an end. On the other hand, the complex religious and nativistic movements that had emerged in Melanesia since the arrival of European colonialists were identified, in Western anthropology, from the late forties, as "cargo cults" by only one—and not always the predominant one—of their many features. Was it pure accident that the first person who used this label in print was neither a missionary nor an anthropologist but an Australian planter and businessman (cf. Lindstrom 1993: 15–23)? This does not mean that the desire of receiving European goods did not play an important role in Melanesian anticolonial movements. Without a doubt, many of them were cargoist. It only means that the reification of these diverse movements as "cargo cults" could only happen because there was a very similar kind of materialist orientation and desire in contemporary Western society. But if my argument is right, it would be an intriguing question to discuss where the revival of interest in cargoism we can observe during the last ten years and demonstrated by this volume as well really stems from.

Notes

1. For another variant of this myth, obviously widespread in Eastern Indonesia, but without the idea that the islanders' source of wealth was stolen by European intruders, see Barnes (1974: 107–109).

2. For an interpretation of Melanesian cargo cults as "experimental ethnographies" see Jebens and Kohl (1999).

3. This tends to be overlooked by critics of the process of "othering" such as Hermann (present volume).

4. Quoted by Wolf (1999: 198).

themes from the state's cargo cult of the modern.[2] This is what I argue happened in Maluku in 1999: local millenarianism was given renewed voice and legitimacy by tapping into and redirecting state millenarianism.

The local process of emulation and redirection was, however, not a conscious act of inversion or subversion, and the theoretical goal of the chapter is to caution against any facile ascription of a hidden logic of resistance to millenarian narratives, in general, and the Halmaheran millenarianism, in particular. It is hardly unprecedented to caution against romanticizing resistance (Abu-Lughod 1990; Brown 1996; Ortner 1995), but the point bears repetition in the context of studies of cargo cults and millenarianism, where the tendency to excavate hidden logics of resistance or narratives of critique is still prevalent. I argue that the millenarian narratives in Halmahera clearly inflect Indonesian state notions of modernity and in the process alter and bend these notions, but I maintain that translating these alterations as being moments of resistance or critique would misread both the tenor and the logic of Halmaheran millenarianism.

Divine Apparitions

Before going into the specifics of this logic, however, I will provide a brief overview of the climate of anxiety that was generated in Halmahera in early August 1999 by rumors of the violence in Ambon. Although Halmahera lies some 500 kilometers from Ambon in the north of what was until October 1999 the province of Maluku (figure 6.1), the events in Ambon were nevertheless of great concern to people in Halmahera, because many people feared that the violence between Christians and Muslims would spread to engulf the entire province and possibly the whole country. As it turned out, their fear was well founded. Fanned by a dispute over the location of the boundaries of a new district in the central part of Halmahera in August 1999, sporadic clashes erupted throughout Halmahera and other islands of North Maluku over the following months. By late October, the death toll was in the dozens and the number of internally displaced people was more than 10,000. Whatever the sociological causes of each individual riot, the riots cemented in the public imagination the view that they were part of a pattern of religious conflict instigated by outside provocateurs. In late December 1999 suspicion and paranoia was endemic, fueled by constant rumors of imminent attack by the religious Other. In the predominantly Muslim district capitals of Ternate and Tidore, Christians were being attacked and forced into internal displacement after a pamphlet had raised the specter of a plan for the Christianization of North Maluku (Bubandt, forthcoming), while in Tobelo Christians attacked and killed several hundred Muslims after rumors of an alleged "Bloody Christmas" attack by Muslims had galvanized their violent resolve. As violence continued into the year 2000 and the death toll on the island climbed to several thousand, the North Malukan conflict threatened to destabilize the political security of the whole country when thousands of Muslim protesters during a demonstration in Jakarta on January 7, 2000, called for a *jihad* to stop what they saw as a Christian massacre of Muslims. The arrival of Laskar Jihad troops from Java and Sumatra to Maluku and North Maluku in April 2000 was not only a national embarrassment for President Abdurrahman Wahid; it also further buttressed religious opposition and complicated the reconciliation process that began in 2001. When the state of civil emergency that

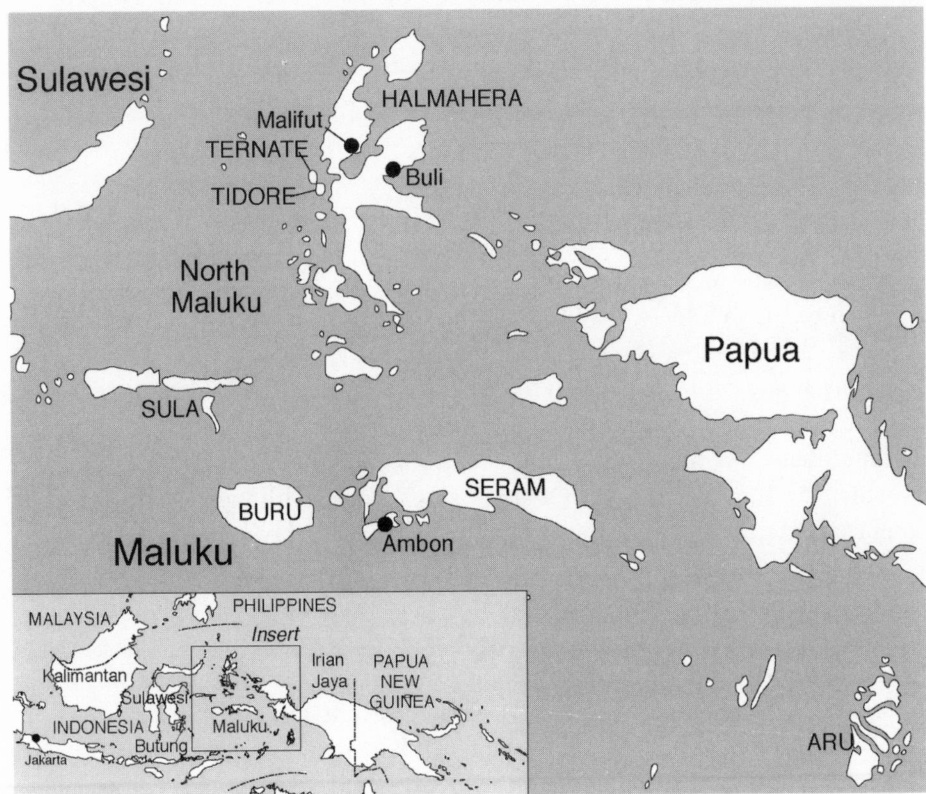

Figure 6.1 Maluku and North Maluku.

had been in place for three years was lifted in mid-2003, the official death toll from for the fighting in North Maluku, the first province to be established after the fall of the Suharto regime in May 1998, was 2,083, and the number of internally displaced people was an astonishing 266,137, roughly a quarter of the total population of the province (ICG 2002: 18). Religion was not the spark for fighting, as international nongovernmental organization reports also point out (ICG 2000: 6). Rather, the conflict was anticipated by and came to make sense within increasingly paranoid imaginings made up of apocalyptic narratives, shadowy provocateurs, and political hearsay.

It was in this setting that tensions rose during the month of August 1999 in Buli, a village cluster with a religiously mixed population of about 2000 on the east coast of Halmahera. Daily media reports from the unrest in Ambon were augmented by rumors that described the violence in Ambon in horrific detail and claimed the number of casualties was of catastrophic proportions—there were, for instance, stories of thousands, even tens of thousands, of Ambonese orphans being given away to strangers by their desperate families. As reports of tensions in a number of Halmaheran villages also began to appear, there was a clear sense of apprehension. For the roughly 700 Christians in the village of Buli Asal, this apprehension was substantiated by Christian expectations of an imminent Second Coming of Christ.

In this climate of anxiety, God was spotted on the beach near Buli Asal in early August. A group of Christian women, collecting coconuts for sale on the weekly market, were the first to meet him. His silvery hair reached down to his shoulders, his black clothes tied by a simple sash around his waist. Significantly, the man had a skin infection (known in Moluccan Malay as *kaskado*), a clear sign that it was God, because He always chooses to appear in a humble state, often afflicted with this socially disabling skin disease. As the women approached the man, he asked for a coconut, which he then pierced with a single grass straw. Although he thus displayed extraordinary abilities—repeated later when he showed enormous strength by lifting a large bag of coconuts with one hand—he made no predictions and no prophecies, nor did he reveal himself as the Christian God. Although there was a great deal of confusion and speculation as to the portent of this encounter, people still surmised that the man was in fact God. This assumption was based on a recent history of appearances by the heavenly Father on the island of Halmahera. Only three months earlier, another persona of the Holy Trinity had appeared to a group of Muslim men from a neighboring village. The men had been transporting a stranger by boat to the village, when he suddenly raised his arms to reveal stigmata on his hands. At that moment, a gust of wind had materialized to carry the boat to its destination at great speed. Rumor back in Buli Asal had it that the men—despite being Muslim—had immediately recognized the man as the Christian Savior, and, although the story did not relate the men's own interpretations of this, the Christian community saw the appearance of Jesus in this case as in all others as a harbinger of Rapture. Such appearances were thus not new. Over the past few years, God had appeared to Buli villagers in one form or another many times, but the frequency of appearances seemed to many people to be on the rise. A young woman who cooked for the mining exploration team that camped near the village had, that same week, experienced several visions of a woman holding out a baby boy to her. But each time she reached out to take the baby she presumed was Jesus, she had fainted.

The increased frequency of divine appearances accorded with the heightened sense of expectancy and anxiety that had grown not only in Buli Asal or Halmahera but throughout much of Indonesia since the onset of the economic and political crisis in October 1997. This climate had been further intensified in Buli Asal by the outbreak of sectarian violence in Ambon in January 1999. The violent clashes had died down for a few months in the middle of the year, but the latest appearances of God coincided with a savage renewal of violence, intensely covered by the media, in early August. Thus, by the end of the year, the death toll in the Ambon violence had risen from 450 to well above 1,500. In keeping with the notion that the latest appearances of God in Buli were signs of extraordinary circumstances, God lingered in the area—after initially appearing to the group of women collecting coconuts.

A few days later, on August 6, a young boy returned excitedly from a solitary fishing trip to report that he too had encountered what appeared to be God. God had spoken to him, telling him that he was a Bugis man who was on his way to the next village. The man seemed extraordinary, even frightening, to the boy, and when he suddenly brandished a knife, the boy had run back to the village. The information that the man was of Bugis ethnic origin generated an alternative explanation in the village. It was still entirely possible that he was in fact God and merely claimed to be a poor Bugis traveler in order to test the people he encountered. Such trials of faith are quite standard to local visions of God. Often God will test the generosity of those experiencing apparitions by appearing as a poor, decrepit person who initially asks for food before revealing himself. The *kaskado* skin disease, which normally evokes strong rejection, is also part of such a trial of tolerance. Appearing as a Bugis in an ethnically charged situation might just be part of this trial pattern. It was now also possible, however, that the man was a Muslim provocateur sent to Buli Asal to torch the local Church and thus bring the interethnic and religious violence that plagued Ambon to Buli. The knife seemed to confirm this, and the more story of the man's encounter with the boy spread through the village, the more erratic and threatening his behavior became. Salomon, a respected hunter with knowledge of fighting magic, set out to find the man. The idea was that if Salomon was unable to find him, he had probably magically disappeared—evidence that he was indeed God. If Salomon did find him, the man was probably a political agent and, if so, knowledge of fighting magic, of which Buli Asal people like to pride themselves, would be necessary for the fight that might ensue. As it happened, however, the outcome proved to be much more peaceful and mundane, if still interesting.

The man, it turned out, was neither a god nor an *agent provocateur*, but still an unusual person. He was indeed of Bugis ethnic origin and came from the South Sulawesi island of Butung. His tendency to aimlessly repeat the last words of the questions addressed to him (part of the enigmatic behavior that had initially marked him as a divine being) as well as his fits of rage, during which he swore and uttered obscenities obsessively, suggest that he was afflicted by the cultural syndrome known in Indonesia as *latah* (see Geertz 1968; Winzeler 1995). Symptomatically close to La Tourette's syndrome, sufferers of which also often display socially inappropriate behavior such as swearing, compulsive uttering of obscenities, and obsessive physical ticks, *latah* is widespread in Southeast Asia but is unknown in Buli Asal. This explanation, therefore, was of little interest to my informants. To most Buli Asal people, the man was simply "mad" *(pongpongol)*.

Madness may have a number of causes, ranging from spiritual interference to sorcery *(mahapayao)* and witchcraft *(mahagua)*, but it is not usually associated with divinity. It is merely a symptom of one of the many illnesses that plague and interrupt everyday life. The madness of this stranger represented, however, an urgent, hermeneutic problem. His madness could either be the shroud of divinity or the cloak of a hostile political strategy. Madness in this case invited both a spiritual narrative that apotheosized the madman and a narrative of social and ethnic exclusion (see Foucault 1973). As such, the madman on the beach was revealing of the transformative effects of millenarian belief in the province of Maluku in 1999. The two assumptions about the identity of the *latah* man—that he was God or that he was a Bugis provocateur—show the way the violence in Ambon was woven into apocalyptic scenarios about an imminent Day of Judgment. In these apocalyptic scenarios, social divisions were redrawn and radicalized. To understand how this happened, we need to look at the complex background of the violence.

Rumors of the Ambon Violence

The Ambon violence reflected a double set of oppositions. Portrayed in both the national and international media as a religious conflict between Christians and Muslims, the sectarian violence was also founded upon local Ambonese resentment against immigrant merchants from South Sulawesi, who as peddlers of anything from plastic kitchenware and clothes to shark fins and bêche-de-mer had cornered much of the regional trade. In addition to being conspicuous traders of cheap but highly desired consumer goods, the migrants from South Sulawesi were also resented (and envied) because they made up a significant proportion of the police force in Maluku. The popular label for this resentment, found throughout much of eastern Indonesia, is "*bahaya BBM*," the danger of BBM, "BBM" being an acronym for the three major ethnic groups of South and Southeast Sulawesi: the Bugis, Butung, and Makassar people. Despite the fertile grounds for an "ethnification" of the unrest, the religious aspects of the violence received most attention, and throughout Maluku the violence came to be read as a religious conflict, a reading inspired in no small measure by the media. In light of the even distribution of Christians and Muslims in the province, there was much anxiety that the violence—at this stage conceived almost exclusively as religiously motivated—would spread to the rest of Maluku and pit Christian and Muslim neighbors against each other. For the national media, the religious aspects of the violence echoed the politicization of religion surrounding both the general election in June and the debate leading up to the presidential election in October 1999. The violence in Maluku seemed therefore to realize the specter of a religious civil war, and this was the tone of media reports in August. This tone merely confirmed local apprehensions in Halmahera that the Ambon violence was contagious and that its spread, as part of an apocalyptic renewal, was ultimately inevitable.

The suspicion that the stranger on the Buli Asal beach might be a rogue Muslim troublemaker reflected the fear of contagion following reports of religious clashes in Halmahera as well. Buli Asal is at the southern extension of a compound of three neighboring villages, two of which are Christian and the third Muslim. All Buli to whom I spoke in August—Muslims as well as Christians—were adamant that violence between these villages was unthinkable, because intermarriage and a common mythological link to the past caused them to regard each other as brothers. The possibility of outside provocation was, however, a constant theme in the news reports about the Ambon violence, and this produced some anxiety, because it introduced the possibility that dark, unknown forces would instigate the violence everyone thought impossible. The rumors of provocation circulated mainly in the media. Thus, the military radio reported in July 1999 that they had confiscated Israeli-manufactured weapons among the groups fighting. There were also rumors of boatloads of expatriate Dutch Malukan killing teams arriving in Ambon at night from Holland and disappearing before dawn. Their supposed aim was to reignite the Malukan independence movement (RMS), which still has many supporters in the community of Malukans who were given political asylum in Holland in 1950 (Chauvel 1990). Both reports were later denied by the army radio, but conspiracy theories still ran deep in most people's understanding of the violence. Many Indonesians were thus convinced of some level of provocation—even outright instigation—of the violence in January by sections within the army in an attempt to sabotage the national elections in June, a charge that was explicitly stated by Abdurrahman Wahid, then head of the Muslim organization, Nahdlatul Ulama, and later president of the country. Muslim leaders in Ambon charged that boatloads of Ambonese hoodlums had provoked the violence. These Ambonese gangsters had made up the core of private guard organizations in the Jakartan entertainment and gambling industry until they were forced to leave the capital after an outbreak of violence in the Ketapang district of Jakarta in December 1998. The gangsters were associated in two rival groups, one Christian and one mainly Muslim, and they were supposed to have taken their conflict back to Ambon with them. Possibly, the rumors said, they were paid to do so, either by people from the political youth organization, Pemuda Pancasila, who had connections to former President Suharto, or by an Ambonese member of the national parliament. Again, Abdurrahman Wahid was one of the people pointing the finger. From its inception, the Ambon violence was in other words an issue in national politics. The many conspiracy theories were integrated locally in Maluku and became part of the dynamics that generated the violence, because each group saw itself as the victim of instigation and provocation.

In their report on the violence, Human Rights Watch have termed the two main theories on the origins of the violence "the separatist theory" and "the gangster theory" (Human Rights Watch 1999), but for the population of Maluku the realm of rumors and theories were not so clearly distinguishable. Rather, they fused into narratives that made local sense. In Buli Asal, people knew that some instigation was probably involved, and they had enough access to the electronic media to be able to see that the Ambon violence was intimately part of national politics both before and after the national elections in June 1999. The suspicion of a conspiracy behind the violence emanating from within the political opposition was clearly an open challenge to the (then still) ruling Golkar Party under President B. J. Habibie. As it filtered down to the regional and local level, this sense of a political conspiracy came to be a narrative of local conflict. It is in this light that the suspicion that the man roaming the beachfront near Buli was a rogue Bugis agent provocateur should be seen. Throughout most of Maluku, people of Bugis origin form a large body of the police force, and alleged police brutality engenders strong resentment against the Bugis and Butung communities, who also control much of the local and regional trade. In 1996, a young Bugis police officer had shot and killed the village head of the Muslim part of Buli with his service revolver over a trivial argument about fasting during Ramadan. This had stirred strong anger toward the Bugis population in the area, most of whom had moved to the district capital to be protected by the police.

Interpreting the violence in Ambon as an ethnic confrontation between the Ambonese and immigrants from Sulawesi (BBM) seemed thus to ring true with a local history of resentment toward the Bugis and Butung people. Opting for an ethnic rather than religious interpretation of the violence was also determined by the feeling in Buli that an explicit assumption of a religious reading of the conflict would threaten their own sense of identity, cutting the Buli community in half. Ideally then, Buli people had to reject the image of a religious war in Ambon, if they wanted to uphold a sense of community.

Ambon and Armageddon

The refusal of the religious aspects of the Ambon violence was problematic, because it was challenged by a powerful narrative that saw the violence as a portent and actualization of an apocalyptic battle between Christians and Muslims. During 1999, this narrative was disseminated in Christian congregations throughout Halmahera by prophetic letters and cassette tapes. One of these stories told of Ria's encounter with Jesus, told by Ria herself on a cassette tape that was copied from person to person and that I copied from the minister in a neighboring village. The minister had obtained it herself at the previous church council meeting. On the tape, Ria, a sixteen-year-old student, related how Jesus had appeared to her on January 20, 1999—a day after fighting broke out in Ambon. Ria was from the island of Halmahera, in the north of Maluku, but stayed with her grandmother in Ambon while attending high school. Ria and her grandmother had sought refuge from the fighting in a military barracks when Jesus woke her up just after midnight. Jesus had told her that the year 2000 would mark the beginning of a new era, but the time before this renewal would be marred by bloodshed and fighting. Much calamity was still to come, but Jesus had a task for Ria: he would show her heaven, and it was her duty then to tour the Christian communities in the Ambon region and tell them of his Coming. Over the following six nights, Ria was taken to heaven. In heaven, she learned that the earth was still full of sin. It was the duty of all people to choose the narrow path of righteousness, since all other paths lead to hell. She was shown the nature of divine punishment for sinners. Hoodlums were tied by their hands and feet, while the lips of those who had engaged in idle talk and gossip had been padlocked. The most severe punishment was, however, reserved for Muhammad, the holy prophet of the Islamic faith, who for eternity was doomed to turn a large wheel, and was denied food and drink. The sin of Muhammad was unforgivable, Jesus informed Ria, for he had disputed the authority of the Christian God. Whereas all Muslims were thus barred from entering paradise, Jesus assured Ria that all Christians who had died in Ambon were already enjoying the pleasures of heaven.

Ria's prophecy was clearly slanderous, even blasphemous, to Muslim ears. The people circulating the tapes therefore took great care to whom they played Ria's story. Coming so early in the conflict, her story gave a particular reading of the violence that incited the Christian communities to see it as a harbinger of the Second Coming. Ria herself helped spread this interpretation, because Jesus assigned her to tour the Christian communities wracked by violence and tell her prophecy. Ria took this divine assignment very seriously and did tell her story to many of the congregations afflicted by the violence.

The Year 2000 and Indonesian Modernity

The inflammatory incorporation of Muslims into the millenarian narrative was new, but otherwise Ria's encounter with God repeated a standard Halmaheran idea about sinners and their punishment in the upcoming apocalypse. Rumors of the end of the world have emerged in Halmahera at intervals since at least the eighteenth century, but they were particularly intensive during the period of conversion to Christianity after 1866 (Bubandt 1995). In Buli Asal, such rumors have appeared repeatedly since I began fieldwork in 1991. Buli apocalypticism is expressed in Christian concepts and emphasizes the unworthiness of the locals to be accepted into the new kingdom of God because of their supposed stubborn maintenance of pre-Christian beliefs and practices associated with witchcraft *(mahagua)*, sorcery *(mahapayo)*, divination *(failál)*, and the worship of ancestors *(smengit)* and animal spirits *(suang)*. The stress is therefore on the destruction of their world and the death of all Buli sinners, which is bound to accompany the Second Coming.

The climate of expectation characterizing Buli apocalypticism is, however, a far cry from the frantic atmosphere that one has otherwise come to expect of cargo cults or millennial movements. "Millennial fervor" would be far too strong a word to characterize the climate in Buli. There is no clear millennial core group and thus no distinct social imprint of these millennial beliefs, just as there is no prophet and no doctrine. The stories about God's appearance, whether in local apparitions or in regional testimonies, provide instead a tonality of millennial possibility to everyday life, but one that is neither dominant nor uncontested. This "tone" to social discourse in the village is sometimes voiced seriously, at other times parodied, derided, or ignored.

The recent violence in Ambon had, however, injected a heightened sense of anxiety, and at times even terror, into the social climate that made the work of interpreting the signs of the present for their message about the future more urgent. In this heightened climate of expectation, there were, however, few guidelines. Buli apocalypticism does not spring from any elaborate cosmology, nor does it result in any sustained social movement. Instead, it is linked to fragments of local mythology that are simultaneously believed and derided as expressions of ancestral stupidity. What characterizes the accounts of God's appearances and other signs of the Second Coming is above all their lack of explicit meaning or clear message—a lack that neither local myth nor Christian biblical texts are able to remedy. As the appearance of God on the beach illustrates, divine apparitions are always enigmatic in their deficiency of meaning. If God speaks at all in these encounters, it is always in brief code. Thus, the work of assigning meaning to these portents of the apocalypse has ample interpretative room.

Some interpretative guidance has however emerged from an unexpected quarter. In recent years, the timing of this apocalypse has become synonymous with the year 2000—a date to which the Ambon violence seemed to be eerily timed and that it thereby seemed indirectly to confirm. As I have described elsewhere (Bubandt 1998), the association of the Christian apocalypse with the year 2000 is not merely based on a Christian narrative, but is the incorporation of development rhetoric by the Indonesian state that—until the recent economic crisis—spoke of the year 2000 as the time for an Indonesian economic "takeoff" and the beginning of an era of modernity and globalization. This state millenarianism is itself, no doubt, related to the traditional millenarianism of Javanese cosmology.[3] The New Order government, whose rule ended so abruptly in May 1998 in the wake of the Asian economic crisis, transformed this millenarianism into what Richard Franke (1972) calls a "cargo cult of economic development." In this developmentalist ideology, state legitimacy came to rest on its ability to ensure continuous economic development by attracting foreign loans and investment to stimulate domestic growth without succumbing to a "laissez-faire capitalism."[4] Patrick Guinness notes how there is a marked emphasis on material improvement in New Order development ideology and notes that the modern consumerism engendered by this emphasis has changed the material conditions for understanding identity and ethnicity in Indonesia: "Television, newspapers, pop music and magazines, motorized transport, western dress, school or civil uniforms, refrigeration, fast foods, and many other elements of contemporary consumer society have introduced new elements into the cultural diversity of Indonesian society" (Guinness 1994: 269).

Modernity as Cargo

It is thus fairly obvious that the ethnic prejudice exhibited by Malukans against Bugis, Butung, and Makassar traders is fueled by resentment of their better access to desired consumer goods, which they sell to locals throughout eastern Indonesia. This, however, does not make the resentment "cargoist," and there is much to be said for Ton Otto's warning against the tendency to find cargo cults everywhere, because such percolation empties the concept of all analytical usefulness in Melanesia (Otto 1999), while uncritical use often remains too naively innocent of the discursive genealogy of the concept (Lindstrom 1993). As the contributions to this volume clearly establish, this usage is colonially charged as well as both methodologically and epistemologically problematic.[5] Nevertheless, although the analysis of ethnic prejudice in Maluku is not helped by a reference to "cargo cults," some illumination of the millenarianism inherent in religious interpretation of the Maluku violence may, I will argue, be achieved by a passing use of the term "cargo cult" in a loosely analytical sense. I do not use the term in its formal ethnographic sense. Thus, my contribution to the critical reevaluation of cargo cult consists in moving the term beyond the geographic boundaries of traditional Melanesianist gate keeping. Although the danger in this is to aid the discursive construction of "cargo cults everywhere" (see Lindstrom 1993: 183; and present volume), the redeeming feature in this move is that it enables one to employ the critical analytic potential of cargo cult on aspects of the modern condition (see Dalton, present volume). This "export" should, however, be carried out with circumspection, because, as I argue toward the end of the chapter, the analytical propensity to see "cargo" as critique or resistance carries specific dangers of its own.

In taking cargo beyond Melanesia, I follow the lead of Jonathan Friedman, who uses "cargo" as a comparative analytical term that describes "a certain essence of the externality of social selfhood" (1994: 184). "Cargo" is the objectification of an imagined vital outside source to a local sense of identity. In this sense "cargo," or what Friedman argues might be called "post-cargo" (1994: 184), is an aspect of a specific type of (post)modern identity formation in which "the maintenance of self [depends] upon a flow of life-force from the outside, on the stable gaze of the authoritative other" (Friedman 1994: 249). In the Malukan and Indonesian context this "authoritative other" is the modern West *(barat)* or America, imagined icons of the modern world *(dunia modern)*. My point is thus, first, that the cargoist aspects of Indonesian millenarianism are tuned less to the acquisition of consumer goods than toward the expected arrival of an imagined, fetishized "modernity." This fetishization of modernity, which was particularly evident within Indonesian state rhetoric up until the fall of the New Order regime in 1998, is part of a global phenomenon that Michael Taussig calls a "third-world cult of the modern" (Taussig 1987: 278). Taussig uses this term to describe the magical faith in Western medicine among Putumayo peasants that exists despite a poor record of recovery in the health clinics. He suggests that the belief in the power of modern medicine is as magical as the belief in traditional medicine. The same faith in the magic of modernity is also evident in political ideas of development and national progress.

This leads me to my second point, namely, that the cargo cult of modernity in Indonesia perhaps derives less from a local millenarian tradition than from a reinterpretation of modernist millenarianism itself. The millenarian aspects of modernity are linked to its utopianism, expressed in the notion of progress and in what Jean Baudrillard calls an "aesthetic of rupture": "a freeing of subjectivity and a ceaseless quest for the new" (Kumar 1995: 95). Postcolonial governments have, of course, a tortured relationship with modernity, in view of their need to distance themselves from modernist colonial thought, on the one hand, and, in the case of Indonesia with its large Muslim population, from the moral decadence and political libertarianism of the late-modern West, on the other. But the bureaucrats who inherited the Dutch East Indies after the independence struggle were deeply influenced by modernist thought nonetheless (Holtzappel 1997), and they formed the linchpin in the utopian vision that modern Indonesian nationhood promotes.

The Simulacrum of "America"

The modern utopia with its emphasis on the plasticity of the human being, egalitarian order, and the transparency of society is highly reminiscent of the cargo cult, which also operates with an aesthetic of rupture, a reconstruction of space and time, and a utopian idea of sociality.[6] As a number of critical theorists have already pointed out, the Western fascination with Melanesian cargo cults may reflect cargo cult-like constructions of desire and hope within Western modernity itself, whether this hope and desire are related to utopian ideas of romantic love,[7] millenarian Christianity (N. Cohn 1970; McGinn 1995), the utopian project of discovery and colonialism (Huizer 1992: 109), the millenarian aspects of the notions of history and progress (Campion 1994; Tuveson 1972), or utopian capitalist consumerism.[8] After the end of World War II and the inauguration of the Bretton Woods accord, many aspects of cargoist capitalism have been exported as part of the "development project" (see McMichael 1996). Indeed, the construction of postcolonial nation-states as "third world" hinged on a projection of these nation-states as desiring of modernity. Part of the process of globalization might then be described as the troubled and complex internalization of this cargoist desire by such states.

Indonesia may serve as a case in point. Here the process of modernization is often conceptualized in terms that portray modernity as a category of cargo. In his article on the cargoism of Indonesian conceptions of development, Franke thus relates an experience he had in Central Java in the early 1970s: "A district staff member points his thumbs upwards—an Indonesian sign of approval—and exclaims: 'Wah, America, you people are really making it all possible.' By 'America' of course he means the foreign countries which have been pouring in funds since the establishment of the Suharto government, and by 'it' he means the new typewriters, adding machines, two-storey shopping centers, cars, motor-cycles, and even his superior's new jeep" (Franke 1972: 372). In the cargoism of modernity in Indonesia, "America" may thus at certain times function as an icon of modernity. This was the case for a Javanese district official in the early 1970s, and this is—with some modification—the case for many Christian Malukans in the late 1990s. Ria's prophecy was only one of several that I encountered in August 1999. Another was a letter in which Martina tells of her vision of Jesus. Jesus visited Martina three nights in a row in March 1999. He told her of imminent natural catastrophes that would presage the end of the world and instructed her in the proper precautions that believers should take to ensure their salvation. This involved holding hands and singing specific psalms praising the arrival of the Lord. On the second night, the prophecies of Jesus became more cryptic. He appeared to Martina holding a bucket. From the cement floor of her house, Jesus drew a bucket full of water. As he emptied the bucket in front of Martina, the water turned into small pieces of paper, each with writing on them. The wind immediately began carrying the pieces of paper away, but Martina managed to hold on to a single piece, inscribed on which was a single word: "America." Martina's vision ends here without any explanation as to the meaning of the inscription. The proper interpretation was, however, given by the ministers who circulated Martina's letter and the other prophecies in August: as the religious clashes between Christians and Muslims escalated into full-scale civil war, "America" would intervene to help the Christian community.

Local apocalyptic narratives in Maluku have for some time reversed the optimistic rhetoric of the state and turned modernity and globalization into ominous aspects of an imminent end to the world. The Ambon violence has been incorporated into these apocalyptic ideas of the end. In

Martina's and Ria's narratives the year 2000, which New Order rhetoric had established as the time for the arrival of modernity (see Bubandt 1998), was transformed into a time of destruction and renewal, of which a titanic battle between Muslims and Christians is the harbinger (Bubandt 2000).

The same type of transformation from national optimism to local pessimism is also evident in the notions attached to "America" as an icon. Despite the New Order government's emphasis on national self-determination and its critique of Western capitalist influence, America nevertheless functions, at least for some political technocrats and many of the sharply rising number of middle-class consumers, as an icon of modernity. The production and circulation of such ideological constructs were in fact basic to New Order rule. Using Baudrillard's concept of "simulacrum," Ariel Heryanto (1999a) contends that New Order rule was supported by its production of simulacra of fear such as "communism." One might argue along similar lines that "America" is a simulacrum of modernity and functions to bolster the New Order cultivation of specific ideological ideas about "progress" and "development" (Heryanto 1988; Van Langenberg 1986). This is a "third world" transformation of Baudrillard's observation that America is a hyperreality, a realized utopia (or dystopia, as the case may be), in which all the myths of modernity have become American myths (Baudrillard 1988). According to Baudrillard, America represents to the European observer "the original version of modernity," of which Europe with its past and traditions must forever be content to be a poor replica, a "dubbed or subtitled version" (Baudrillard 1988: 76). This sense of seeing the utopia of modernity realized elsewhere is even stronger, I would argue, in a marginal "third world" location such as Maluku, where developmentalist ideology has long since become internalized. Here "America" is a holographic third world image of the West, pasted from the millennial imaginings of modernity within Indonesian state rhetoric and adapted to a local version of Christian apocalyptic cosmology. "America" as it was embossed on the note in Martina's dream is thus a Christian objectification of both modernity and "the West."

Heryanto goes on to argue that the production of political simulacra ultimately subverted New Order authority by providing the context for parody (1999a: 163; see also Tsing 1993). In Martina's prophecy there is no parody, but there is at least a twist to the Indonesian state's "cult of the modern." Thus, in Martina's encounter with Jesus, "America" is not a simulacrum of modernity that supports state notions of development; instead, "America" (and its military power) becomes a Christian type of cargo associated with the breakup of the nation and the end of the world. This association between America and world destruction was firmly established in North Malukan memory during the last days of World War II, when American troops strafed and defeated the forces of the Japanese navy who had occupied eastern Indonesia for three years (Ricklefs 1981: 187). The memory of war has had a profound impact throughout the Pacific and has often been reported as influential in the transformation of millenarian movements (Keesing 1992; Stritecky 2001). The Gulf War was similarly interpreted in apocalyptic terms in Halmahera as well as elsewhere in Melanesia (see Robbins 1997: 13). The experience of fear and amazement associated with the wonders of American military might during and after World War II should therefore not be underestimated and probably prepared the ground for the reception in Halmahera of state developmentalist discourse. Modernity is first and foremost a characteristic of "the West," of which "America" is both the wondrous and frightening icon in Malukan eyes.

The ambivalence of "America" as an icon of modernity stems not only from its being simultaneously cargo and military salvation, but also from the experience that such salvation is attended by a great deal of destruction. "America" is associated with the same expectations of commodities, Christianity, and violence that also make modernity such an ambivalent entity among Christians in Halmahera.

Critique, Resistance, and Other "Chicago Cults"

The millenarian motives I have described achieve much of their symbolic form by mimicking modern, national discourses. It would be tempting to interpret this mimicry as part of a discourse of parody, critique, and defiance, even resistance. Such an interpretation would, however, be misleading. The mimicry of Malukan millenarianism does not harbor any sustained parody or critique of modernity or Western consumerism. Malukan millenarianism borrows from the state's cargoism of modernity, but it critiques neither state nor modernity. The last decade of the twentieth century saw an emerging critique of the resistance metaphor within anthropology.[9] The same period, however, also witnessed a renaissance of resistance studies, particularly in the field of what has recently been termed "occult economies" (Comaroff and Comaroff 1999), in which witchcraft alongside other "occult" practices such as sorcery, magic, and millenarianism are interpreted as "apt discourses" on globalization, capitalism, and other of "modernity's malcontents."[10] Though there is much to be said for these studies, I find that, despite their disclaimers, they are in danger of overly celebrating the grand-scale resistance aspects of local action to the detriment of detailed attention to the micropolitics of such action and beliefs (see also Ortner 1995). In seeing the continued viability of "occult economies" as being due to their capacity to speak to and against modernity, globalization, or capitalism, the conditions of possibility of these "occult economies" are reduced to their role vis-à-vis the supposedly more profound sociological realities of modernity and globalization. This view appears in other words to reintroduce a functionalist perspective on the so-called occult. "The new functionalism," as Marshall Sahlins (1993: 13) charges, "consists of translating the apparently trivial into the fatefully political." No one can accuse witchcraft or millenarian beliefs of being trivial, but there is as much danger in seeing fateful politics in the exotic as in the trivial. The danger is, to my mind, to deemphasize—once more—the interpretations of local actors of their own actions and beliefs and to see such actions and beliefs instead as thin veils of a greater and truer reality.[11] Perhaps "cargo cults" belong to the same type of phenomenon as "witchcraft," "millenarianism," or "devil fetishism" that an anthropology of critique and resistance has consistently construed to be "really" about something else (Taussig 1980)? In addition to being aware of the chauvinist and colonial legacy of the term "cargo cult,"[12] we need to be just as much on guard against the dangers of a postmodern or late-modern heroic ethics in our critical use of "cargo cult." In seeing cargo cults or other exotic phenomena as critiques of Western culture or bourgeois consumerism, whose critique are we really voicing?

According to John and Jean Comaroff, the historical reconstruction of hidden narratives of defiance from the colonial archives is what anthropology is all about. Discovering the defiance of the "occult" is a way of revealing the apparently exotic as an active engagement with the modern world and should be part of anthropology's escape from exoticism. The reconstruction of the hidden narratives of defiance, they maintain, is part of a common charter for anthropology and is therefore far more than what they call "a Chicago-cult" (Comaroff and Comaroff 1992: 45). Comaroffian anthropology is full of important insights, and the Comaroffs' attempt to blur the distinction between magic and modernity is laudable, but the question whether the perspective on cargo cults (or witchcraft or millenarianism) as cultural critique is indeed not "Chicago-cult" more than anything else still needs to be asked. Is it not, as Michael Brown suggests, primarily the anthropologists' own conscience that is being allayed when we describe acts of resistance? Thus, finding grass-roots resistance and defiance everywhere is perhaps a way, as he puts it, to "reassure ourselves that the pursuit of what might seem to be esoteric ethnographic detail is really a form of high-minded public service" (Brown 1996: 730). This is not to deny that millenarianism or cargo cults in some cases may harbor aspects of defiance and resistance. The problem lies in the tendency to take such aspects, which remain exterior to and hidden from the lived reality of millenarianism, as the social raison d'être for the "occult."

I thus might construe the Malukan appropriations of the "cargoism of modernity" as parody and incisive critique. Perhaps the optimism of state ideas about modernity was being criticized as it was turned into apocalyptic pessimism in Maluku? Such a reading is appealing but underestimates the ideological impact of state discourse (even after the fall of Suharto not all has changed), and would also deny the reality and transformative capacity of the millenarian motives themselves. The millenarian narratives were real (although contested). They were not constructed or perceived as "critiques" of state rule, modernity, or globalization, and there was little claptrap, parody, or irony in people's waiting for "America." Seeing the millenarian beliefs about the violence as "statements of defiance" would ignore the extent to which the people I knew in Buli were terrorized by them. There were no heroics in the millenarian reception of the visions of Jesus or of the apparitions of God—only ambivalence and angst. Making their angst into "statements of defiance," "apt discourses," or "cultural critique" might make me feel good, but it would not, I believe, do justice to their experience of the violence. The millennial motives that came to be central to the Malukan experience of the violence were themselves lived, complex social realities that had transformative, if often unexpected, effects.

These effects cannot be reduced to having a single significance or meaning for the people involved. Buli people were thus ambivalent about the millenarian motive. On the one hand, many people were attracted to it "poetically." As Charles Jones (1962) suggests, the near universal occurrence of millenarian beliefs may at least in part be due to their inherent narrative appeal. In Buli Asal, the millenarian reading of the Ambon violence thus seemed to correspond to a general apocalyptic tone in local expectations toward the future. Whereas the previous apocalyptic scenario saw the local Christian villagers as the sinners about to be punished at the upcoming Day of Judgment (see Bubandt 1998), the millenarian expectations associated with the Ambon violence tended to displace the problem of sin onto the Muslim community. This displacement of sin from Self to "Other" carried, no doubt, some appeal in itself. On the other hand, Buli people were opposed to the religious explanation because it meant a violation of their own sense of ethnic identity. This identity was itself in large part the result of New Order reifications of culture and tradition that strategically downplayed religious affiliation (see Kipp 1993). Constituting Muslim Buli people as "Other" was thus inherently problematic. The ethnic interpretation was appealing to many people because it harmonized with their resentment against Bugis traders and police officers. The two interpretations stood in a tense relation to each other, a relationship that became increasingly strained as most of the Malukan population opted for the religious, millenarian interpretation that promoted the spread of the violence from Ambon to the rest of the province.

Millenarian motives were not alone in accounting for and promoting the violence. The various social groups nationally and regionally understood and utilized the violence in very different ways: the political opposition in Jakarta, for instance, saw the violence as instigated by the old guard around Suharto and used it as a way to discredit the "status quo" government that ruled until October 1999. Meanwhile the local Ambonese elite used the violence in its own ways as part of a regional struggle for political power (see van Klinken 1999). But where elite manipulation forms part of the social landscape of the violence, it does not in and of itself explain the explosiveness of the emergence and perpetuation of the violence in Maluku. To understand these dynamics, it is necessary to turn to the local, Malukan experience of the violence and explicate its narrativization. As I have tried to show, it is only by paying attention to this experience and its narrativization that an understanding of the transformative dynamics of violence is possible. By being inscribed into a millenarian scenario that pitted Christians and Muslims against each other, the violence was accelerated. As part of her assignment from Jesus, Ria for instance preached what Norman Cohn (1970: 286) calls "phantasies of a final, exterminatory struggle" to the Ambonese communities that had experienced the first outbreak of violence in January 1999, thereby providing a narrative that made sense of the violence and that no doubt fueled further violence. The millenarian reinscription also had profound effects on the spread of the violence from Ambon to Halmahera after August 1999. The process I have described is essentially the sedimentation of a millenarian logic during August 1999. This logic, which anticipated "a final, exterminatory struggle," legitimated the "preemptive" strikes by Christians on Muslims throughout Halmahera in December 1999, in which hundreds of people were killed within the span of a few weeks (AsiaNow 2000). Although the symbolic form of this logic was borrowed from state discourse, the tone was not one of critique, but one of anxiety, confusion, and—as the violence appeared to become inevitable—terror.

One point remains, though. The village cluster of Buli never experienced any violence. Of the more than twelve districts in Halmahera, the district of Maba with its capital of Buli was the only one that escaped sectarian violence, despite the prevalence of millenarian discourse in the villages. The possible explanation for this, in regional terms, unique situation are varied and complex—after all, accounting for why violence did *not* happen is at least as difficult as explaining why it did. The relative isolation of the district; the intensity of cooperation between government officials and community leaders of both faiths to control the circulation of rumor as well as the influx of outsiders; and the absence of the particular ethnic groups that had been the main protagonists in clashes elsewhere—in particular Tobelo and Makian people—were no doubt conducive to maintaining the peace in an extremely tense situation. The ability of the community to prevent religious dualism from gaining the upper hand by actively cultivating a localist and ethnic discourse that ostracized outsiders but unified the community across religious boundaries may also have played a role. I have suggested that there were compelling local reasons to opt for an "exemplary dualism" based on ethnicity, despite the narrative appeal of the millenarian narrative that constructed a religiously based dualism.[13] Elsewhere in Maluku and North Maluku, religiously mixed communities had also sworn never to fight their "brothers" next door. Buli was one of the few places where the communities managed to keep that promise.

Conclusion

The aim of this chapter has been to focus on the often-ignored link between violence and millenarianism. Communal violence clearly reflects the surrounding political situation and speaks to aspects of both power and hegemony. It is equally true, however, that violence is sometimes informed—indeed produced—by the millenarian logic of prophecy. Political action and violence were thus in Maluku continuously inscribed within a millenarian narrative. This millenarian inscription both legitimated and promoted the violence. Millennial discourse was in other words constitutive of the violence and its unfolding in Maluku (see also

Kapferer 1997). Violence thereby became the political praxis of millenarianism. The unexpected escalation and savagery of the violence are linked to the increasing legitimacy and monopoly of the religious interpretation of the violence, which in turn was increasingly associated with a millenarian scenario of an apocalyptic battle between Muslims and Christians.[14]

Ethnic oppositions clearly played into and motivated the conflict, and in many contexts ethnic and religious oppositions fused into an image of an ethnic and religious "Other." As I have shown, this fusion was impossible in Buli. There ethnicity acted instead as an alternative explanation of and point of reference in relation to the Ambon violence. The appeal of the religious explanation lay in its millenarian narrativity, a narrative not attached to ethnic opposition. The central role of both ethnicity and religion in the current climate in Indonesia has a particular political history. It can be traced to the uneven and often contradictory political construction of ethnicity and religion during the New Order rule, when these forms of identity were both showcased and suppressed, depending on context. The growing appeal to religious rather than ethnic identity currently witnessed throughout Indonesia is no doubt related to an increasing politicization of religious affiliation during the 1990s and particularly during the "reformation" period after May 1998 (Hefner 2000, 2002). I have argued that a further reason for its appeal was that the narrative of modernism, which remained dominant in Indonesian state rhetoric despite the global crisis of modernity, fertilized (and thus implicitly legitimized) the millenarian scenario associated with a religious identity to the detriment of others. The narrative of religious opposition transformed the cargo of modernity into the postcargo of identity formation and, in the process, became an active force in reshaping the communal violence.

The origin of the millenarian interpretation of the Ambon violence was local as well as Christian and "modern." It would thus be possible to situate the millenarian logic within a local apocalyptic tradition in northern Maluku that is traceable in the colonial archives back to the Nuku revolt in 1780 (Andaya 1993; Bubandt 1995). One might also opt to highlight the Christian motives in the millenarian narrative and see them as part of a strategy to assert a new identity based on religious affiliation in a politically unstable post-Suharto context, where religion has become the most significant marker of identity. In this chapter, I have for the most part followed a third strand in the genealogy of millennial motives, claiming that they shared more than a passing similarity with the millenarianism of modernity propagated by the New Order state discourse. My argument is that the millenarian interpretations not only reflect local tradition or Christianity, but are part of a discourse of mimicry of the "cargoism of modernity" promulgated by official state rhetoric and disseminated by the national media in Indonesia.

In line with the attempts of other contributors to this volume to deconstruct the links between cargo cults and modernity,[15] I suggest that modernity itself is a millenarian project and that these aspects of modernity are further embellished by "third world" developmentalism. The type of cargo cults one encounters in the rhetoric of third world nation-states incorporates, transforms, and amplifies the millenarianism inherent in modernity. In the Malukan narratives, I suggest, "America" has come to be a simulacrum of millenarian modernity. America in a sense is the cargo of modernity. Perhaps the fashioning of America as a simulacrum of modernity (and the West) often associated with apocalypse is not restricted to Indonesia, but is a global symbolic phenomenon, visible also in Iranian ritual burnings of "Stars and Stripes" and "Uncle Sam" cardboard figures during the revolution as well as in European fears of "McDonaldization" or American cultural hegemony. The political semiotics of each of these instances are different. As Michael Billig suggests, the global flows of images, ideas, and products associated with "American culture" mean that "America" may be flagged not as a particular place but may be "universalized as the world" (Billig 1995: 129). This "banal" reflection in language of a new form of geopolitical hegemony is, however, not straightforward. In some intellectual circles in Europe, "America" may be the sign of a particular and dreaded version of a globalized world, while in many "third world countries" the notion of "America" is metonymic of the West, indeed of Europe (Coronil 1996: 54). In Indonesia, rich elites conspicuously consume things "Western" or "American," as part of a new "Asian life style" (Heryanto 1999b: 169), whereas Christian villagers in North Maluku look to "America" as both an icon of Western global dominance and an instrument of cosmological retribution. I suggest it is necessary to pay attention to such processes of indigenization of notions of the global. The unfolding of the violence in Maluku shows how notions of the global are being domesticated to act as powerful icons for explaining and promoting local events, but without becoming allegories of resistance. Detailed inquiries into the role that the dynamics of domestication of the global play in the unfolding of political events on both a local and national level are, I would argue, an important dimension in remaking the discipline into "an anthropology of contemporaneous worlds" (Augé 1999).

Notes

A number of people took it upon themselves to read the chapter, comment on the argument, and correct its most glaring mistakes. For their patience and the incisiveness of their interventions, I wish to thank Bob Tonkinson, Martijn van Beek, Andreas Roepstorff, and Ton Otto, as well as the anonymous reader from the University of Hawai'i Press.

1. North Maluku was until late 1999 a regency in the province of Maluku and was thus, on the whole, governed from the provincial capital of Ambon. As a result of the decentralization policies implemented after 1999, however, North Maluku was declared a separate province in October 1999, as the first in a long series of regencies throughout Indonesia.

2. I use the term "cargo cult" in a loose and metaphorical, rather than a strict analytical, sense here. I will discuss and justify this usage later in the chapter.

3. See B. Anderson (1990), Helman (1988), and van der Kroef (1959).

4. See Guinness (1994: 303), Heryanto (1988), and Mackie and Macintyre (1994).

5. See also Hermann (1992b), Jaarsma (1997), Lattas (1992b), and McDowell (1988).

6. See Kempf (1992), Lattas (1998), and McDowell (1988).

7. See Crapanzano (present volume), Illouz (1997), and Lindstrom (1993, and present volume).

8. See Huizer (1992: 112), Otto (1999, and present volume), and Trompf (1990).

9. See Abu-Lughhod (1990), Brown (1996), and Keesing (1992).

10. See Comaroff (1985), Comaroff and Comaroff (1993), and Geschiere (1997, 1998).

11. See also Englund and Leach (2000).

12. See Hermann, Kaplan, and Lindstrom, all in the present volume.

13. On exemplary dualism, see Anthony and Robbins (1999: 267): "In exemplary dualist worldviews, contemporary socio-political or socioreligious forces are transmogrified into absolute contrast categories embodying moral, eschatological, and cosmic polarities upon which hinge the millennial destiny of humankind."

14. This argument is supported by field data from Halmahera. Although I believe the actors in the Ambon violence were as influenced by these millenarian interpretations as their northerly neighbors in Halmahera, this will have to be confirmed by people who know the Ambon area better than I do. See van Klinken (2001).

15. See Dalton, Lindstrom, Otto, and Robbins, all in the present volume.

CHAPTER 7 Government, Church, and Millenarian Critique in the Imyan Tradition of the Religious (Papua/Irian Jaya, Indonesia)

Jaap Timmer

AROUND THE same time as the commemoration of the fiftieth anniversary of the proclamation of Indonesia's independence (August 15, 1995), after thirty-four years of New Order administration and twenty-five years of five-year development plans, Imyan speakers in the village of Haha commemorated the forty-eighth anniversary of the arrival of their missionary hero. Where the government stressed national independence as a national victory and local civil servants regularly gave speeches about the New Order government's goal of bringing welfare to remote locales, the Imyan appeared to be convinced that it was more important to dwell upon moral and Christian achievements because the Gospel was brought to them.

The Imyan, numbering more than 1,200, are the Imyan-Tehit speakers of the northwestern part of the administrative subdistrict of Teminabuan, southwestern Kepala Burung, Papua/Irian Jaya. The subdistrict has a relatively dense population of about 9,000 people, of whom some 1,500 are Buginese and Butonese from south Sulawesi and about 200 are Javanese transmigrants. The Imyan live in the villages of Sasenek and Sodrofoyo, nestled in the lush green hills in the northwestern part of the subdistrict and the villages of Haha, Tofot, and Woloin to the south. The southern villages are located near the swampy mangrove tidal flats of the upper Seremuk River. While the northern Imyan cultivate a variety of tubers, bananas, and peppers, the people living near the coast mainly harvest sago. Together with the Yatflé, Sawyat, and several Maybrat groups, the Imyan consider themselves Nasfa, people of the hills. The Nasfa share a tradition of male initiation called *wuon,* a ritual central to concepts of social relations, identity, power, and wealth. The Imyan people are tied together in a so-called *sorsorat* customary network of collaboration and ritual practices centered on *wuon*. These practices are now defunct, because of Protestant missionary activity and government interference, but in their reflections on past, present, and future identities many Imyan hold *wuon* central.

Considering commemorations of pioneer missionaries who have become "heroes" of a local Christian mythology among people of the D'Entrecasteaux Archipelago and Epi islanders in central Vanuatu, Michael Young (1997) shows the extent to which national narratives are interwoven in Melanesian Christian celebrations. Reenactments of the arrival of the heroes appear most significantly as narratives that people tell to themselves to make or remake their local identity. Young concludes that "if commemorations of missionary heroes can be construed in any way as 'narrating the nation' then they are in a markedly Christian key" (1997: 124).

In another investigation of narratives of nation, Jeffrey Clark characterizes Papua New Guinea Highlanders' worldview as "Melanesian Gothic" to indicate the extent to which contemporary Melanesian worlds are "based on the Bible and its laws, morality and millennial prophecies" (1997: 71). Clark points out that, in contrast to prenationalistic Europe, these worlds also comprise "a universe in which computers, videos, Toyotas, and international flights are observable and available (if not to all!)" (1997: 71). It is in this world that Highlanders imagine the state and the government, and new forms of consciousness arise. For Huli people, as Clark notices, these new forms of consciousness are as yet precursors not to nationalism, "but merely to a form of ethnicity which unites Huli-an unity which was once expressed in the mythology and rituals of ground fertility ... in potential opposition to the state" (1997: 89).

In Papua, the landing of the first missionaries on Mansinam Island in Cenderawasih Bay in 1855 (see Kamma 1976: 53) is throughout the territory celebrated as a nationalist event. People emphasize that these missionaries blessed Irian Jaya to become God's chosen land, reaffirming ideas about ancient sacredness that differ from community to community. In general, experiencing a history of oppression and exploitation, many Papuans tend to relate the event to the glorification of Papua or their own territory as a Christian land opposed to Indonesia's Islamic majority (Timmer 2000b: 53–54). The Imyan case that I discuss in this chapter shows that such a Papuan or Imyan unity is not only an instance of Melanesian Gothicism, but also leads to local political struggles that either strengthen or undermine positions of individuals and descent groups. Debates about village leadership, reflecting both local histories and people's reactions to the church and the government, mark the social conditions in which millenarian critique arises and the cultural forms it takes.

Imyan messianic stories stress the excellence of the Imyan past in terms of a completion (cf. Mimica 1988); the biblical end of all things appears as a restoration of the ancient unity between the sky and the earth. Their millennial narratives heap criticism on ineffective church rituals that fail to deliver material and spiritual goods as well as on the government, whose promises of development do not easily materialize. These stories indicate that the Imyan attach growing importance to finding effective ritual means to restore completion of which a free West Papuan state with Jesus Christ as its president forms a part.

The cases I present below are meant as a contribution to the discussion that Joel Robbins started during the Cargo, Cult, and Culture Critique workshop in Aarhus (see Robbins, present volume). Because cargo cults, millenarian belief, and related religious movements continue to be important to Melanesians themselves and raise issues of power, inequality, and cultural change that interest anthropologists today, Robbins argues that there is no point in doing away with the category of cargo cults. Here he concurs with Ton Otto who, in his critique of Lamont Lindstrom's (1993) focus on Western discourse about cargo cults and its roots in a Western metadiscourse about desire, proposes to examine the immense archive on cargo cults for its power to raise fascinating questions about the force of cultural models (Otto 1999; see also Otto 1992a).

It appears to Otto that "the greatest theoretical promise lies in a further sophistication of a praxis approach which combines the analysis of acting individuals with that of changing cultural models and historical circumstances" (Otto 1999: 94). I aim to contribute to this approach by showing some recent shifts in the field of Imyan cultural domains or traditions of knowledge.[1] I focus on the tradition of the religious that has taken on local notions since the Imyan encountered mission Christianity, condemning "traditional religion" and bringing new forms of guilt and fear in terms of sin and the fate of sinners. These notions have developed into a discrete realm of the religious that the Imyan gloss as *gereja*. *Gereja* comprises ideas and practices related to a clear church organization, fixed Christian rituals, and a body of knowledge contained in the Bible. The most significant aspect of the *gereja* tradition of knowledge is the typical Christian millenarian promise and related apocalyptic expectations that largely revolve around the revelation of St. John the Divine. Imyan eschatological scenarios not only suggest that tomorrow will not be a continuation of today, but they are also moral messages about the Imyan people's own community.

The other tradition that I discuss is *pemerintah,* which, among other meanings, comprises local ideas about the Indonesian New Order state ideologies of national development *(pembangunan)* that classify the Imyan as second-class citizens in particular in the context of development projects.[2] In many respects, *pembangunan* condenses ideas about "the state" and provides a discursive framework for conceptualizing and managing their relationship with the government.[3] The *pembangunan* policy as it is executed most profoundly through the implementation of development projects takes hold and is instantiated in the local setting in terms of lack of sociality. Because *pembangunan* promises wealth and a better future, it gives shape to Imyan desires that are believed to be hard to realize because of the community's shortcomings. These beliefs sprout from a particular dynamics of negotiating difference that is triggered by decades of insults from government agents and condemnations by missionaries and present-day church leaders.

Both the *pemerintah* and *gereja* traditions trace their origins to outside influences but have developed distinctively in interaction with each other and with existing "traditional" traditions of knowledge. In this complex dynamic of cultural practices of Imyan villagers in the context of local and global power relations, *gereja* and *pemerintah* have become specific conceptions of ways of modes of activity.

In the field of competing ontologies, a newer tradition called *agama* (religion) is becoming increasingly powerful as it opposes or supports the other traditions and is mainly perceived and lived by the Imyan as a cosmology that positions them in a personal, local, sacred (and largely secret or hidden) world. *Agama* in fact belongs to the church and the New Order Pancasila state ideology but is perceived as originally Imyan. *Agama* is a pillar of the Pancasila ideology and belongs to the policy that promotes a double conversion; Indonesians must declare membership to one of the five religions recognized by the government—Buddhism, Catholicism, Hindu-Bali, Islam, or Protestantism—and pledge allegiance as a citizen of the Indonesian state. As laid down in the first principle of Pancasila, all citizens are expected to believe in a singular God *(Tuhan Yang Maha Esa)*.[4] If people convert to one of these five religions, they fulfill one of the main duties of every Indonesian citizen. The policy is especially designed for "underdeveloped primitive peoples" in remote places (*masyarakat terasing;* see Koentjaraningrat 1993). These peoples have yet to accept religion *(belum beragama)* because they still hold "superstitions" *(kepercayaan)*. It is not surprising that most indigenous people in Papua are considered belum beragama. Effectively opposing and undermining this classification, the Imyan say that their "traditional" religion is *agama*. Perhaps even more powerful is the fact that the Imyan *agama* arouses expectations for the millennium (see Timmer 2000b).

What millenarianism among the Imyan shares with Melanesian cargo cults, cargo movements, or Melanesian religion in general is a "keen awareness of limitation, a refusal of self-satisfied tendencies to cultural inertia" (Jorgensen 1994: 130). In the Imyan case, this keen awareness is reflected in questions of renewal and redirection of group life values: a concern over deterioration of morals that obstruct the building of a good Christian community that is prepared for Christ's coming (and related prosperity or "cargo"). The Imyan expect the cargo to come when their relationship with the dead is restored after Jesus has inaugurated the Kingdom on Earth, that is, when they sky and the earth become one and the Imyan can again engage in direct exchange with sky deities and the dead. Imyan stories of power and divine forebears begin at the beginning of things and end at the end of time; godlike forbears maintained close relations with the other worlds of power and end with the return of Jesus Christ at the end of time.[5]

Below I address the question of human cultural practice in the context of power relations in order "to discover the social conditions in which [millenarian] critique arises, the cultural forms that it takes, and the effects that it has within societies in which it is practiced" (Robbins, present volume). I discuss the reactions of Imyan people to Indonesian development projects and a village-based struggle for power highlighting the use of traditions of knowledge.

Mungbeans and Autonomy

In 1996, the government implemented a new project within the framework of a national IDT (Inpres Desa Tertinggal, or "Underdeveloped Village Presidential Instruction") program for aiming to reduce the "social and economic disparity" of Haha villagers, whose lives are considered "seriously left behind by progress" *(tertinggal parah)*.[6] The new project consisted of the production of mungbeans as a cash crop in Imyan villages. After several informational and instructional sessions, Haha villagers had slowly begun to work for the project. The government provided free of charge the beans to be used as sowing seeds. If this initial phase was successful, they would then continue using a part of the initial harvest as sowing seeds or buy new beans in the town of Teminabuan using the funds provided by the IDT program. After two days of instructions by two Ambonese men from the department of agriculture of the district government, some twenty men and fifteen women worked four days to prepare a garden for the mungbeans. When the garden was ready, they collected two ten-kilogram bags with beans for sowing, cleared the garden, planted the beans, and regularly weeded the new crops for two months. Right from the beginning, some villagers were critical of the project, saying that it would never last long because of the time-consuming work needed to get a good harvest. The work was simply too hard, they said.

When, after a month, the garden promised a good yield, others began to add that it would be virtually impossible to find an outlet for the product because already for several years Javanese immigrants in the district were selling beans. Haha villagers would only be able to compete with them if they lowered the price to such a level that no one would be motivated to carry the heavy loads to town. During these discussions, everybody seemed to have forgotten that the government controls the cooperative that would pay a fixed price for the beans and also that the church cooperative had decided to add 10 percent to this price.

People started expressing serious doubts about the project after a prayer session at Amos Mejefat's house. As head and clergyman of the village, the forty-nine-year-old Amos used this session to remind people about the promises made to them and that those working in the mungbean garden should continue trying to finish the job, collect the money, and thus set an example to others. After a severe speech, he stimulated them by suggesting to set up a competition with surrounding villages that were also engaged in the IDT beans project. His attempt to keep a close watch on the fulfillment of the project, as he was told to do as representative of the government, was unsuccessful.

Harvesting the beans took three days, and when they were dry, placed in bags, and readied for transportation, nobody felt like carrying these heavy loads to town (a fifteen-kilometer walk through a muddy forest). People gathered in the empty garden to discuss the matter. Amos was also there and told the people that the hard work of carrying bags was not an acceptable excuse, in particular not to the government officials who would show up the next week to evaluate the progress of the project. Yuwel Mejefat, a forty-eight year old, stood up and explained that it is not the hard work, but that people found it stupid to sell this beautiful product to "Indonesians":

> Why should we sell this stuff for little money to people who already have enough money to feed their children? Why feed the Indonesians in town

> and in the city of Sorong? We get very little money in return and stay hungry. If we collect the money then we have to walk back to town, buy beans, and rice at the market, thereby enriching the outsiders. With their big salaries the government employees will buy the beans and feed their children. Forget about this project and feed the beans to your family. We have already eaten about a quarter of the harvest and our children love it. Over the past week my children eat beans every morning and they feel healthy. They do not fall asleep in class, as they tend to do when they only get some cold sago jelly for breakfast. Therefore, we should not feed the Indonesians but ourselves instead.[7]

Yuwel's brief for keeping the consumption of mungbeans for themselves met with wide approval. It was clearly not the time for Amos to deny Yuwel's argument, and he walked home murmuring about *pemerintah*. When I visited him a few hours later, he told me that he would not support the now widespread enthusiasm for making new gardens to get more beans.

> It may sound good that all villagers should enjoy this good new food, but it does not make sense. We should be concerned with work, *pembangunan*, and God. Read St. John 6:27, where it says: "Labour not for the meat which perisheth, but for that meat which endureth unto everlasting life." As long as Jesus' Kingdom is not here we should serve the government, which is also given by God. Yeah, but as you whites know and the villagers will probably never understand, God will reward working for the government. *Pembangunan* also includes becoming good Christians. Just consuming the beans, you will not get anywhere.

During the inspection session by the IDT team a few weeks later, Amos had to pull out the stops to explain to the officials in front of the villagers that the mungbean project was too time consuming. Haha villagers already had too much on their minds: harvesting sago to feed their families, getting their children to school, attending church services, hosting prayer services at their houses, and meeting such obligations as marriage payments—paying part of the bride price—and paying fines—which the government imposes for violations of its regulations. None of the villagers wanted to let Amos down in front of the officials. Showing discontent among them in front of the powerful "Other" was simply not done. The conclusion of the leader of the IDT team was as usual: Imyan villagers are too lazy to plant and harvest mungbeans and too dull to understand that they would get *pembangunan* by merely selling beans at the market in town. The Imyan villages would remain backward, no matter how great the efforts of the Indonesian government.

The villagers' renunciation of selling mungbeans to Indonesians and their emphasis on the importance of consumption for their own physical and mental strength should be seen as a negation of *pembangunan*. It is an example of a tendency of closure, a negation of the confusing "Other," a turning away from the separate world of outsiders, who are seen to come to Imyan land to utter insults and to carry out policies that culturally and economically deprive Papuans. Drawing on *pembangunan* cases elsewhere in Indonesia, Tania Li illustrates that "the separation of state and society produced through the exercise of planning enabled a community to find new and stronger ways to define 'itself' and contest state plans that threatened to appropriate crucial resources" (1999: 316). Li shows that this capacity for action or agency is not constituted outside but within the framework of state and society. In that respect, *pembangunan* (and *pemerintah*) should be seen as a terrain of struggle, as the routine and intimate compromises through which relations of domination are lived.

The Imyan case indicates the level of compliance achieved at the local level and shows that development involves complex cultural work at the interface between development projects and those they target. The majority of villagers tend to see work not as a moral duty in terms of *gereja* or *pemerintah*. In line with the traditional domestic mode of production, not the work in the gardens but the local consumption of the mungbeans is seen as solidifying the foundations, autonomy, and individuality of Imyan society.[8]

If critique of the government and the church is widespread in the village of Haha, we still need to explore the reasons for the marked difference between the majority's withdrawal into autonomy and Amos's self-representation as someone who supports the power and promises of the government. In later clashes with villagers about the collection of money for the upcoming Christmas celebration, Amos and others who support him continued to reiterate the dogma of *pemerintah* and *gereja* to safeguard their position. The way they incorporate these new institutions in their lives suggests that the New Order and Christian doctrines are largely convincing to them. Their appeal to *gereja* and *pemerintah* is integral to their involvement in local politics.

Competing Ontologies

People's reaction to the actual practice of *pembangunan* and the villagers' emphasis on local production and autonomy relate to certain ontological dilemmas that the Imyan are dealing with. In expressing a perceived disordered condition, the Imyan distinguish most clearly between four traditions of knowledge:

- *Adat:* "custom," or the bygone order that in certain contexts includes *wuon* lore and imagery related to the now-defunct male initiation cult and *lait* (pervasive death-dealing evil powers).
- *Gereja:* church and mission.
- *Pemerintah:* colonial and postcolonial governments, modern world, Pancasila state ideology, media, and school.
- *Agama:* cosmology informed by both mission Christianity and local myths and ideas about sky deities.

Depending on the context, people make meaningful connections between these traditions of knowledge. These connections appear to reflect the fact that apparently different traditions of knowledge can assume similar contextual meanings, allowing alternation between different worlds of meaning and possibility. In many instances, this alternation highlights a concern with knowledge, in particular the powerful knowledge that was possessed by ritual leaders and employed during *wuon* rituals.

Wuon was a ritual central to conceptions of social relations, identity, power, and wealth. In the Imyan cosmology, cargo or blessing *(berkat)* is the focus of Imyan ideas about the powers of *wuon* and the sky beings *(ni mlasa)*. During rituals, a sky deity named Klen Tadyi takes the ritual leaders and the novices in a flying canoe *(kma sene)* to the other world where *ni mlasa* dwell. To ensure a safe return, the canoe is tied to a large tree with a rope. Once contact is made with *ni mlasa,* the initiators and the novices bargain for the riches hidden in the forest, the waters, and the palace of the sultan at Tidore, North Moluccas.[9]

The ritual leaders exploit their contact with sky beings in a number of ways. For example, they can ready all the fish in a river for easy capture by noninitiated men, women, and children. In the fishing ritual, still performed in the 1960s, the ritual leaders positioned themselves at the headwaters in preparation for a competitive struggle with Klen Tadyi. Others stood downstream along the banks of the river waiting for the loud sound of Klen Tadyi indicating his surrender to the ritual leaders. Klen Tadyi then prepared the catch for collection by cutting the fish tails and tying the shrimp feelers together. Soon after they heard the sound, the people would see this yield float to the surface. All natural riches that Klen Tadyi controls and gives to man are seen as *berkat.* Similarly, Bernard Juillerat reports recent Yafar (West Sepik) exegeses of myths that "did not need much touching up to identify European goods with game, a scarce product in a subsistence economy" (Juillerat 1996: 536).

The Imyan establish correspondence between Christian lore and *wuon* because they see both doctrines as interplays of secrecy and sight. The teachers and novices depart into the woods to obey the "unseen Other," the sky beings of which Klen Tadyi is the most important. During their encounters with the sky beings, lay people merely hear the spirits' voices. Only upon the return of the novices to the public grounds do the people get visible evidences of the presence and workings of the sky deities. Images drawn with chalk on the torsos of the newly initiated men are the most significant of these signs; they are seen as the signatures of Klen Tadyi and remind people of the first time Klen Tadyi left his mark on Bauk, the first Imyan novice to be successfully initiated in the secrets of *wuon*.[10] This mark, together with a range of stories about the hardships endured during the rituals, creates the recognition of the divine powers of the sky beings whose celestial salvation *(berkat)* will only come through offering clothes, lives, and the integrity of people.

The outsiders labeled as whites *(na welek)*, Westerners *(orang Barat)*, or "Dutch" *(Belanda)* are accused of having withheld the originally Imyan *wuon* secrets *(kahan)* in order to prevent the Imyan from gaining control over their own fate. The Imyan lost the *kahan* as the result of a disaster that happened during the second initiation organized by Bauk. It forced the departure of Olinado, a manifestation of a sky deity, Klen Tadyi, taking the *kahan* to the West. The loss of power through Olinado's departure (as the result of ancestral transgressions) appears to structure all subsequent events. Olinado's journey to the West produced a cultural order in the world that, however, was only to be discovered when the Imyan encountered the "Other."

For the Imyan, the loss of *wuon* entails an estrangement from the sky beings and triggers the feeling of having lost control. This situation warrants the search for truth of people's own predicament in order to transcend it. The Imyan feel that their community has been in debt for a long time following the loss of the key powers of *wuon*. This loss led to negligence of the sky beings and an increasing distancing of the living from the dead. This broken relationship has buried the sky beings and the dead in oblivion. The Imyan believe this is why humans cannot establish something good in this world and will not succeed in being unitary and sociable again.

In these theories, the concerted efforts of missionaries and government agents to abolish "pagan" practices including the *wuon* initiation cult are considered crucial. The related loss of knowledge is believed to have impoverished the Imyan and has created a divide between Papuans and whites and "Indonesians." Only the recovery of that knowledge or regained access to powerful knowledge in general will reform the situation.[11] In particular, *wuon* rituals are now considered effective if they result in the establishment of close contact with ancestral and nonancestral spirits who may bring riches, food, and blessing (*berkat*) for the living. Because it is the most powerful means for gaining access to wealth and power, it is not surprising that *wuon* forms part of a tendency to produce internal differences in Imyan society.

Village Politics

Amos Mejefat's reaction to his people's refusal to produce mungbeans for the good cause of *pembangunan* shows that at the local village level *gereja* and *pemerintah* appear to provide meaningful identities such as "good Christian" and "good citizen" characterized by morality and charity. These identities appear to be easily opposed or undermined by reference to *adat* and *wuon*. Underlying much of the discussion of *pembangunan* among Haha villagers is the fact that a significant number of villagers oppose the ruling elite, which allies with the truths and rules of *gereja* and *pemerintah*. The opposition suggests that the present-day tide of increasing confusion and deterioration of morals can only be turned through adherence to traditional leadership holding exclusive access to secret *wuon* knowledge. To show how this conflict highlights some crucial aspects of the role of the traditions of *adat*, *gereja*, *pemerintah*, and *agama* in Imyan society, I need to sketch briefly the history and social structure of the village of Haha.

The Dutch government and the missionaries in the late 1940s forced people to leave their settlements in the hilly interior and move to open spaces or to the coast. Some ten descent groups moved down to the coast to build clusters of houses between the gently sloping mountain range and the mangrove forest with vast sago-palm forests, streams, and meandering rivers.

Local memory holds that Queen Wilhelmina of the Netherlands ordered her citizens in the Teminabuan subdistrict to move down from the hills and build the village called Rinkasin and that Trithoin Kemesrar was appointed by her as the first village head *(kepala kampung)*. Because of a conflict that arose between clans belonging to the Woloin descent group and the clans belonging to the Mejefat group, Rinkasin split into two villages. Trithoin Kemesrar decided to move to a new settlement called Teltolo, and the other group moved to what is now the village of Woloin. Teltolo was a concentric cluster of houses near the bank of the

Mario Creek that leads to the Seremuk River and was built in the 1950s by the four clans that continue to live together in Haha: Mejefat, Kemesrar, Wolobié, and Klaflé.

As part of New Order development, a *desa* system was introduced in the 1970s, and the new *desa* of Haha comprised the village of Woloin, Tofot, and the former Teltolo. In accordance with the national Village Law Number 5 ("Undang Undang No. 5 Tahun 1979 tentang Pemerintahan Desa"), all settlements in the Teminabuan subdistrict were grouped into ten *desa* (MacAndrews 1986: 38). Teltolo became the seat of the new village leader *(kepala desa)*. Lagging behind developments in other provinces of Indonesia, the regional *desa* system was reformed in the late 1980s. It was considered more effective if funds could be distributed over smaller units. Reorganization resulted in thirty-one administrative units for the Teminabuan subdistrict. Woloin, Tofot, and Haha became separate *desa*. Around the same time the settlements rearranged according to an image of a "civilized" human society. Typical Indonesian village houses with iron sheet roofs and plank walls now line a main road passing through the village. The church, the school, an office, and a meeting hall are situated in the middle of this oblong layout.

On the social and local political level, the most striking aspect of the recent changes is the differences that have arisen between old and new elites. The rift between these elites splits the village both politically and geographically in half. It opposes the majority of the old elite living on the western side (*kampung bawah,* where the sun sets) and the new elite living at the eastern side (*kampung atas,* where the sun rises). The new elite largely consists of people of Mejefat descent, and the old elite is centered on a few leading Kemesrar people.

The important figures of the Mejefat elite are Amos and his brother, Elias, aged forty-seven, who is the head of the school and holds a leading position in the church council. The traditional Kemesrar elite is represented by Lourens Kemesrar, age fifty-eight, one of the remaining initiation leaders, and his son-in-law, Seppy Kemesrar, age thirty-seven, who traces his descent to some famous warriors. The opposition of the old elite of ritual leaders and war leaders takes the form of imagery of the good old days when *adat* was still prized and the traditional order provided stability and welfare. As a result of growing concern with lost knowledge and increasing importance attached to the *wuon* techniques for getting "cargo," over the past few years Kemesrar faction sees more chance of success in the village. Because God is one of the Imyan sky beings and Christian lore is traditionally Imyan, the church is most easily accepted as being able to perform the same role as *adat,* but because the church is in the hands of the new non-*wuon* elite, opposition against them comes in terms of "the good old times" promoted by the children and grandchildren of initiators and war leaders.

By contrast, during the first decades of colonial and postcolonial regimes, there was a tendency to negate tradition, do away with pagan rituals, and get involved in modern projects. During this period most Imyan attempted to learn "the Other's" language in order to be able to attend schools and to become religious teachers. The spread of Malay in particular is recalled as a determining factor that helped to create the current elite. Amos was the first Imyan to attend the boarding school in Teminabuan in the mid-1950s and to return to his land after being graduated as village preacher from the Dutch mission school in Miei. In the mid-1990s, Amos and Elias used a "real," "civilized," and "official" form of Indonesian in their sermons and public addresses, a decision meant to suggest to listeners that they knew what they were talking about. Alongside the employment of the meanings of the *gereja* and *pemerintah* traditions and the "backward" Kemesrar people, the Mejefat also employ the institutions in which they hold dominant positions. For example, they may exclude opponents and their family members from active participation in church activities such as Holy Communion, forbid prayer meetings at people's houses, and postpone children's confirmations (*sidi*).

However deep and unsettling the regular disputes between the factions may run, there is no element of discord powerful enough to break all the ties between them and produce two separate villages or to lead to really dangerous outbursts of hate. The politics are subtle and careful, avoiding aggressive conflict and accusations of tyrannical avarice. In struggles of power at the local level, the glosses that evoke certain meanings belonging to different traditions of knowledge are used to strengthen or undermine powerful positions of individuals and descent groups. The Mejefats regard themselves as more civilized than those who want to revive and seriously examine *wuon.* The latter group consists of the potential adherents of the flourishing new tradition of *agama,* and they are seen as threatening because they are inclined to escape the *pemerintah* and the *gereja* ways of running the village. The debates between these factions over moral and historical rights to lead the village also reflect the importance attached to the clan identity through origins, precedence, and such practices as *wuon* initiation. Haha village has become not only a venue for political struggle between the Kemesrar and Mejefat factions, but also a critical site for reflection on cooperation and morality.

Agama and the Efficacy of Knowledge

The concern with lost *wuon* knowledge sustains the Kemesrars' distinctiveness and their superiority. The traditional differences between "*wuon*-related" and "non-*wuon*-related" clans in Imyan society are both maintained and undermined by using new forms of knowledge from outside (*pemerintah* and *gereja*). Alongside the internal conflicts, a major local concern is the decades-long denial of the Imyan people's competence in learning and performing in modern colonial and postcolonial contexts. This concern is in fact a crucial part of a larger and still more intrusive concern with denied identity and lost certainties. In stories about the millennium, people relate this concern to ancient topographies that characterize the essence of their past lives. The core of this essence is the knowledge by which the Imyan could get close to "cargo."

Informed by the concern with knowledge, the Imyan often negotiate the differences and the powers of cultural Others in a search of lost elements of an (imagined) ancient order. Therefore, the dynamics of the traditions of knowledge among the Imyan reflect openness to outside ideas and structures and an experimental approach to finding potent new customs. In that sense, everything that the Imyan do is always provisional and regarded as perhaps closer to the solution, but not close enough. The new tradition, labeled *agama,* which is born out of the frustration sketched above and is driven by Imyan preoccupations with the possibility of Jesus Christ's return, illustrates this.

As indicated above, the Imyan have labeled a new revolutionary doctrine as *agama*. Significantly, *agama* also comes to the fore in Papuan cargo cults. For example, in the Tanah Merah region, the local leader Simson called his movement "Agama Kubur" (religion of the graves). The movement was active in the early 1940s. Simson's doctrine explained that the Gospel had been mutilated so that the Dutch could keep all the goods that they obtained from the Cyclop Mountains by an underground sea route (see Kamma 1972: 286). A leader of a millennial movement in the Wandamen area claimed to have been in contact with the land of the spirits and called his doctrine "Agama Syariwari" (Kamma 1972: 287).

The *agama* that the Imyan envision consists of a blend of *wuon* and Christian doctrine that may help to disclose the truth. This theology gives prominence to an Imyan world of sky deities related to the sultanate of Tidore and thereby undermines the discourses of the missionaries and state. *Agama* criticizes the state and missionary Christianity for denying access to the powers of Imyan sky deities, enriching Europeans, and empowering Indonesians to form the oppressive New Order regime. The return to local beliefs in *wuon,* in combination with Christian doctrine, will reveal white and Indonesian power and restore to the Imyan their stolen future.

Imyan *agama* never explicitly refers to any form of *pembangunan,* and Indonesia does not play a role. The "cargo" that is part of this package comes from the West, Olinado's destination. Indonesia is edited out and as such the millennium among the Imyan can be read as a way to explore and define the political economy of their relationship with the West. By reinscribing a sharp distinction between local and Indonesian perspectives on *pembangunan*—a process triggered by the harsh and disrespectful presence of "Indonesia"—the Imyan prevent *pembangunan* from making sense. As belonging to what threatens their world's integrity, the Imyan intentionally disregard "Indonesians" by relegating them to the hell scenario contained in the end-time stories.

Besides being a potentially successful way of escape from outside forces, the Imyan search for community can be understood more clearly when we realize that it resembles the community of initiates who retreated in the forest for months in order to learn the *wuon* lore. The participants were sworn to secrecy. Whatever the secrets may be, the secrecy is the search for a community that excluded "the Other," the ones who do not know the secret, or the ones who do not properly handle the secrets. The first are traditionally those members of society who were excluded from initiation: women, children, noninitiates, and whites who have received the secret core of *wuon* from the Imyan but refuse to return it or share the powers and wealth that it involves. The latter includes "Indonesians," in particular the Javanese elite, who elaborate on the knowledge and technologies developed by whites on the basis of the kernel of power and knowledge (*kahan*) that came from Imyan land.

Imyan responses to the government and the church discourses reflect their observation that the demands of both institutions lead to chaos that can only be corrected by reversion to old traditional powers and politics. This interpretation transforms Imyan land and its people into powerful grounds and potentially powerful individuals. In this way, the Imyan build, maintain, and defend boundaries in a world that they not only experience as confusing and threatening, but also shape it as such in order to discriminate against "the Other." In that sense, the Imyan do not avert the threats from outside or inside their community; they embrace them. This entails the reproduction of cultural values whereby there is an increasing emphasis on the margins, boundaries and the distinguishing qualities of the "Imyan," and, by extension, the national traits of (West) Papuans. Running through these attributes is the Imyan conviction that the past was the truth, completion, and it lay hidden to them but is now exploited by "the Other," to return to its origin only during the millennium.

Their concern with knowledge and completion is the main reaction of the Imyan people to the colonial and Indonesian governments that incessantly have told them that they are backward and primitive and that it is impossible for the Imyan to build a communion mode of cooperation, collaboration, and charity. In their discussions of the ways to establish such a community, the Imyan do not solely refer to the powers that come through successful contact with sky beings, but also express the feeling that since they started to disregard the "other world" their own world appears to be forgotten by the rest of the world and disrespected by themselves.

The gods have left, and the people are in debt. Giving and reciprocity do not make sense, now that the primordial and most essential exchange has been discontinued. Only through engaging in exchange with the dead through *wuon* rituals could the gods be propitiated for the evil that had been done. Yulianus Woloblé commented on the oblivion of the gods as follows:

> Look, it are people like Reverend Marcus [the major first Mennonite missionary who worked in the area in the 1950s] who urged us to do away with *wuon* and tell us our other world is not true but evil. Seems that he wanted us to lead us astray [*kasih sesat*] because those things were too powerful. He was lying to us. No problem. But the problem is that I don't even know where it is. It are the old people who know these things but me and my friends, let alone my children, wah, it's long past, it is sunk in oblivion [*dilupakan*]. Because there are no gods anymore people stay at home when they are sick. The health center is too far and too costly and will there be friends who care? Since we have left the gods behind us and believe in God, everybody feels alone and appears to get an attitude of need [*sikap minta*].

Indeed, in particular when people are ill they grow frustrated over the lack of *wuon* specialists and the virtual impossibility of doing real effective rituals that involve their own ancestors, let alone the powerful sky beings. If, on top of that, a praying session does not help to improve the situation, uncertainty is blamed on what the others did and do: the Dutch who took and destroyed *wuon* and the Indonesians who further work on putting Papuans in a structural state of oblivion so that they will be unable to come into power.[12]

It should now be clear why the Imyan consider the collective tasks proposed by the *gereja* and *pemerintah* as false. The Imyan are sure that what the church and the government attempt to do with seemingly endless speeches, sermons, and project after project is to artificially pump up the noncommunity. Some go even further and say that this is part of conscious policy aimed at keeping Papuans busy so that they will not think of ways to get back the powers that are rightfully theirs. They see that the attempts of the church and the government to restore collectivity are empty because without involvement of the beings in the sky it is all meaningless and inauthentic.

Elsewhere I have described the symbolism that is derived from the Book of Revelation as it informs the excitation when people talk of the need to create the condition of sovereignty for all under the democratic and fair leadership of Jesus Christ (Timmer 1998; 2000a: chap. 6; 2000b). This movement toward the New Jerusalem often appeared to me as an apotheosis of Jesus and the Scripture and as such an intended symbolic move. This move in turn, it was hoped, would trigger others, making everybody to have faith in Jesus, thus summoning the energies deemed necessary to shatter the Indonesian state, bring justice, and give the Papuans an autonomous state.

Conclusion

I have shown that in two senses there is inequality between different traditions of knowledge. The first is inequality that grows from imbalances in the field of power: Haha society's internal struggle is fueled by Kemesrar attacks on the positions of power of certain Mejefats and the Mejefat elite's attempt to maintain their leadership positions; the other, directed toward the outside, is a shared concern with knowledge and hope vested in the millennium. In that sense, the precedence of *wuon* over *gereja* and *pemerintah* is a response to colonial and postcolonial incursions. The response is a search for power and prestige in the "foreign" and shows continuity with precolonial strategies, when the Imyan searched for the elements of the foundations of wealth and health that were sought in the sultan's palace on Tidore.

The knowledge that the Imyan need is not easily accessible. In the ancient *wuon*-related geography the search was oriented toward the power of *ni mlasa* and the cargo located in Tidore, and in practice this meant close scrutiny of people, knowledge, and material items that came either directly from Tidore or through indirect trade lines. Presently, the outward search or attempt to grasp the Other's system encompasses an even larger world. Again though, those elements representing the powerful *topoi* (places or foci of power) in the modern geography and that come within reach of Imyan are subject to their scrutiny. The persuasiveness of the Kemesrar arguments also comes through the suggestion that only they have command of the knowledge for getting access to the topoi of power. Having access to certain bodies of knowledge thus also determines the inequality between traditions of knowledge.

Pemerintah (supporting Mejefat power) and in particular its *pembangunan* symbolism, money, and projects is still a candidate for hegemony among the traditions of knowledge. Oriented toward the church, the school, and the government, many Mejefats mimic the order that provides identities that bear the government's seal of approval and, perhaps more of a motivation, because it offers money and prestige. But behind the cover of all the conversations about the past, the rules of *wuon,* and the discipline of *adat,* Kemesrar people tell of a truth that is grounded in the present-day Indonesian sphere. In terms similar to *pemerintah* discourse and "Mejefat-speeches," they tend to talk more of the wrongs of tramps, rebels, thieves, Satan, witches, and sinners than of the practical matter of reinstalling *wuon.* In this sense both *wuon* and *pemerintah* traditions of knowledge overlap and mutually inform each other.

This meshing exists because both parties hunger for change, that is, change that they themselves can control and therefore requires intervention based on "traditional" principles. This shows the level of compliance achieved by decades of *pembangunan.* The ontology of the *pemerintah* tradition at the village upholds in many respects the highly valued *adat* principles in much the same way as *wuon* ideologists. Both parties want order, and in this longing they share the concern with *wuon,* in particular as it is now safely categorized as *agama.* It thus seems likely that in the future *wuon* will gain precedence over all other traditions. But, in line with the millennial movements among the Urapmin (Papua New Guinea), the Tupí (Brazil), and the Guarani (Paraguay) whom Robbins (this volume) discusses, *agama* among the Imyan appears not to lead easily to the wished-for renewal of everyday life, but rather to an increasing distancing from the government and the church.

Modification of Jakarta's policy as it is currently unfolding under Megawati's government may well change this. In particular, when there is a chance that Indonesia's easternmost province will gain more autonomy, the tradition of *pemerintah* may be able to shape the ambitions of the young. Because the Imyan concern is with knowledge, power, order, and completion, under a new, perhaps extensively autonomous provincial government as promised by the 2001 law for special autonomy,[13] the tradition of *pemerintah* among the Imyan may develop into an ontology that is compatible with present-day *agama*. People may begin to see significant overlaps between these two traditions that may be further developed along courses of reasoning driven by hope and new ambitions. On the other hand, the current climate in Indonesia is also increasingly dominated by nationalist rhetoric allowing the military to have significant political and economic power, in particular in outer provinces such as Aceh and Papua. This appears to the Imyan to possess a large degree of disorder. As a result, certain degrees of orderliness may also remain to be sought in the tradition *agama* and *wuon*.

In any case, Christianity among the Imyan has taken on specific local colorings in response to Imyan philosophies, interests, and expectations and will continue to inform interpretations of what happens inside and outside the Imyan worlds in more existential ways than the other traditions of knowledge.

Notes

Research for this article was carried out among the Imyan from November 1994 to June 1996 and from December 2002 to January 2003; I am grateful to the Imyan people who befriended and worked with me. I gratefully thank the hosts and other participants of the "Cargo, Cult, and Culture Critique" workshop at Aarhus for stimulating my thoughts about signs of the millennium among the Imyan. I also thank Hank Nelson, Rupert Stasch, and an anonymous referee for their useful comments on a previous version of this article, which remains entirely my own responsibility.

1. Local categories such as *gereja* and *pemerintah* result from decades of engagement with Christianity and the colonial and postcolonial governments. The resulting cultural changes have led to the emergence of certain categories that in people's talk appear as recurring glosses with distinctive sources and histories and particular sets of meanings and moral guidelines. I see these sets of meanings as "traditions of knowledge," reminiscent of the analyses in the politics-of-tradition literature (for example, Jolly 1992, 1997; Linnekin 1992) but largely following Frederik Barth's anthropology of knowledge, developed in *Cosmologies in the Making* (1987) and further elaborated in *Balinese Worlds* (1993). The categories I deal with in this chapter appear as expressions of heightened cultural self-consciousness that have emerged in confrontation with new institutions and new external others (R. Foster 1995; Otto 1991; Otto and Borsboom 1997).

2. *Pembangunan* is that complex of top-down programs such as village formation, development and resettlement programs, and industrialization with the aim of bringing welfare to Indonesian citizens. The programs come in the form of "Replita" (Rencana Pembangunan

Lima Tahun), or five-year development plans, that materialize modestly in such places as Imyan.

3. "The state" is also associated with vivid memories about evil military operations in the 1960s and 1970s and the unsettling feelings that arise from the threat of military forces that are ever present in such Indonesian centers as Sorong, Fak-fak, Biak, Jayapura, and Ambon.

4. The Pancasila state ideology is intended to safeguard national unity. The first principle (belief in one God) is said to guarantee harmony between the different religious communities in the Indonesian archipelago. Although this doctrine advocates religious tolerance, it masks a growing distrust between Christian Papuans and Islamic immigrants from elsewhere in Indonesia.

5. Such new indigenous theologies resemble what Andrew Lattas, in his analysis of the incorporation and transformation of Western beliefs and practices in New Britain Bush Kaliai narratives, has described as "attempts to develop new epochal principles, new ontological schemes for organizing human sociability; this is done by developing new practices for disclosing the world, for working secrecy, for understanding those absences that render the world present in a particular way" (Lattas 1998: xxvii).

6. The IDT program is supported by the World Bank for development of "isolated" villages. For a discussion of the paradox of development involved in this program, see Timmer and Visser (2000).

7. Neal MacLean notes a similar attitude among Papua New Guinea Highlanders who do not want to grow peanuts to make others strong (MacLean 1994: 675). He uses this example to introduce a discussion about a tension between freedom and autonomy, a theme that is also central in the present chapter.

8. Compare Maclean (1994) and Otto (present volume), emphasizing that work does not have a central ideological position in Melanesia.

9. See Timmer (2000a: 119–122, 298–300).

10. It is interesting to note that the signs are now also taken as evidence that the Imyan could already read and write long before the whites came to teach them these skills. Most informants added that Bauk was in possession of a book (the Bible) which was taken to the West. They argued that after the book was lost the Imyan people lost their writing skills. From then on, they could only write (draw) marks on the breasts of the novices with chalk.

11. The knowledge with which the Imyan are concerned is "knowledge" in the nonrestrictive sense. It comprises the information, beliefs, magic, ritual, and techniques need to fruitfully engage the world (cf. Barth 1993: 306–308). Compare Otto, emphasizing that knowledge is a focal point in Melanesian interpretations of Western wealth and power (present volume).

12. Indonesian propaganda as it effectively works through schooling, books, newspapers, radio, and television for decades has indeed put much effort at putting official positions on matters of political sensitivity, largely by suggesting that the history of Irian Jaya/Papua is an age-old struggle (*perjuangan*) for unity with Indonesia. In a situation in which the army plays a crucial role to control the population, it is not surprising to see widespread written histories that tell of heroic military battles in which Papuans play heroic roles. See, for example, Sejarah Perjuangan (1989) and compare Ballard (1999: 153).

13. "Undang Undang No. 21 Tahun 2001 tentang Otonomi Khusus bagi Provinsi Papua." See Sumule (2002), and Timmer (forthcoming).

PART III

CARGO AS LIVED REALITY

CHAPTER 8 Encountering the Other

Millenarianism and the Permeability of Indigenous Domains in Melanesia and Australia

Robert Tonkinson

In this chapter, I explore aspects of Melanesian and Aboriginal reactions to the advent of Europeans, in an attempt to account for a major contrast: the frequent and widespread occurrence of millenarian phenomena in Melanesia and their comparative rarity in Australia. The question guiding much of this enquiry is why should Melanesian reactions to Europeans and their material trappings have so often entailed concerted attempts at explanation and incorporation whereas—in the vast Western Desert region, at least—Aborigines reacted with equally strenuous efforts at exclusion and the maintenance of strongly separated domains?[1] My major focus is on indigenous religious systems and worldview, for it is in these realms that the most interesting explanatory possibilities reside. Although the different modes of environmental adaptation involved offer obvious contrasts, I am mainly interested here in the role of spiritual forces and the communicative possibilities they offered human actors and in the extent to which beliefs in these spiritual forces provided avenues of empowerment. Notable differences in the nature and role of spirits of the dead in the two regions also help explain contrasting indigenous reactions. I draw much of the Australian material from the Western Desert region, and my primary temporal concern is with early reactions to contact rather than more recent manifestations of change, where in the Australian case some evidence exists for millenarian ideas.

After this brief introduction, I assess the case for and against the occurrence of millenarianism in Aboriginal Australia, concluding that the evidence for millenarian responses among Aboriginal people is, at best, flimsy. The bulk of the chapter attempts to account for notable contrasts in the reactions of Melanesians and Aborigines to the advent of Europeans and their technologies. This element of difference deserves exploration, though its scope is so immense that only tentative conclusions are possible. The concluding discussion concerns issues of power, causation, and agency that highlight significant contrasts in the intellectual systems of the two cultures, especially in relation to beliefs in spiritual beings.

Whereas millenarian movements (labeled "cargo cults")[2] have featured prominently in Melanesia, their virtual absence in Aboriginal Australia challenges assertions about the universality of millenarianism (Otto 1992a: 2). One important comparative study of indigenous movements in Oceania that directly addressed the "presence-absence" question was that of Valentine (1963). His dichotomy between western Melanesia (where cargo cults are prevalent) and the rest of Oceania (where they are not) rested on strong historical and cultural contrasts between the two areas and centered on two key variables: "race relations" and certain characteristics of the indigenous political systems. One need not venture beyond Melanesia itself, however, to search for answers, although the huge scholarly interest in cargo cults there has tended to obscure the great diversity in reported reactions to European intrusions. These cults were not a universal feature of Melanesian reactions, and there was clearly a great deal of variation in their content. Despite assertions that cultural heterogeneity in the region largely precludes useful generalizations (Chowning 1977: 2), some universally occurring basic themes exist (cf. Sillitoe 1998). There is also sufficient similarity in Melanesian modes of adaptation, political structures, values, and worldview (particularly apropos concepts of power and causation) to lend weight to the generalizations made below.

In Aboriginal Australia, too, there were basic continuities in cultural themes *and* important regional variations. The northern tropical region, which includes Arnhem Land, is significantly different in certain respects from the interior deserts. Indeed, the role of prior contacts with Macassans and Papuans in the north may well be relevant in assessing possible cosmological changes and contrasts between that area and the desert in the colonial period.[3] In a discussion of attempts by Yolngu people in northeastern Arnhem Land to incorporate Europeans, Morphy suggests that, for example, in the reformulation of boundaries subsequent to contact with Europeans, women have gained access to sacred knowledge that is part of a strongly bounded "inside" or Aboriginal domain relative to all others, including non-Aboriginal people (Morphy 1983, 1991). Bos, also writing of social change among the Yolngu, contends that "The Dreaming ... has had its content considerably expanded in order to continue to provide a relevant ideological framework for social practice" (1988: 435). These examples, plus the recent work of Swain (1993), strongly suggest a significantly permeable "Dreaming" domain (see Stanner 1979) in parts of northern Australia, making it unwise to attempt to generalize for the entire continent.

Millenarianism in Aboriginal Australia?

Anthropologists generally agree that millenarianism was not characteristic of Aboriginal reactions to alien intrusions, but there has been some discussion concerning reported "nativistic" and "utopian" movements in Australia.[4] Several points are germane here. First, if the criteria put forward by Norman Cohn (1970) are accepted as those minimally necessary for any given movement to be classified accurately as millenarian—namely, that it be collective, terrestrial, miraculous, imminent, and total—then they were very rare indeed in Aboriginal Australia. Second, in the Melanesian literature there are some strong suggestions that such phenomena predate direct contact and that much "cargo cult" activity occurred quite soon after first encounters with Europeans;[5] but in Australia there is no evidence to suggest that early Aboriginal reactions along the frontier of European expansion included millenarian elements. Third, and probably not coincidentally, initial efforts to convert Australian Aborigines to Christianity resulted in widespread failure (cf. Woolmington 1988). Unlike most of their Melanesian and Polynesian neighbors, Aboriginal people proved strongly resistant to such overtures and impositions, and conversion to Christianity has been a slow and still-ongoing process (cf. C. Anderson 1988; Kolig 1988). As Kolig notes, "Christian missionary impact most certainly appears to have remained extremely slight" and "Christian moral and philosophical canons have remained peripheral to the way Aborigines perceive and organise their existence."[6]

I am unconvinced by Borsboom's (1992) contention that there is strong evidence for millenarianism among Aborigines. Such manifestations have been reported only rarely, and even where there appear to be some parallels with Melanesian cargo cults—as, for example, with the Elcho Island movement reported by R. M. Berndt (1962)—Berndt expressly denied that it was millenarian in character, choosing instead to label it an "adjustment movement." Because Berndt had previously carried out intensive research in the New Guinea Highlands and had written at first hand about "cargo cults" there (Berndt 1952/1953; 1954), his conclusions are not easily assailed.

In Borsboom's favor, it is possible to discern similarities between aspects of the Elcho Island movement and certain millenarian phenomena: for example, the essential rationality of the movement when viewed from a Yolngu perspective and the leaders' goal of forcing the Europeans into reciprocity: in return for revealing their most sacred paraphernalia, they hoped to obtain jobs, education, economic security, and greater autonomy. In an analysis undertaken in the light of profound changes occurring among the Yolngu since the time of the movement, Morphy demonstrates convincingly that the principles employed by the movement's leaders for negotiating with white Australians *predated* the movement (Morphy 1983: 112).

Despite these parallels, the case for millenarianism is unconvincing for a number of reasons. For example, both Berndt and Kolig are skeptical of the millenarian character of the movements they describe. Borsboom understandably singles out for special consideration the "cult" described by Petri and Petri-Odermann (1970, 1988), because of all the Australian cases this most strongly suggests a millenarian orientation. This account, however, appears to rest on quite slender evidence (the testimonies of two men) and is marred by factual errors in its discussion of origins, regional developments, and intercommunity relations.[7] It is also significant that Petri and Petri-Odermann hedge their discussion with qualifying statements: they begin by affirming the rarity of nativistic and millenarian movements in Aboriginal Australia and conclude by noting that the emergence of syncretistic cults, such as the Jinimin-Jesus cult, "appears to have begun only after Australian policies towards Aborigines had become widely liberalised" (Petri and Petri-Odermann 1988: 394), that is, in the post-1960s era.

The claim that arguments for the absence of millenarianism in Aboriginal Australia derive from a dominant view of the culture as static, incapable of change, and inimical to "individual creativity, charismatism [*sic*] and innovation" (Borsboom 1992: 11) is unsubstantiated.[8] To my knowledge, the only anthropologists to promulgate such a view in the last half-century were Strehlow (1947) and Lommel (1970). Borsboom quotes a similarly unsupported claim by Swain and Rose (1988: 1) to the effect that assumptions of a rigid and unchanging Aboriginal religious life are "still commonly held," but this is, in my view, as erroneous as their inference that anthropological theory has only recently turned its attention to cultural dynamics and change.[9] In much of Aboriginal Australia, individual creativity and innovation are denied to the instigator, but these achievements do not, from an emic perspective, devolve to the group, contrary to what Borsboom suggests (1992: 20). Rather, they are credited ultimately to the spiritual realm of the Dreaming as the source of power and of all new knowledge (Tonkinson 1991: 20).

Also, in light of the strongly egalitarian ethos among mature adults of the same gender in Aboriginal societies and the strength of sentiments against any public displays by men or women that could be construed as egotistical or "lacking shame," the absence of charismatic or prophetic personalities (frequently associated with cargo cults) is scarcely surprising. In view of all that we know of Aboriginal social life, especially the strong constraining force of kinship and the highly contingent and contextual basis of leadership over most of the continent (cf. Meggitt 1962; Hiatt 1986), the challenge would instead be to explain how such personalities could successfully gain the approbation of others and sustain a leadership role over time.

Before turning to a discussion of contrast between the two regions, a final point needs to be made about the Australian situation—namely, the importance of distinguishing between millenarian and syncretic or accommodatory phenomena in relation to the aftermath of Aboriginal-European encounters. Whereas the evidence for clearly millenarian elements in Aboriginal reactions right up to the present day remains slight, the possibility of contamination of indigenous religions by Christian ideas has long been suspected, most notably in connection with nineteenth-century southeastern Australian cosmologies featuring "sky-god" beliefs.[10] There is also strong evidence of religious syncretism occurring in the present century.[11] Another important example concerns the incorporation into Aboriginal "traveling" rituals of elements drawn from a variety of non-Aboriginal, nontraditional sources, including Christianity and historical events postdating contact with Europeans.[12]

Under certain circumstances, then, its carriers have opened out the Dreaming concept in an attempt to accommodate and rationalize significant changes. In the Kimberley and desert regions, these more visible manifestations of an altered consciousness are relatively recent, coinciding with a period of uncertainty and trauma. Employment prospects for Aboriginal people in pastoral areas evaporated, forcing them from their home territories into towns, where social problems centered on alcohol and related violence rapidly escalated. Deeply alarmed, many Aboriginal people appeared to have begun a search for radically different coping strategies, in which both "traditional" religion and Christianity would play important roles. Rather than "syncretistic," much of the response in the Kimberleys, as in parts of the Western Desert, is better described as accommodatory or, as Widlok (1997) suggests, parallel, in that commitment to, and belief in, both Christianity and the Dreaming Law coexist in the same person, but not as a synthesis of elements drawn from both systems.

Accounting for Difference

From a wide range of historical and other sources, it is possible to piece together some patterns of indigenous reactions to the new arrivals, though most available accounts of "first contact" in Melanesia and Australia come from the European side of the frontier. In coastal areas of both regions, where the arrival of the first Europeans was a sudden event, the newcomers were frequently identified as returning spirits of the dead (cf. Reynolds 1981; Trompf 1991). Such explanations for these strange, "human-like" beings had plausibility, especially for the many coastal peoples whose lands of the dead were offshore; however, making sense of such beings in the light of existing conceptions of ancestral spirits posed very different problems for indigenous witnesses. Reported reactions in both areas included alarm, surprise, and considerable curiosity. Perhaps the great fear allegedly shown by many Aborigines relates to the unprecedented nature of this event: for them, the dead, once finally put to rest by ritual, stayed there forever.[13] In both areas, though, the indigenous people soon revised their interpretation. In inland areas of Australia, there is fragmentary but clear evidence that news of the Europeans, items of their technology, some of the animals they introduced, and words of their language preceded their arrival, sometimes by a considerable period (Reynolds 1981). The same is undoubtedly true of inland regions of the larger islands in Melanesia.

The much higher incidence of millenarian movements in Oceania than in Australia has been attributed to demographic and sociohistorical differences: sedentarism and higher population densities in Melanesia contrasting with mobile, small, scattered Aboriginal bands, as well as the postcolonial status of the Aborigines as a small, powerless, encapsulated minority (Borsboom 1992: 22–23). In a similar vein, Rose points out that the two contexts are radically different: "one an invasion of conquest, dispossession and eradication, the other an invasion of political control and economic manipulation" (Rose 1994: 176). These factors are undoubtedly relevant, but are they sufficient to provide a satisfactory explanation? I think not and will therefore examine some other possibilities. An important concern is whether the encounter with Europeans made it inevitable that indigenous people would look to the domain of religion for inspiration and assistance—and to then attempt some kind of syncretistic response involving millennial elements—to assist them in coping creatively with unprecedented change. If, as I have argued here, millenarianism has been absent from the frontier era in Australia, the answer is negative.

The religious understandings of Aboriginal Australians structured their entire society and permeated every aspect of their lives. Theirs was quintessentially "a living faith, something quite inseparable from the pattern of everyday life and thought" (R. M. Berndt, quoted in Stanner 1965: 213). The key cultural concept, the Dreaming, provided multiple, indissoluble linkages between people (as flesh and spirit), the land and its natural resources, and the spiritual realm.[14] In ideological terms, the Dreaming was a fixed and immutable blueprint for social reproduction, guaranteed to the living in return for continued obedience to its dictates (Stanner 1979). As Stanner also notes, Aboriginal religious belief "expressed a philosophy of assent to life's terms" (1965: 213)—set by the rules and values believed by Aboriginal people to have been laid down in the Dreaming era and guaranteeing society's continuance if followed faithfully. This dominant attitude is one of acquiescence to, and living within the bounds of, a world and society long since fully realized. It stands as the antithesis of eschatological belief and millennial strivings toward salvation in a world transformed, with a "new heaven, new earth" (Burridge 1969a).

Cultural conservatism was the inevitable result of what, from the available archaeological evidence, were many millennia of largely undisturbed existence (Gould 1980). During this time, Aboriginal societies were most likely in a state of dynamic equilibrium, characterized by continuous change of some kind and maintained despite considerable climatic and ecological variations. The Aborigines appear to have been isolated on their island continent until, in comparatively recent times (but predating the Europeans), Macassan and Papuan visitors appeared in the coastal north and northeast of the continent, respectively. Both these groups had a discernible impact on aspects of Aboriginal cosmologies and technologies, but their arrivals appear not to have precipitated any major economic or structural transformations (cf. Macknight 1976; Mulvaney 1989). The fact that such contacts were intellectually and culturally accommodated suggests both a flexibility in the responses of north coastal Aboriginal societies and a much smaller scale of difference between the Aborigines and their northern neighbors than that between the Aborigines and the later European invaders—as well as different sets of motives and intentions.

In light of all the foregoing factors, it is difficult to imagine Aboriginal people welcoming incompatible, alien elements into their religious system. A widespread and prolonged rejection of Christianity is but one aspect of this boundary maintenance. Yet Aboriginal resistance to the incorporation of European ideas and principles went hand in hand with their ready acceptance of European artifacts, suggesting an active process of selection from the available array of ideas and materials. Their refusal to accommodate or absorb these alien ideas and principles into the religious system in no way signals fossilization, inflexibility, or an inability to generate viable adaptive strategies. Rather, reactions of intellectual resistance strongly suggest that such exogenous influences have been appraised, judged inadequate, and therefore rejected—or at least kept at arm's length, beyond the conceptual bounds of the Dreaming.

Of the more notable points of comparison between the Aboriginal and Melanesian regions, two variables that invite analysis are the dominant modes of subsistence (tropical horticulture as against hunting-gathering) and the cultural valuations placed upon material wealth (see Otto, present volume). The Melanesians were swidden horticulturists and pig-herders, who in most cases also hunted and gathered foods in the wild. Although theirs was basically a subsistence economy, important cultural values underwrote the production of food surpluses, which many men used in a competitive struggle for prestige and preeminence. Essential elements for success in this struggle were the acquisition and judicious exchange of wealth (pigs, pearl shells, and so forth) and the creation and retention of support networks, for example, through marriage; a man's ability to command wealth was paramount (cf. Schwartz 1976). A related element that lent excitement and vitality (and fear and danger) to social life was feuding or outright warfare, fueled by strongly held values associated with warriorhood, retributive justice, and, in intergroup relations, a continual striving toward balance between competition and sociability (cf. Sillitoe 1998).

Melanesians everywhere appear to have been intrigued and excited by the European newcomers and their seemingly great power and material wealth, but anthropological assessments are far from homogeneous. Some scholars suggest that the advent of Europeans may not have come as a shock to many Melanesians, whose reactions, even if they were surprised, were "also tempered with nonchalance" (M. Strathern 1990: 26). Whatever the initial reactions, the historical and anthropological record suggests that a dominant indigenous response was to engage intellectually with the explanatory problems posed by the Europeans: if not their sudden appearance, then doubtless their subsequent behaviors, especially in regard to exchange relationships and the perpetuation of chronic inequalities in wealth and status. Once confronted with the newcomers, the Melanesians sought both an acceptable explanation for these aliens (and their seemingly great wealth) and inspiration or direction for strategies to engage productively with them. This quest was associated with the emergence in many areas of cargo cults, which earned the region a certain notoriety and for a time challenged anthropology's explanatory powers.

Early European explanations and the reactions of colonial administrators consigned these movements to the realm of the irrational. A 1923 account of "the Vailala Madness" suggested that the natives became "automaniacs," responding in a deranged manner to an overwhelming European impact (F. E. Williams 1976a: 354). As Williams also mentions and later studies have shown, however, such cargo cults entail attempts to understand and accommodate the newcomers and their material wealth in terms of preexisting knowledge and expectations. The Melanesians sought to encompass and absorb Europeans within indigenous systems of meaning, even as such meaning systems were being irrevocably transformed by the encounter (Lawrence 1964): hence their propensity to reexamine their mythology, to discover encoded within it an explanation for both the whites and their cargo and the reasons why it had been denied to them, the unlucky, though deserving, indigenes (Burridge 1960, 1969a). Burridge provides illuminating accounts of the reinterpretative process, and of the distress caused by the failure of Europeans to observe expected reciprocal behaviors, and their ignoring of fundamental moral principles associated with exchange. Sahlins has also highlighted the transformative potential built into such frontier interaction: existing cultural categories take on new values, which alter cultural meanings and, in so doing, transform "traditional" structures (Sahlins 1981, 1985). The moment of contact creates a massive disjunction, in the sense that thereafter the past can be read from the present only in terms of a consciousness of unique, unprecedented difference and of a new timeline—"tradition" can never again be, or mean, the same thing. In a useful refinement of Sahlins's approach as applied to Lawrence's intellectualist perspective, Mosko interposes a dialectic between the expressed symbolic messages of actors and "their concerted projects, or missions" (1991: 270).

Lawrence, in his classic account of cargo cults in the Southern Madang District of Papua New Guinea, discerned the rationality of indigenous responses and highlighted the continuities with traditional religious values and epistemology that underlay and motivated those responses (1964). The successive cargo beliefs he so impressively detailed exemplify a continual process: Melanesians sought to arrive at satisfactory explanations for these exogenous forces and find the key that would unlock the cargo secret, which the whites were allegedly intent on keeping from them. An instructive example is Lawrence's account of how Yali, the movement's leader, orchestrated a "pagan revival" after a visit to Queensland, where he had witnessed the whites' care of animals in zoos and display of them in museums. This led him to the conviction that the missionaries had lied about one important aspect of Christianity: in addition to Adam and Eve, there were other totemic ancestors, revered and protected in ways similar to his own people's treatment of their ancestral totems, and no doubt therefore as ritually powerful. According to Lawrence, Yali concluded that the still elusive key to European material wealth probably lay in this withheld knowledge (1964: 173–178; see also Mosko 1991).

The crux of Lawrence's argument lies in his description of the Melanesian cosmic order, particularly his account of the significance of material wealth, where the centrality of ritual as productive technology is established, as are the consistency and rationality of Melanesian cargo movements (1964). An interesting point of comparison with Aboriginal culture is discernible here, because in both cases religious knowledge and ritual as technology—in fact, as the dominant "mode of production"—are valued very highly. The principle of human intellectual discovery is discounted as a source of important knowledge in favor of myths and, in the Aboriginal case, a belief in the spiritual realm and its withdrawn creative beings as the ultimate source of all knowledge. In Australia, however, the spiritual imperative was more global in its scope and significance than in Melanesian cosmic orders: Aborigines believed that the continuance of all life and the natural world itself depended on the performance of ritual and obedience to the dictates of what many of them today commonly refer to as "the Law" (cf. Tonkinson 1974: 7). Mundane material and extractive technologies were, in Aboriginal worldviews, taken-for-granted means to an end that was made possible primarily through human agency—namely, religious activity—and in particular via rituals controlled by mature males. The creative epoch provided both the blueprint for human possibilities and the parameters within which they would be realized (cf. Stanner 1979). Whatever European material goods may have symbolized, and however readily they were utilized, the explanation for their existence was not couched in terms of the Dreaming. In the Western Desert, at least, objects introduced by Europeans seem to have been perceived as totally outside Dreaming-defined notions of origin and purpose (Tonkinson 1991: 160–182). These discrepant Melanesian and Aboriginal reactions to European material goods are explicable largely in terms of the very different potential they represented. For desert Aborigines, possession of such items had utility value but, because they were relatively short-lived and susceptible to demand sharing or appropriation by kin, their utility for prestige enhancement was minimal. For the Melanesians, on the other hand, European artifacts rapidly became the focus of much competitive effort, albeit principally in the pursuit of "traditional" social and cultural goals (cf. Shineberg 1967).

Another factor of possible relevance to the question of millenarianism is the contrast in modes of adaptation with respect to labor inputs (see Otto, present volume). For Melanesian horticulturists, subsistence required much harder work than in hunter-gatherer societies and, at times, involved backbreaking tasks unknown to the Aborigines. The appeal of ritual as a productive technology in the Melanesian's pursuit of material ends is entirely understandable. Apropos the Paiela people of Enga Province, Biersack suggests that the concept of effortless achievement predated the Europeans, whose arrival and access to goods with little or no apparent work served to confirm this possibility (Biersack 1990). The contact event is the climax of Paiela history, a millenarian sign that is instantly comprehensible and assimilable to local understandings (Biersack 1991b). Resting upon a charismatic tradition and a strongly millenarian worldview, the Paiela political system is open and actively appropriative of exogenous powers and has "absorbed the White man and appropriated him for its millenarian purposes" (Biersack 1991a: 23).

It is significant that the Paiela stress transformation rather than reproduction as the norm. In the case of the Paiela, then, Western technology is "millenarian praxis," part of a history that they themselves define and shape, so its adoption does not signal "'culture fatigue' or, worse, cultural divestiture at the hands of dominant outsiders" (Biersack 1991b: 274). Westerners and their technologies confirmed Paiela conceptions and thus were easily accommodated because the Paiela, in effect, had been expecting them. Biersack also shows how, in the postcontact period, indigenous understandings about cash, cargo, labor, baptism, prayers, and so on were effectively syncretized—"inspired by exotic notions yet informed and motivated by local millenarian principles" (Biersack 1990: 10).

Similarly, Marilyn Strathern contests the notion that Melanesians were preoccupied with "making sense of" the Europeans and their technologies (1990). In her view, Europeans presented a particular kind of image, and, because images frame or contain events, they do not have to be explained by reference to events outside them, hence the surprised yet nonchalant Melanesian reaction to the newcomers. Because Melanesians continually take themselves by surprise through the performances and artifacts they create, the arrival of Europeans would thus have been another such accomplishment and therefore not "uniquely untoward" (M. Strathern 1990: 31). The Europeans, as beings in disguise, might not have been a big surprise, because the Melanesians perhaps thought that through their powerful actions they had produced them. Therefore, accounts by Europeans of amazed or terrified behavior at first contact could be interpreted as Melanesian reactions to their own creative powers. In Strathern's view, "cognitive disorientation/dissonance" theories of cargo cult generation are inadequate, because "we do not have to suppose that Melanesians thought they were dealing with beings whose decontextualisation presented a problem" (M. Strathern 1990: 33). She suggests that a significant feature of Melanesian societies is the slightly unexpected nature of the enactment of social life, wherein "all events were staged to be innovatory" (M. Strathern 1990: 41). Lindstrom, however, reaches a different conclusion from his survey of anthropological analyses of cargo cult phenomena: "Melanesians ordinarily seek to be inspired, rather than creative" and "normally change their societies by organising cults" (Lindstrom 1993: 59).

My reservations about Strathern's depiction center more on the aftermath than on initial contacts and reactions. It may be true that the Melanesians did not have to "make sense" of the European invasion, "explain" the aliens, or put the event into its "social context" (M. Strathern 1990: 33). Yet a huge practical problem remained: how to induce their creations—if this is indeed how some Melanesians regarded the Europeans—to behave like moral humans and share fully their great wealth. Their failure in this regard, and the growing realization that power relations favored the Europeans, would surely motivate the Melanesians to search for ways that would yield them the wealth they felt was theirs by right of achievement. In other words, Melanesians may have thought that they controlled the event, but certainly not the structures of power and gross inequalities deriving from it. Millenarian manifestations can thus be viewed as their customary, chosen means to attempt, or reattempt, to gain the necessary control.

If it is true that Melanesian social life was structured to engender an element of unpredictability and surprise among its actors, as Strathern contends, and that "Melanesians ordinarily expect and strive to change their lives in a total and disjunctive manner" (Lindstrom 1993: 60), these characteristics stand in bold contrast to the Aboriginal case. In Australia, stability was heavily stressed and was of paramount importance to those mature adults entrusted with the faithful reproduction of the founding design for social life that was derived from the Dreaming. The whole cultural domain was constructed so as *not* to produce surprises and to deflect or disguise human innovation through an overriding emphasis on spiritual control of power and knowledge. A myriad of overlapping and interlocking systems of classification, social category, and kinship effectively, and paradoxically, anchored a nomadic people very firmly to territory. These institutions would thus have added greatly to the prevailing sense of a highly integrated, secure, and predictable existence, despite the vagaries of everyday life caused by social discord and the forces of nature.

In the Melanesian case, there is no doubt that aspects of the capitalist economic system struck a responsive chord in those regions, where entrepreneurial skills were intrinsic to the repertoire of the aspiring "big man" (cf. Finney 1973). The clearest correspondence between the contacting societies was that of tilling the soil, an activity easily recognized by the colonizers. Europeans could thus easily appreciate Melanesian ties to place and the economic importance of land. In Australia, however, no land was tilled, and there were no such resonances between two vastly different economic systems. The invaders seemed totally ignorant of the profound cultural significance of territory to Aboriginal people. To the Europeans, one piece of land should have been as good as another for nomads, and it is no surprise that settlers along the frontier should have so often employed a dehumanizing chain of reasoning (nomad → parasite → vermin → eradication) in rationalizing their attempts to "solve the Aboriginal problem" with violence.

Aborigines were exclusively nomadic hunter-gatherers whose mobility demanded a minimal material culture, and there was no craft specialization. In the Western Desert, my primary region for comparison, society was largely noncompetitive and excluded consideration of secular material technologies and artifacts from matters of individual status and prestige. A combination of an egalitarian ethos and very strongly developed inhibitory emotions, notably "shame/embarrassment," minimized greed, grandiloquence, and forceful public oratory. The principal values used to assess individual social worth were a willingness to share, the ungrudging fulfillment of obligations and responsibilities toward kin, and, more generally, an unquestioning commitment to "the Law." Of course, these ideals were not always realized, but strong cultural emphasis on inclusivity, boundary permeability, and cooperation were undoubtedly reinforced not only by regional social homogeneity, but also by an inescapable ecological imperative: the unpredictability, paucity, and patchiness of rainfall (Tonkinson 1998a).

Despite a dominant ideology of stability and nonchange, social life was rendered dynamic by the variety and fluidity inherent in nomadism and by constant transmission and diffusion of information and objects. The religious system allowed for the creation, acquisition, and incorporation of newly revealed knowledge without difficulty—yet such innovations needed to be congruent with existing structural forms for their successful absorption. Change occurred, often gradually and nearly always seamlessly, as the innovations of today were rapidly transformed into the timeless verities of the Dreaming, in contrast to the dramatic and abrupt way claimed by Lindstrom and others for Melanesia. The available evidence suggests that Europeans were simply so far outside Aboriginal experience and the encompassing worldview of the Dreaming that they could not be accommodated within either the Law or the Dreaming, which encase and exemplify these forms of permanence. With the physical eviction or eradication of the Europeans impossible, the only alternative was for the Aborigines to consign them conceptually to a distinct, separate, and inassimilable domain, that of the "whitefella." Aboriginal worldviews, integrated and held firmly within the framework of the Dreaming and focused so strongly on a fixed and immutable past that is reproduced in the present and anticipates the future, were evidently not conducive to millenarian responses.

In my long association with the Mardu (a now commonly used collective label for several neighboring dialect-named groups in the Western Desert of Australia), dating from the early 1960s, what has impressed me deeply is the absence of any attempts to speculate about or ponder the origins, characteristics, or material technologies of the whites. The foundations of their worldview, the notion of an all-powerful beginning that set in place for all time the major lineaments of society, fostered an ideology of the immutability of social and cultural forms such that neither debate nor philosophizing about them was conceivable. In spite of the full onslaught of Westernizing influences, I have never heard a Mardu person expressing in any private or public context doubt or skepticism about the abiding truth and reality of the Dreaming. Despite almost a quarter century of missionary assaults on the indigenous religion and society as "the work of the devil," this remains so and indicates that, for a time at least, they successfully insulate core aspects of their cultural domain from that of the whites.

As if seeking, however, to find some point of comparison or contact between these two dichotomized domains, every now and then people would note matter of factly that much of what the Europeans possessed was prefigured in the Dreaming and was therefore accessible to living Aboriginal people. For example, my enthusiastic description in the late 1960s of the Boeing 747, which could have accommodated the entire population of Jigalong with ease, left my audience totally unmoved—with only a quiet but firm reminder from one older man that the power of flight, being characteristic of dream-spirits, was unremarkable. It was as if I had forgotten that, every rainy season, giant dream-spirit serpents carried hundreds of people on their backs during visits to major rainmaking sites in the desert. Interestingly, crayon drawings made for me by one of the senior men of dream-spirit "vehicles" constructed from sacred objects, were clearly modeled on aircraft, right down to the depiction of propellers. This suggests that *conceptualizations* of such objects were fluid and open to European influences.[15]

The refusal of the Mardu to syncretize the two cultural domains, however, is exemplified in aspects much more significant than material objects. Elsewhere, I have discussed how the Mardu, reacting to the settlement situation, strongly invoked a conceptual separation of the domains of European and Aboriginal space, the former exemplified in the word *maya* (house) and the latter in *ngurra* (camp).[16] The whites engineered and maintained physical separation between the two areas, and this imposed boundary would have provided a metaphor to describe the social and ideological separation of these domains. In the remote mission settlement of Jigalong, Aboriginal acceptance of European control of bureaucratic dealings with the nation-state went hand in hand with active resistance to missionary intrusions, physically and ideologically, into the Aboriginal domain.[17]

At no time in the period since first contact with whites, however, have the Mardu exhibited anything resembling millenarian sentiments or behaviors. They appear to take very much for granted alien material and social forms. As noted above, in relation particularly to artifacts, they unhesitatingly adopt, adapt, and refashion useful foreign objects to indigenous purposes. They exhibit no trace of wonderment at things technological, and no interest in discussion or debate about origins or modes of production. In recent decades, however, they have been impelled by historical and social forces to pay greater attention to the outside world in order to engage with it more fully and effectively.

Conclusion: Accounting for Contrasts

An important parallel exists between Melanesian and Aboriginal cosmic orders in both the privileging of religious knowledge and the notion of ritual as technology. The question with which I began highlighted Melanesian reactions aimed at explanation and incorporation, contrasting with those of desert Aborigines focused on exclusion and dichotomization. Where can one look, in addition to the many possibilities discussed above, for any further keys to difference?

This search leads back to questions of indigenous conceptions of power, causation, and agency in the two intellectual systems. Melanesians seem to share a basic characterization of power as inherently variable, susceptible to augmentation, and vulnerable to assault through human agency—and sometimes as finite in quantity (cf. R. Kelly 1976: 40). In Aboriginal Australia, the existence of sorcery beliefs and, for example, the curative, protective, and enhancing power of red ochre, suggest that Aboriginal conceptions similarly allow for individual agency in manipulating certain kinds of power for either good or evil. What, then, of the origins of and control over power emanating from the spiritual realm? Here, some clear differences can be identified. For example, in Aboriginal Australia magic and sorcery, which are predominantly individual activities, generally appear to entail the manipulation of powers derived from forces not directly attributable to the spiritual realm. In Melanesia, however, although some forms of sorcery also rely entirely on sympathetic magic, in others agents such as deities, ghosts, and ancestors are implicated (Lawrence and Meggitt 1965: 17).

Viewed emically, Aboriginal social reproduction was unambiguously a human responsibility, carried out via collective ritual activity. Yet the continuing flow of power from its source in the spiritual realm (controlled by the creative beings) was considered to be largely automatic—as long as humans obeyed the dictates of the Law. Among the Mardu, individuals were not empowered to engage directly with the spiritual realm. The importance of the individual (with the possible exception of diviner-curers) did not include being able to initiate communication with that realm. Rather, as a passive recipient, any adult of either sex was a possible conduit for the transfer of innovatory power via spirit-beings acting as intermediaries between the Dreaming and society. Such beliefs served the cause of dynamism and innovatory activity without advantaging individuals in a manner likely to threaten either the ideological hegemony of the creative powers (cf. Bern 1979) or the strongly egalitarian ethos that pervaded everyday life (Tonkinson 1988a).

To a scholar of Melanesian religions, a striking feature of the desert Aboriginal case would be the absence of spirits of the dead as major agents within the cosmic order. Beliefs in their existence and social importance were ubiquitous in Aboriginal Australia, but there they were not involved in human affairs once their departure from the living had been effected via mortuary ceremonies. They completed the life cycle by returning, in most cases, to their place of origin, and remained there forever, having no further direct social impact. In traditional Melanesian religions, whether stronger cultural emphasis was placed on spirits of the recently dead or long-dead ancestors, these beings figured prominently in the relationships of humans to the rest of the cosmic order. Most of people's religious dealings with the spiritual realm were conducted via these ancestors, among whom they lived in a single social universe and to whom they looked for assistance in all manner of activity, in response to propitiatory, offertory, or coercive communicative acts (Lawrence and Meggitt 1965). Their continued involvement in human societal life, for good or evil, appeared to have been a universal given in Melanesia, whereas in Aboriginal societies their impact was usually temporary and their presence in the affairs of the living transient.[18]

Melanesian cosmic orders were at the same time more circumscribed and bounded and more varied than those of the Aborigines, which everywhere appear to have been underlain by the central idea of the Dreaming. In culturally heterogeneous Melanesia, this boundedness is not surprising, especially in view of the prevalence traditionally of intergroup conflict and a cosmic order in which enemies are prominent. No adequate account of Melanesian society would be possible without considering instability and conflict and how they are kept in check. The Melanesian stress on the intercessory powers of ancestors of the dead could readily be linked to the prominence of intergroup conflict. Although Aboriginal mythology is also rife with events that include conflict (albeit interpersonal rather than intergroup), it appears that nowhere in the continent, even in Arnhem Land, did intergroup conflict attain the cultural prominence it had in Melanesia. Strongly manifested values favoring conflict minimization and resolution were reflected in a variety of customary behaviors and ritual practices, such as the *makarrata* of northern Arnhem Land.[19] These practices were largely group oriented and, as imperatives handed down from the Dreaming, entailed no direct appeals to any spiritual agencies. Everyday social life, lived in emulation of the positive aspects of the lives of the creative dreaming beings, was structured to be largely predictable and stable, the antithesis of surprise and contingency. The social contract was between humans and the withdrawn creative powers of the Dreaming, thus precluding the much more immediate give and take of Melanesian dealings between humans and spirits of the dead.

When Europeans made their appearance in the desert, it would have been extremely difficult for the Aborigines to make religious sense of them when the flow of knowledge was one way, from the spiritual realm via the human intermediary into society and when direct appeal to that realm was impossible. Neither the coming nor the arrival of these alien beings was foreshadowed in the Dreaming, or even hinted at in ways accessible to the Aborigines as they confronted the invaders. There were no spirits of recently or long-dead ancestors living permanently near, or even accessible to, the living and thus available to perform an intercessory function between the two groups.

In contrast to the Melanesian case, such a divinatory, explanatory, or remedial role was not available because of very different cultural emphases. The key spiritual beings that act as intermediaries for Melanesians were culturally unavailable as a resource for Aborigines, thus tightly circumscribing or rendering impossible personal appeals or maneuver in relation to the inhabitants of the spiritual realm. In light of the dominant Aboriginal attitude of acceptance or assent to the things of life and the total absence of skepticism or philosophical enquiry as to the verities of received dogma, there was no alternative to the categorization of whites as an inexplicable phenomenon, assimilable intellectually only as a completely separate category, existing entirely outside the Dreaming.

The invasion of "whitefella business" into the desert Aboriginal domain has been relentless, but it has accelerated markedly since the 1970s. Once "self-management" became the dominant government policy in Aboriginal affairs, many responsibilities for dealing bureaucratically with the outside world were thrust upon often unprepared communities. The battle to keep the two domains apart since then has been a losing one. Today, they live with electricity, television, telephone, faxes, e-mail, supermarkets, four-wheel-drive vehicles, workshops, and so on, and children are being educated in a basically Western system (Tonkinson 1999). What is not yet clear in regions such as the Western Desert, however, is whether the serious erosion of barriers protecting the indigenous religious domain from invasion will precipitate a noticeable decline in the power and relevance of that domain, as was so often the case in insular Melanesia in the heady early days of Christian fervor—and sometimes in association with millenarian movements—or, more probably, as has often been reported for much of Melanesia, it emerges in a synthesis with an "indigenized" and ultimately powerful Christianity (cf. Tonkinson 2000: 187).

Notes

For their helpful comments on drafts of this chapter, I thank Myrna Tonkinson, Holger Jebens, Lamont Lindstrom, Mark Mosko, Mary Patterson, David Trigger, and Thomas Widlok.

1. In a comparative article contrasting Melanesia with Aboriginal Australia, Catherine H. and Ronald M. Berndt single out millenarian movements, because "virtually nothing of the sort seems to have taken place until quite recently, and then in a very diluted form" (1971: 72–82). As they note, Aboriginal mythology could have underpinned such movements, had social and political conditions been right; instead, the Aborigines moved from colonial domination to political involvement without any intermediate millenarian stage. The Berndts typified the New Guineans as perhaps just as religious as the Aborigines, but certainly more politically restless and individually self-assertive and geared to a more hostile social environment. "They fought back aggressively; and, when that approach failed, they turned to 'supernatural' validation to assert their own right to the goods and esteem and political recognition that they wanted" (C. H. Berndt and R. M. Berndt 1971: 79).

2. It should be noted that this term has proved controversial among many anthropologists and has been objected to by some Melanesians; in the view of one critic, its use "is tantamount to an invocation of colonial power relationships" (Hermann 1992b: 69; cf. Peter Buck 1991; but see also Dalton, present volume); further, as Mosko (1991: 294n) notes, the labels "cult" and "millenarianism" carry "many ethnocentric and pejorative connotations of irrationality and exoticism." Lindstrom provides an excellent overview of the major issues (1993; esp. chap. 3, "Cargo Cult Culture"). The term "millenarian" is also problematic for some anthropologists, who claim that this element is not universally present in the Melanesian movements (Trompf 1991: 193–196).

3. See Thomson (1933), R. M. Berndt and C. H. Berndt (1954), R. M. Berndt (1962), Meggitt (1966), Mulvaney (1989: 22–28), and Keen (1997).

4. For example, Eliade (1973), Koepping (1988), Kolig (1989), and Swain (1993).

5. See R. M. Berndt (1952/1953), Biersack (1991a), and Lindstrom (1993).

6. Kolig (1989: 90). It is true, however, that when we consider quite recent times, there is some evidence of the kind of Aboriginal commitment to Christianity that warms missionaries' hearts. For example, the Christian revival movement that began on Elcho Island in 1979 and swept from northern into western Australia is indicative of the emergence of a newly confident and Aboriginal-controlled "church." Although certainly charismatic, it contained many distinctively Aboriginal elements and was syncretic but not millenarian in character. Bos sees it as "an attempt to adjust ideology in a way that makes contemporary social realities comprehensible and provides a framework for social action, while leaving the Yolngu with some cultural integrity" (Bos 1988: 433).

7. The year Petri and Petri-Odermann learned of the new "cult," I was doing field research at Jigalong Mission, suspected by them to be the epicenter of anti-European feelings and nativism, but saw no evidence, then or later during intensive investigation of Aboriginal religious life there, of such "cult" activity. The source of the strong antiwhite, antianthropologist sentiment alluded to by these researchers was undoubtedly the Pindan group (discussed by them in the same article) and desert Aborigines in areas further south. Petri and Petri-Odermann state that, "according to the Native Welfare Department (WA), there is a cult called *gurunu* in Jigalong which has become a nativistic cult" (1988: 394). Because no cult of this

name existed at Jigalong, the reference was possibly to the well known *gurangarra* ritual, which, however, as Petri and Petri-Odermann (1988: 394n) and Ronald Berndt (1951) note, and I also found, was strongly traditional in form and lacked any features indicative of syncretized alien elements. To the contrary, attempts by the Pindan group to syncretize Aboriginal and European practices were the cause of major tensions between them and the more tradition-oriented Jigalong Aborigines (Tonkinson 1974: 66).

8. Koepping similarly claims that authorities on Aboriginal religion have concluded that "Aboriginal religion, and therewith Aboriginal thought, is incapable of adjustment or change, or innovation or creativity" and alleges that researchers had decided "that Aboriginal thought categories are immobile" (1988: 400). However, there is abundant evidence that anthropologists have long recognized and explicitly differentiated between Aboriginal ideologies of stasis and immutability and the realities of a dynamic traditional religious life (cf. Stanner 1966; Maddock 1969, 1972; Tonkinson 1970, 1974, 1991).

9. Swain and Rose (1988: 4). See, for example, H. G. Barnett's influential work, *Innovation: The Basis of Cultural Change*, which was published decades ago, in 1953, yet was by no means the first major anthropological study dealing theoretically with cultural dynamics.

10. Compare Swain (1993) and Hiatt (1996). Compare Swain, who asserts that the European invasion in this region precipitated a restructuring of cosmological principles (1993: 125). I find this claim dubious, not only because, as Swain himself notes, Aborigines showed little interest in Christianity, but also because in many Aboriginal cosmogonies, including the vast Western Desert, many major creative beings end up as precisely locatable heavenly bodies (stars, constellations, "black holes," and so forth) that are in no way construable as "a dislocated Utopian innovation" (Swain 1993: 128).

11. For example, Calley (1964) on the Bandjalang.

12. Compare Kolig (1981), Glowczewski (1983), and Widlok (1992, 1997).

13. Regardless of whether beliefs in reincarnation were present, in some areas whites were identified as particular relatives whose return signaled their prior knowledge of the country's resources but whose failure to recognize their living relatives, speak the language, or use traditional skills was attributed to forgetfulness (Reynolds 1981: 26–29).

14. The ancestral creative epoch is not universally equated by Aboriginal people to dreaming or the Dreaming or Dreamtime. In northeast Arnhem Land, for example, the appropriate term, *wangarr*, "cannot be translated literally as Dreamtime, and indeed some Yolngu feel that the connotation of 'Dream' is inappropriate: *wangarr* is not a dream but reality" (Morphy 1998: 68; compare N. M. Williams 1986: 25).

15. In another example, two sacred stone objects prompted me to remark aloud that one was shaped like a meat cleaver and the other a pistol. This occasioned a forceful "why are you surprised?" reaction from a couple of the men present, conveying their utter conviction that the creative beings had possessed such things first. Their ethnocentrism neatly reverses the situation, crediting ancestral beings with the invention of items of ostensibly European technology.

16. Compare Tonkinson (1978, 1982, 1988c).

17. Compare Tonkinson (1974). For an excellent account of the salience of these domains in an Aboriginal community, see Trigger (1986, 1992).

18. In the Western Desert, there is fear of malevolent spirits, but these are not spirits of the dead. Mardu say that, prior to the Dreaming, these beings (*malbu*) enjoyed sole occupancy of the land until most were vanquished by the immigrant creator beings of the Dreaming, who also bequeathed strategies for dealing effectively with those that remained.

19. Compare Warner (1937) and R. M. Berndt and C. H. Berndt (1988).

CHAPTER 9 Talking about Cargo Cults in Koimumu (West New Britain Province, Papua New Guinea)

Holger Jebens

After an apparent decline during the 1970s and 1980s, anthropological interest in cargo cults seems to have reached a new peak in the past decade.[1] Though obviously sharing this renewed interest and testifying to this recent upsurge, various authors have contributed quite convincingly to the deconstruction of cargo cults as an analytical concept. Deconstructive and self-reflexive exercises, however, are preceded by an earlier critique, which had questioned the existence of cargo cults as separate cultural and social entities and stressed the term's negative connotations as it had first been used by the agents of colonization in order to reject all those social movements that were perceived to be a threat to Western hegemony (see the introduction to the present volume). In various ways, this "colonial usage" does now seem to be reproduced in indigenous discourses, when Melanesians themselves appropriate the term to derogate their opponents.[2] Here "cargo cultism" continues to be an ideological weapon of exclusion: the cargo cultist is always "the Other."

In this chapter I will present an ethnographic example of such indigenous cargo cult discourses. I will do so with reference to Koimumu, a comparatively large coastal village, located in the eastern part of the Hoskins Peninsula in West New Britain and neighboring to Rapuri, where Charles Valentine lived in 1954 and 1956.[3] The inhabitants of the area speak Nakanai, an Austronesian language (Johnston 1980). My subject is the indigenous representation of the so-called Kivung and the "creed of Batari": the Kivung—not to be confused with its namesake from East New Britain—was reputedly founded after World War II by a white Catholic priest with purely Christian and economic objectives, before being subsequently changed. Villagers picture this change as both a transformation into a cargo cult and a return to ideas and practices that had been propagated prior to the war by Batari. Born in Vovosi, north of Koimumu, he has been referred to as a "cult leader" by such Western authors as Lucy Mair (1948) and Peter Worsley (1957). It might be recalled that, according to Mair (1948: 66; as cited by Worsley 1957: 206), Batari had "scored a strong point on one occasion when a crate named 'battery' was unloaded from a ship—but not delivered to him." It is beyond the scope of this presentation, however, to compare Western and indigenous narratives about Batari or, for that matter, the Kivung systematically. Rather, I will focus on the way people are talking about cargo cults *in* Koimumu and surrounding villages.

Although Western interpretations of cargo cults can be seen as attempts to cope with the cultural Other, this objective is by no means a Western monopoly. Moreover, the very practices and beliefs that have been labeled with the contested term can, in principle, be understood to constitute similar attempts on the part of the Melanesians.[4] Accordingly, the primary aim of my analysis of indigenous cargo cult discourses is to gain an understanding of how cultural otherness is coped with in them.

I

When, in May 1996, I heard the name "Kivung" for the first time, it came as a surprise. During an informal conversation I had just asked Joe Sogi, the man who had introduced me to Koimumu only a few days before, if he could remember any of the predecessors of the present priest. Sogi's answer included the following: "There was Pater Berger. He started the Kivung family, which then turned into a cargo cult and ended just like that. People wanted to learn something about the 'way of the whites' *(sindaun bilong waitman)*[5] and about 'our way' *(sindaun bilong mipela)*. ... However, it didn't work. Then the Whites introduced local government councils and quarrels emerged because the Kivung opposed them and the paying of taxes. Some adherents of the Kivung went to prison and the council won."[6] This statement should prove to be exceptional, because throughout the first few weeks of my fieldwork in Koimumu the Kivung was hardly mentioned. I generally preferred not to touch upon this topic myself and concentrated on such tasks as drawing a village map, taking a census, and recording genealogies, not conducting any formal interviews at all. In June, however, when Paul Gar, the alleged big man of Koimumu, had just listed names of his clan, the Kevemuki, I announced that in the future, after completing my genealogies, I would like to learn something about the "Kivung family." Paul replied immediately and with a heightening degree of agitation:

> The government repeatedly took us to court about this and so we stopped it. Lima and his people have changed it. It was brought up by Berger. We did what Berger told us to do. It was good. Later Berger went away and we stopped. We didn't do any cargo cult. Cargo cults have been done by others, like the people in Bali, Gloucester, and Arawe. There was no family Kivung there. This existed only in Talasea and Bialla. There were no cargo cults among the Western Nakanai. The government repeatedly accused us of doing cargo cults but we did not. Others were against us and they blamed us without reason. "Cargo cult" means to bring food to the cemetery, to get money from the cemetery and cargo from the ancestors. This was done not by us but by others. We were just worshipping. We were against premarital intercourse, sorcery, and theft. We built new houses for people who were newly married; we built a store and a big house in Vavua. Encouraged by Pater Berger we planted coconut palms, we sold copra and we received cargo from Rabaul. ... We did just that and that was good. Cargo cults are bullshit. Money and cargo do not derive from the ancestors, money derives solely from sweat. Berger said that, too.[7]

Whereas Paul insisted on the, so to speak, "secular origins" of Western wealth, he did so with a notable questioning undertone: Could I confirm this? Was it really true that money and cargo do not derive from the ancestors?

The founding role of Pater Berger, Christian and economic objectives, change, and finally conflicts with the government—in the following months, I came to regard these topics as "typical" for indigenous representations of the Kivung. They were continually repeated by many informants, albeit with considerable variation in content and elaboration. Some emphasized the importance of cash crops, others the observance of Christian regulations in claiming, for example, that they had married in church and had given up sorcery. It was also noted that, during his first stay in Rapuri, Valentine had supported the Kivung, because "we worked with money, we did not wait for cargo. He saw that himself."[8]

Of the topics that constituted what can be constructed as "a common Kivung narrative," the element of change was certainly the one the inhabitants of Koimumu were most hesitant to talk about. Whenever they did so, they preferred to use the words "exaggeration" or "deterioration" rather than talk about a transformation into a cargo cult, as mentioned by Joe Sogi, or a return to what had been done in the "times of

Batari." Later, "transformation" and "return" should prove to be used synonymously, but more often than not they were left unspecified, unless, for example, I remarked that I still had not grasped their meaning. In response people said that, unknown to Pater Berger or against his intentions, Kivung adherents had finally stopped planting cash crops just to wait for ships with which their ancestors would come and bring cargo. Thus, the *sindaun* of Westerners and villagers would eventually become the same. Outlining a basic history of such successive expectations, Titus Mou from Vavua recalled that, at one point, his schoolteacher was expelled on the grounds that as a white man he would prevent the advent of the cargo.[9]

It is in keeping with Paul Gar's assertion, "We didn't do any cargo cults," that he blames "Lima and his people," all of them inhabitants of Vavua, for having changed the Kivung. In Vavua, however, it was stressed that Lima had done nothing wrong in merely following Pater Berger and that the changes had been initiated in distant villages in the north. This argument—that the Kivung was no cargo cult and, if it turned into one, it did so only elsewhere—was explicitly contradicted when I visited Galilo, the only village that had never participated in any form of the Kivung. Here a request to tell me about the Kivung immediately prompted the following answer: "This is called 'cargo cult.'... One thing they did, was to stay at the cemetery and wait for the ancestors. They thought they would give them money, food and cargo. At night they went to the cemetery, looked at the grave and addressed the ancestors but they did not reply. ... We didn't believe that in Galilo because we know that Christianity doesn't say anything like that."[10]

Both Joe Sogi and Paul Gar link the end of the Kivung to conflicts with the government. These conflicts were attributed very different reasons. Paul deplored the fact that the government had mistakenly accused people of being cargo cultists, and, according to Titus Mou, Kivung adherents believed that once they had accepted the local government councils they would no longer be able to receive their cargo. The concomitant introduction of taxes was reputedly rejected by Lima on the grounds that whoever had no money would be forced to sell his wife to someone who could pay for him—an idea that had also been reported for the Kaliai from the western part of West New Britain;[11] however, whereas Kivung adherents opposed local government councils, others welcomed them because the colonial authorities had allegedly promised that they "will make that something will get in order in the village."[12] Thus, the introduction of these councils split the population into two antagonistic factions, and conflicts between them finally culminated in a large trial that was held at the district headquarters in Hoskins. In the words of Joe Sogi, "Some adherents of the Kivung went into prison and the council won." Yet Lima's brother, a very old man in 1996, regretfully told me that the colonial authorities' promises had turned out to be a lie and that, personally, he would have preferred to try out the Kivung just a little bit longer.[13]

If the transformation of the Kivung into a cargo cult is understood as being synonymous with a return to ideas and practices that prevailed at the "times of Batari," what do the inhabitants of Koimumu and surrounding villages say about these ideas and practices? As with the Kivung, it is possible to construct a "common narrative" that consists of a few recurring elements: having been instructed by a white man, Batari appointed "soldiers" who marched along the coast of the Hoskins Peninsula, and in almost all the coastal villages he ordered single women and men to marry. After he had attracted a large following, however, the invading Japanese put many of his adherents into prison and thrashed him, so he finally gave up his activities.

As with the Kivung, these elements are presented with considerable variation in content and elaboration. In some accounts, Batari claimed to have met a white man who had returned from the place of the ancestors, where they were producing cargo. In another story, Batari said that he had seen them doing this himself when he visited this place, which the priest called "purgatory." Batari's "soldiers" reputedly wore a special waistcloth, which was sometimes said to bear the "mark of the Japanese," that is, a red circle. According to one informant, the "soldiers" were ranked, having their own "lance corporal, sergeant," and "sergeant major."[14] During a conversation with a group of elderly women in Koimumu, one told me that she and some of her age mates, who were also still alive, had married at Batari's orders when they were young girls. Another woman added that, in the course of a marriage row, one might still sometimes hear the wife confronting her husband with the words, "It was not *my* wish to marry you, it was Batari's."[15]

The inhabitants of Koimumu were not only hesitant to specify changes to the Kivung, but also to talk about other ideas and practices that were attributed to the "times of Batari." Again, however, careful and often indirect questioning elicited references to the expected arrival of ships, ancestors, cargo, and, as a result, to assimilation between villagers and Westerners. When we visited Galilo in July 1996, Vavua-born Titus Mou was the first to claim that Batari's adherents had brought food to the cemetery to offer their ancestors—information people in Koimumu did not confirm until almost a year later. Titus was also the first to claim that Batari's followers had imprisoned and mistreated a white priest in Vovosi. Having asked various informants in Koimumu about this—also almost a year later—they confirmed it, though with differences as to the priest's name and where the incident occurred and with varying degrees of explicitness as to the extent of the priest's maltreatment. I also heard, however, that Batari's adherents had stolen the priest's cloth and books, which they subsequently used to conduct their own mass. One of the persons involved was reputedly still alive in Koimumu in 1997, and to this day, I was laughingly told, he would sometimes get drunk and say, "Come on, let's do a mass."[16] Despite such "imitation," Batari may have viewed the white man's religion as preventing the villagers from having access to the cargo and, as a result, assimilating. Thus, according to Peter Tautigi from Koimumu, Batari had promised

> *Bai yu kamap olsem waitman. ... Sapos yu holim lotu, em yu stop. Yu stopim olgeta samting i no ken kam long yu. ... Yu mas bihainim mi, yu ken sindaun olsem ol masta, ol waitman. Yu ting masta i save wok? Ol waitman i no save wok. Ol i sindaun tasol, big man i givim ol long samting. Kaikai i kamap nating. Ol i, i no hat olsem yumi, long wanem, yumi bihainim ol misin, yumi wokim bikpela lotu. Em yumi stopim olgeta rot bilong samting ya. God i no inap long givim yumi long dispela samting.*[17]

> You will live like the white men. ... If you are holding on to Christianity, then you stop. You are preventing everything from coming to you. ... You have to follow me, you can live like the white men. Do you think that the white men habitually work? The white men do not habitually work. They are just living, God is giving them everything. Food emerges just like that. They don't, don't have the hard life that we have, because we are following the missions, we are putting great efforts into worship. This is how we are blocking all the roads that lead to this. God will not give this to us.

In general, the inhabitants of Koimumu either talked about the Kivung or the "times of Batari," without making connections, let alone comparisons, between them. In this sense, the view, rarely formulated, of the Kivung's return to Batari's ideas and practices was an exception, as was the detailed account by Titus Mou, fusing together the two otherwise distinct narratives into a picture of a single continuous movement with the same followers and the same basic intentions, and with only Batari being replaced by Lima. If we accept the existence of such a single continuous movement, people have attempted to explain and change their situation at each stage: Batari elucidates the production of Western goods, the Kivung adherents want to learn something about the "way of the whites" and about "our way," Batari's followers prepare for the advent of the cargo through their "military organization" and their marriages, and the Kivung pursues Christian and economic objectives.

All these attempts at explanation and change appear to be based on assumptions corresponding to certain contemporary ideas I encountered in Koimumu. During an informal gathering in the men's house, for example, people were discussing the fact that the night before I had been asked by a visitor whether Jesus had ever been to Australia and where he had died. Then a man stood up and said, "Jesus wanted to visit all countries, the whole world, but the white men—you know how the white men are—have killed him so that he cannot go everywhere. Had he come to Papua New Guinea, we would have factories as well. We are just like the white men, they are just like us. Why, why, I ask, do they know how to build factories and we don't. I think it's just because of this reason."[18] Throughout the following months of my fieldwork this "killing of Jesus" was not only confirmed by various informants—one of them claiming that Jesus' message had been later changed by his disciples—but it was also held responsible for the fact that "the white men are white and we are black and without knowledge."

Ideas about unrestricted access not to cargo, but to money as its equivalent, were formulated prior to the national elections of 1997, and they focused on the Pangu Party's candidate Brown Bai. While sitting together with a small group of villagers, I heard that one of Bai's old supporters had claimed that whoever produces a colored visiting card with Bai's picture at a bank, would be given huge amounts of money in return. On previous occasions this supporter had already told me that Bai is rich, that he has often been to Rome, where the Pope had given him some secrets and that, according to Bai, "something will happen" if he wins. As soon as the promise of obtaining money in return for showing the visiting card was mentioned, however, one of the young men present spontaneously remarked, "Hey, this is now a cargo cult!"[19]

II

This last remark—"This is now a cargo cult"—leads to the question with which I begin the final part of this chapter: how is the term itself being constructed and put to use within indigenous discourses? Generally speaking, the language of most of these discourses, the Neo-Melanesian

Tok Pisin, can be characterized by a certain "openness" or, to put it differently, by a small degree of specification. If we consider, for example, the alleged promises that through the introduction of local government councils "something will get in order in the village," or that after Bai wins the national elections "something will happen," in both cases the exact meaning of "something" is very much left to individual interpretation. Furthermore, because most of the villagers do not make connections, let alone comparisons, between Kivung and the "times of Batari," they do not appear very much inclined to systematize the different phenomena or to elaborate on detailed definitions of the terms that are applied to them. Although I do not in the least wish to mystify matters, it is probably due to such "openness" or "lack of specificity" that during fieldwork I sometimes felt I was encountering beliefs or expectations "behind the words." In this sense there might at times even have been an "aura of mystery" that tended to evade the analytical grasp.

One can infer, however, that the term "cargo cult" is primarily characterized by negation—that is, by opposition to colonial government, economic ventures, and Christianity. Accordingly, some informants regard the Kivung's transformation into a cargo cult as synonymous with the rejection of local government councils and the abolition of cash crops, while the contempt for Christianity becomes evident in Batari's idea that through the latter "we are blocking all the roads." If participating in a cargo cult primarily means to turn against something or not to do something, the connotation of passivity, of simply waiting for cargo, emerges. The only "active operation" mentioned appears to be the visiting of cemeteries, which Paul Gar said "was not done by us" and which people in Galilo claimed to have been part of Kivung practice. The "negative characterization" of the term "cargo cult" is mirrored by a negative valuation, most evident in Paul Gar's dictum, "Cargo cults are bullshit," and in the fact that people talk about the Kivung's transformation into a cargo cult as a "deterioration." Thus, calling the promise of obtaining money by showing a visiting card a "cargo cult" can be seen as a way of saying that it is stupid to believe in such promises. Accordingly, I heard two candidates for the national elections, one of them Bai himself, referring to their respective competitors as cargo cultists.[20] Such uses of this term are by no means restricted to the political sphere: when I asked a member of the Catholic community in Koimumu for his opinion of a recently founded charismatic prayer group, he replied curtly, "Cargo cult."[21]

It follows from the negative valuation of the term that its indigenous usage in Koimumu does not seem to differ much from what one finds in the existing literature: "The cargo cultist is always 'the Other,'" or—in Paul Gar's words again—"Cargo cults have been done by others, like the people in Bali, Gloucester, and Arawe" (cf. Hermann, present volume). The distance between Self and Other, between Self and cargo cultist can, alternatively or additionally be conceived of not in spatial but in temporal terms, as, for example, when people talk about the "times of Batari." The axiom that the cargo cultist is always the Other implies that I am not one myself. Therefore, its second implication—the Other might apply the term to me—has to be rejected: "We didn't do any cargo cult," or, as was argued with respect to the Kivung, it "was no cargo cult and, if it turned into one, it did so only elsewhere." In my view, the inhabitants of Koimumu hesitated to talk about certain ideas and practices attributed to the "times of Batari," or to draw any connections between the latter and the Kivung, precisely because they did not want to repeat their historical experience of being denoted as cargo cultists by others. At the same time, this hesitation shows that the villagers understand these particular ideas and practices—waiting for ships, ancestors, and cargo, visiting cemeteries—to be emblematic of cargo cults.

When I first thought about cargo cults as an attempt to cope with the cultural Other, I remembered that earlier scholars had written about what they perceived to be indigenous imitations of Western practices.[22] A similar element seemed to be talked about in Koimumu as well: the "military organization" of Batari's marching "soldiers"[23] and the attempt of his adherents to conduct their own mass with the priest's stolen cloth and books. Such alleged "imitation" corresponds not only to assimilation between villagers and Westerners, effected by the hoped-for advent of the cargo, but also to the villagers integrating the Other into their own frame of reference—an integration that appears to be most prominent in what has often been described as "the persistent idea that Europeans actually are ancestors returned from the dead" (Leavitt 1995a: 182; present volume). This integration of the Other certainly implies a process of change on the part of the Self, which has been interpreted as having dire implications and consequences: through the internalization of Western evaluations and the embodiment of one's own cultural domination, it allegedly reputedly culminates in self-alienation.[24] Here change is very much pictured as an externally induced and passively received influence in much the same way as it is done in indigenous cargo cult discourses themselves. We have seen that they are built on an opposition between passive villagers and active Westerners. They are the ones who have instructed Batari in the person of "a white man," who have initiated the Kivung in the person of Pater Berger, and who, of course, have also introduced cash crops, Christianity, and local government councils. This situation points to a logical conclusion: when people refer to themselves as active planters of cash crops, followers of Christianity, or supporters of councils while labeling others as passively waiting cargo cultists—in reference to Koimumu, the Hoskins Peninsula, West New Britain, or even the whole of Papua New Guinea—they seem to be internalizing the opposition between passive villagers and active Westerners while identifying themselves with the latter. In other words, they come to identify themselves with the Other. What else could be the effect of such an identification if not self-alienation?

However convincing the argument in terms of self-alienation may be, I contend that this is only part of the picture. In my view, the villagers should not be seen as just passively receiving what is initiated by the Other, but also as actively influencing the colonial situation themselves. If, for the Kaliai, "gender has become a metaphor for figuring colonialism" (Lattas 1991: 242), then the reorganization of gender relationships through new marriages—an element of "Batari-" and "Kivung-narratives"—might constitute an indigenous attempt to exert just such an influence. Furthermore, alleged imitations of Western practices do not necessarily imply passivity. Following Kramer (1987), I would prefer to understand them as forms of coping with what is perceived to be threatening, as forms of an active mimetic appropriation.[25] Apart from this appropriation of the Other—and apart from the Other's integration—the Other can, of course, also be excluded: as mentioned before, a schoolteacher was expelled by adherents of the Kivung because as a white man he would have prevented the cargo from arriving. In addition, the hesitation of the inhabitants of Koimumu to talk about certain topics could—with respect to these topics—be interpreted as an attempt to shut out the fieldworker.

In claiming that the argument in terms of self-alienation is only part of the picture, I am suggesting a dialectic of passivity and activity that corresponds not only to the mutual influencing of Self and Other, but also to a dialectic of self-alienation and self-affirmation. When, for example, in one of the "Batari-narratives" the ancestors are producing cargo in purgatory, the Other (the purgatory) has appropriated the Self (the ancestors). The Self tends to turn into the Other, thus leading to self-alienation. At the same time, however, the Self (the ancestors) has appropriated the Other (the cargo). The Other turns into the Self, thus leading to self-affirmation. While this mutual influencing of Self and Other shows the dichotomy between these categories to be artificial (cf. Dalton, present volume), at the same time the dialectic of self-alienation and self-affirmation appears to be mirrored in the ambivalence with which the inhabitants of Koimumu view themselves and Westerners: villagers did change what Pater Berger had initiated,[26] but they did not participate in cargo cults. In instructing Batari, starting the Kivung, and introducing cash crops, Christianity, and local government councils, Westerners have brought what could be perceived as various means of ultimately gaining access to cargo, but they are also actively intercepting this access—for example, through their killing of Jesus—"you know how the white men are."

In conclusion, I stress that ambivalence and dialectic cannot be reduced to one cultural domain alone. Religion (in the form of Christianity) and economy, for example, are closely interwoven, first as part of the Kivung and then as opposed after the Kivung changed. The politician Bai is praised for his close relationship with the Pope and for his wealth. Accordingly, the same ideas and practices can, from a Western point of view, appear to be religious, economical, or political.[27]

Also, the people in Koimumu and surrounding villages may hold different, sometimes even contradictory views of Christianity, cash crops, and councils; they may experimentally appropriate and exclude these aspects of Western culture in changing succession or simultaneously. Without neglecting the power differences between villagers and Westerners, I would therefore argue that indigenous cargo cult discourses show that cultural Otherness is coped with in a flexible, dynamic, and creative way. This might add to our fascination with the topic of this volume, perhaps even more than the previously mentioned "aura of mystery," which, judging from their accounts, seems to have captured some earlier authors.

What my interpretation of indigenous cargo cult discourses has deliberately left out, however, is of course a systematic comparison between indigenous and Western ways of coping with the cultural Other. In this sense there are, at least from my perspective, good reasons to continue talking *about* cargo cults in Koimumu.

Notes

This chapter is based on eleven months of stationary fieldwork in Koimumu (West New Britain Province, Papua New Guinea) in 1996 and 1997. My research was part of the project "Constructions of 'Cargo': On Coping with Cultural Otherness in Selected Parts of Papua New Guinea," which was generously supported by the Volkswagen Foundation and supervised by Karl-Heinz Kohl and in which Ton Otto also participated. I wish to thank the relevant institutions in Papua New Guinea for research permits, and I am, of course, most indebted to the inhabitants of Koimumu and surrounding villages for their cooperation, hospitality, and friendship: *taritigi sesele*.

1. See, for example, Dalton (2000c), Kaplan (1995b), Lattas (1992c, 1998), Lindstrom (1993), Otto (1992d), and Trompf (1990). Compare Robbins (present volume).

2. See Lindstrom (1993: 5), Jebens and Kohl (1999: 15), and, in the present volume, Hermann and Otto.

3. See Valentine (1955, 1958, 1960, 1961, 1963, 1965), and Valentine and Valentine (1979).

4. This approach by no means claims exclusive validity in the interpretation of cargo cults, a claim that would run the great risk of leading to just another reduction.

5. Neo-Melanesian Tok Pisin terms are printed in italics throughout this chapter.

6. Quote from fieldnotes written down immediately after the informal conversation on May 26, 1996, in Koimumu. (All translations from Tok Pisin into English by the author.)

7. Quote from fieldnotes written down immediately after the conversation on June 19, 1996, in Koimumu.

8. "Bikos mipela i wok wantaim moni, mipela i no wetim kago. Em yet i lukim" (part of a transcription of an interview with Martin Gar, Otto Puli, Titus Mou, and others, recorded on July 21, 1996, in Rapuri).

9. Interview with Titus Mou and Alphonse Mape, recorded on July 4, 1996, in Koimumu.

10. Translated from fieldnotes written down soon after the interview with Loko on July 26, 1996, in Galilo.

11. Lattas (1991: 239). The rejection of councils among the Kaliai has also been described by Counts (1971).

12. "Bai wokim samting i stret long ples" (part of a transcription of an interview with Togapu, recorded on July 28, 1996, in Rapuri).

13. Interview with Togapu, recorded on July 28, 1996, in Rapuri.

14. Interview with Barth Sesega, Kaose, and others, recorded on May 27, 1997, in Koimumu.

15. Translated from fieldnotes written down soon after the informal conversation with Antonia Dumu and others on May 15, 1997, in Koimumu.

16. "kam yumi wokim lotu" (part of a transcription of an interview with Paul Gar, Maternus Mape, and Cosmas Gar, recorded on September 18, 1997, in Pt. Moresby).

17. Part of a transcription of an interview with Peter Tautigi, recorded on September 2, 1997, in Koimumu.

18. Translated from fieldnotes written down immediately after the informal gathering on June 23, 1996, in Koimumu.

19. "Em cargo cult nau ya" (fieldnotes written down immediately after the informal gathering on June 14, 1997, in Koimumu).

20. These candidates gave their respective speeches in Koimumu on May 17, 1997 (Andrew Talingapore, National Party), and on June 12, 1997 (Brown Bai, Pangu Party).

21. From fieldnotes written down immediately after the informal conversation with Joe Kaveu on June 16, 1996, in Koimumu.

22. See, for example, Allan (1951: 94), Guiart (1951b: 170), Höltker (1941: 189), Lawrence (1964: 144), Pos (1950: 563), as well as Worsley (1957: 11), Steinbauer (1971: 37), and Jebens (1990: 56).

23. The fact that in their retrospective accounts villagers use such terms as "soldier," "lance corporal," "sergeant," and "sergeant major" should, however, not be overinterpreted; these terms imply an understanding of the relevant phenomena that did not necessarily prevailed in the past, too.

24. See Lattas for "internalization" (1992d: 74), "embodiment" (1991: 233), and "self-alienation" (1992b: 28). See also Lattas (1998) as well as my critique of his work (Jebens 2002).

25. Compare Dalton (present volume). Although it is beyond the scope of this chapter to compare Western and indigenous cargo cult narratives, I would argue that to see the latter as mere imitations of the former does imply a tendency to view people as the passive victims of external influences. The perceived similarities between the two sorts of narrative might to a certain extent be misleading, and indigenous use of the term "cargo cult" might in fact only seem to be a reproduction of Western use (see the introduction to the present volume).

26. The idea that Pater Berger's initial teachings have later been changed by Kivung adherents, reappears in a similar form, when it is claimed that the disciples of Jesus have distorted his message.

27. Thus, I agree with both Dalton and Leavitt (present volume) when they argue against distinguishing between cargo cults and more "pragmatic" movements.

CHAPTER 10 From "Cult" to Religious Conviction

The Case for Making Cargo Personal

Stephen C. Leavitt

STUDIES OF contemporary religious life in Melanesia have had to address a series of critiques of the "cargo cult" literature, critiques that raise questions about Westerners' distorted attempts to understand what the Melanesians are doing. One challenge is to work out a constructive basis for assessing Melanesians' persistent use of cargo ideas in their visions for social change. In that spirit, my aim here is to identify some dominant themes from the critiques of the cargo cult literature with the hope of suggesting some bases for continuing research on the topic while at the same time addressing the central problems these critiques point out. One theme that emerges, especially from earlier critiques, deals with the pejorative connotations of "cult" activities as either "irrational" behaviors of primitive peoples or as signs of mental instability or cultural collapse. Such arguments, the critics point out, prevent much inquiry into the movements' political aspirations or the local cultural constructions upon which they are based.

A second, more recent, theme addresses Westerners' imposition of Western cultural categories onto Melanesian behavior and experience. Our understanding of the cargo cult phenomenon relies, at its most benign, on our unwitting imposition of our own cultural categories regarding social change, mental stability, and the like to Melanesian contexts based on very different ways of understanding Self and collective action. At its most nefarious, our understanding seeks to justify Western domination and quell Melanesian resistance by pathologizing political activity as a way of keeping tight control of the colonial process. At both extremes, the critics argue, analyses of cargoistic phenomena are predicated fundamentally on our own Western constructs, severely distorting what they attempt to describe.

As an extension of this theme, articulated most successfully by Lindstrom (1993), the notion that our preoccupation with cargo phenomena has its basis in our own deepest dilemmas, so that the resulting cargo cult discourse, in both academic writing and popular mythology, has a certain zeal that fundamentally distorts our picture of Melanesians and their contemporary aspirations. Lindstrom argues that the topic of cargo in Melanesia has, over the years, provided fertile ground for a whole series of projections by Westerners of all stripes. He presents a credible genealogy of the concept of "cargo" in Western discourse, showing how earlier writers assembled a range of political and religious activities that were all "essentially alike" into a phenomenon called "cargo cults" (Lindstrom 1993: 33). Accounts used such terms as "madness" and "hysteria" to gloss these activities. Later anthropologists, concerned more with the details of local culture, began suggesting that cargo phenomena were reflections of a fundamental Melanesian worldview. Lindstrom refers to that trend in analysis as a "nativizing" of cargo that "establishes an awful equation between cargo cult and Melanesian culture" (1993: 42). He summarizes the trends in anthropological thinking as moving from an emphasis on the crisis of acculturation (as with the Ghost Dance in North America) to an emphasis on cargo orientations as simply contemporary renditions of Melanesian culture patterns. His point is that, throughout its history, "cargo cult" is something framed by Western desires in defining the terms of representation as much as anything actually happening in Melanesia. He shows as well how popular conceptions of Melanesian societies have been dominated by cargo cult themes so that, for many Westerners, if they have heard of Melanesia at all, they have heard there are cargo cults there. The result of all this is, of course, that our views of Melanesians remain hopelessly entangled with conceptions that have nothing to do with Melanesia at all.

But if one is to take from these critiques the message that the topic of "cargo" is not worth pursuing at all, then, in my view, a more intimate and compassionate understanding of Melanesians' aspirations may be lost. Consider Lindstrom's discussion (in the present volume) of the cargo "shopping lists" that so often appear in both popular accounts and ethnographic studies of cargo movements. Lindstrom summarizes, "Cargo lists, one can suspect, record our own desires as much as they do what Melanesians may actually have wanted" (present volume). Westerners coveted refrigerators in the twentieth century; hence the frequent appearance of refrigerators in cargo lists. Lindstrom suggests that on Tanna, at least, the local people themselves were quite "vague or cagey" (present volume) about what they actually desired. His implication is that, because of our own cargo desires, little can be learned about Melanesians from cargo details. But the details *do* matter. Unlike the Tannese, the Bumbita Arapesh of the East Sepik Province (Papua New Guinea), with whom I worked in 1984–1986, spoke quite specifically about what they wanted. They talked of telephones—not refrigerators—with phone lines emerging from graveyards. They talked of picket fences, of piles of boxes, of unending food, of lawns and tin roofs. One man spoke broadly of smooth things with sharp angles, spreading his hands across my table in a gesture of reverence. The goods mattered. They mattered not only for what they were but also for what they conveyed about gifts from cherished relatives and their affiliations with Europeans. Critiques of cargo accounts should not be allowed to discredit the principled ethnographic study of things Melanesians care very deeply about.

The real challenge is to articulate a strategy for addressing cargo ideas—which have persisted throughout Melanesia—that minimizes the distortions articulated by these critiques. It is naive to suggest that anthropologists can put together a style of analysis that avoids any injection of our own preoccupations and concerns, but it is possible, I believe, to pursue a line of analysis that attempts at least to address the problems raised by the critics. I shall argue here that one approach is to focus squarely on trying to describe individual Melanesians' experience as they strive to accommodate the changes brought by the colonial system. The goal should be fundamentally ethnographic, in the sense that one refrains from making global generalizations about "cargoism" across the culture area. Each local community, even as it attaches itself to cargo ideas spread across whole regions, articulates a specific ideology rooted fundamentally in local cultural categories. Furthermore, individual cult adherents put their own personal stamp on the ideas they espouse so that describing the experience of cargo participation requires detailed discussion of individual cases, with close attention paid to what the person actually says (see also Jebens, present volume).

My work with the Bumbita Arapesh sees cargo ideas resonating not only with people's views of their relations with their own kin, but also with the deep sense of personal loss that comes from dealing with death, with the transformed basis for social relations in the loss of tradition, and with a sharp sense of self-reflection in the face of change. All of this is the stuff of deep religious conviction that the "cargo cult" frame of discourse tended not to acknowledge. In what follows, I shall outline in detail some of the critiques of the cargo cult literature and then illustrate my own view of a productive avenue for analysis by presenting the outlines of Bumbita Arapesh religious convictions drawing on cargo themes.

The Critique of "Cargo Cult"

Some critiques of the cargo cult literature focus on the implied contrast between relatively developed or "rational" societies with those who were more "primitive." This has set up a contrast between the West and the rest that has persisted in even more recent discussions of the cargo topic. One more vehement critic, Andrew Lattas, focuses on the work of F. E. Williams, who had sought to explain outbreaks of "madness" in terms of the loss of native culture. Lattas points out that the patterns of Western response support Western domination in the colonial context. He argues, for example, that attributing mob behavior to emotional proclivities (as Williams did) "pathologizes" potential collective resistances to colonial power (Lattas 1992b: 7). Psychological analyses were framed in ways that supported colonial interests. Trance behavior, for example, became labeled as "insanity" only when used to oppose Western interests (Lattas 1992b: 6). Another articulation of a similar critique is put forward by Jeffrey Clark (1992), who discusses explanations of cargo cults, wild-man behavior, and hysteria that relied on a notion of psychological trauma to explain the acts. Associated with many of these explanations is the idea that rapid social change has undermined traditional worldviews, with its introduction of new systems of control. Clark writes, "Such explanations no longer convince, mostly for their neglect of the dynamic and flexible nature of Melanesian religion, and for their conflation of innovative attempts at social transformation with the disease symptoms of a 'sick' society" (1992: 16). Both Lattas and Clark have addressed cargo themes in their own work, focusing on the specifics of local concepts arising out of distinct culturally patterned views of body and social relations. Their position is that only through an articulation of such fundamental bases of local cultural forms can an analysis avoid reinventing a self-interested dichotomy between colonizer and colonized.

Other criticisms focus less on the hegemonic character of Western discussions of cargo phenomena and more on the unwitting impositions of foreign categories on local constructs. In a brief but influential 1988 article in *Pacific Studies,* Nancy McDowell points out a wide range of complications raised by attempts to articulate what a cargo cult is. She suggests, in fact, that "cargo cult" is not a viable category of social movement; the term is profoundly misleading and should not be used. Her statement is the most forceful in a series of recent criticisms and centers on several points: first, when viewed in the context of Western values, the focus on cargo (or material gains) is condescending or derogatory, especially in the popular imagination. Focusing on a people's desire to get cargo risks portraying them as crassly materialistic and exploits the "exotic" nature of their beliefs. The truth is, she argues, that Melanesian cargo beliefs reflect broad constellations of cultural ideas about the nature of social order, power, history, and the person. They have a lot to do with many more things than cargo. Furthermore, lumping cargo cults into the category of "millenarian movement" leads one to ignore the important local cultural premises on which the cults are based. The ideas underlying cargo thinking in fact underlie Melanesian approaches to business, Christianity, and a host of other social activities, many of which are not religious at all. It is better to see cargo movements as expressions of local understandings about how things change. So McDowell argues, for instance, that cargo and other social movements reflect an "episodic" (as opposed to an "evolutionary") notion of history. According to her, from the Melanesian point of view, if you want social change, you have to bring about a grand transformation. Hence the variety of apocalyptic movements. In addition, focusing on the religious cargoistic ideology of cults tends to obscure the fact that Melanesians have had legitimate concerns about colonial domination and unequal distributions of wealth. Cargo activity is simply the Melanesian way of conducting large-scale political action to effect social change.

McDowell's arguments bring the critics' legitimate concerns into clearer focus. Looking at religious movements without fully appreciating local epistemological frameworks risks distortion and unnecessary pigeonholing. There is, however, a danger too in turning away from the central concept of cargo to look to "episodic notions of history" or "legitimate political action" for explanations of these social movements. The fact remains that the social movements are deeply religious and dramatically apocalyptic. The transformation sought is powerful in local minds precisely because it is *not* just like the usual run-of-the-mill social change. And the fact remains that cargo is the central and most powerful concept. It is not just that cargo cults are examples of Melanesian social phenomena; it is more accurate to say that Melanesian social phenomena, including Christianity and business, are often cargoistic. What does that mean? It means that the central goal is still to get Western cargo, the cargo is controlled by human spirits, and redemption lies in finding the way to get the spirits to hand over the cargo.

Recent sociological research has also focused on similar problems with discussing categories of social movements more broadly. In recent years, sociological studies have shifted from a primary focus on resource mobilization—the pursuit of political and material goals in the context of the political structure of society at large—to an approach addressing "the construction of meaning, consciousness raising, the manipulation of symbols, and collective identities" expressed in social action (Morris and Mueller 1992: ix). The editors of one recent volume on social movements describe the trend as an attempt to develop a "social psychology" that complements resource mobilization approaches (Morris and Mueller 1992: ix). It is a way to "bring culture back in" to social movement research (Hart 1996: 87). The idea here is that "social problems are not objective phenomena"; rather, they are always perceived from within a culturally constructed worldview (Klandermans 1992: 77). People's motivations have to be understood in terms of their prior views of Self and society. In building a vision for an improved world, social reformers seek transformations in their most basic sense of their relation to the community. As William Gamson puts it, "Participation in social movements frequently involves an enlargement of personal identity for participants and offers fulfillment and realization of self" (1992: 56). When people mobilize to create a transformed society, they are at the same time using the movement to refashion their sense of who they are. Because a transformed identity is often a goal in its own right, a movement's ability to tap into participants' basic self-definition can contribute significantly to its success (Melucci 1989). Hence, the sociological literature as well has focused on the potential for strong analyses in the careful articulation of local cultural categories, especially those tacit ones underlying the most fundamental ideas of Self, body, and society.

The critics have made some important points and have at the same time offered avenues for productive research based on detailed articulations of local ideas. In fact, much of the more recent work on the topic of cargo, with its emphasis on discursive practices and narrative structures, exemplified by the work of Lattas (1992d, 1993) and Clark (1992), critics themselves, has reestablished the point that cargo ideas are reactions to particular conditions of power and domination built into the postcolonial paradigm but framed in local discourse. These are not simply pathological reactions, Western projections, or expressions of a general Melanesian culture.

Nevertheless, calls for greater attention to local discourse are not sufficient. If "local discourse" refers simply to local symbolic forms and decontextualized local statements, our research runs the risk of reproducing broad sweeping generalizations not unlike those that got the concept of "cargo cult" in trouble in the first place. So, for example, although McDowell's point about cargo cults going the way of totemism, vanishing under scrupulous attempts to categorize them accurately, directs researchers to resist generalizations at the expense of ethnographic subtlety, her gloss of Melanesians living in a world of "episodic" versus "evolutionary" time does little to help us understand the subtleties of local points of view. Similarly, whereas Lattas promotes greater attention to local symbolic forms, his analysis nevertheless persists in applying a general "subjugator versus subjugated" frame for bush Kaliai relations with Europeans. In a detailed critique of Lattas' publications on the cargo theme, Holger Jebens identifies an "underlying persistency" of a "dichotomy between oppressors and oppressed" in Lattas' work that appears to have "prevented him not only from contextualizing his data sufficiently but also from looking for facts which might have contradicted his theses" (2002: 196). In my own view, one effective way of tempering our tendency to reframe Melanesian cargo aspirations in terms of categories we ourselves find compelling is to devote more space to the actual statements of individual adherents in specific contexts. To that end, in my own work I have sought to address the points raised by the critics by discussing facets of Bumbita Arapesh cargo beliefs in terms of individuals' personal experiences.

Cargo Themes in Religious Conviction

One implication of the above discussion of the critiques of the cargo cult concept is that it is necessary, but not sufficient, to convey the character of religious conviction in cargo ideas by outlining the particular cultural frames upon which those ideas are based. In addition, our work can strive to convey the deeply personal character of these beliefs. If we accept the view that, for many Melanesians, cargo ideas are at the heart of a religious eschatology, we must also accept that these ideas will be applied, as religious ideas often are, to addressing the fundamental dilemmas of human experience. Among the Bumbita Arapesh, cargo beliefs are part of an entrenched ideology through which individuals work with feelings of grief over personal loss (Leavitt 1995b, 1995c), grapple with implications of the end of the colonial administration (Leavitt 1995a), and strive for new visions of Self and place (Leavitt 2000, 2001).

My focus on individual experience begins with the recognition that Bumbita cargo beliefs are based not only on local cultural constructions, but also on deep personal convictions about themselves, their moral positions, and their relationships with close kin. Although scholars have long recognized that cargo beliefs draw on elements from traditional beliefs, there has yet to be full recognition that the ancestors with whom people seek communication and for whom they perform their rituals are not distant and anonymous supernatural beings; they are the spirits of fathers, brothers, and other close relatives. They are the spirits of people whose loss has left deep scars, of people who have been the focus of emotional conflict.

Bumbita cargo beliefs arise out of one central tenet: the conviction that the ancestors, or spirits of the dead, will bring the cargo and bestow it upon the living. For the Bumbita, ancestors are the spirits of close deceased relatives. They have traditionally interceded on behalf of the living by providing power to grow yams, catch pigs, and perform sorcery—if the proper rituals were carried out. The living may communicate with the dead through dreams and occasionally through visions, but such communication is often fleeting and unsatisfactory. Also, the ancestors have acquired a sinister, powerful, and mysterious aspect by virtue of being dead. Consuming flesh from a corpse is the essential component for men to acquire the magical power to kill others through sorcery. The spirits of the dead may protect sorcerers by making them invisible. At the core of the concept of "cargo" lies the prospect of material wealth, which in immediate terms means living like Europeans. Acquiring cargo also means the attainment of a kind of paradise. As the Bumbita see it, the Europeans' world is one without anguish and pain, without sickness and hunger, and without any form of social conflict. Finally, it is the act of "bestowing" that is the most important feature of aspirations for cargo. Acquiring the cargo means receiving it as a gift, a gift from the dead. The Bumbita view of the colonial experience is grounded upon their sense that material wealth has been provided to the Europeans but withheld from them. The Europeans have gotten access to the cargo and can communicate with the dead, yet for the Bumbita themselves, the dead remain largely silent. It is this that leads them to ask the inevitable question: why?

The answer to that question leads to what is at the heart of Bumbita cargo aspirations. The appearance of Europeans required that individual Bumbita actors respond, and they did so by applying conventional categories. At the same time, though, the pragmatics of the historical encounter shifted the symbolic ground upon which the ideas were framed, creating new valences to traditional relations of exchange, changing Bumbita culture even as people sought to preserve it. Specifically at issue was how to interpret the exchange relations implied by the European presence. Following a broadly based Melanesian pattern, the Bumbita make a sharp distinction between the mediated exchange that creates competition or public debt and the unmediated sharing of substance that underlies parents' relations with children. Were Europeans potential competitors in the sphere of competitive exchange, or could they be framed in the sphere of unmediated exchange relations of close kin? With the threat of failure in the prospect of competition, and with the paternalistic idiom of the colonial presence, there was no choice but to associate Europeans closely with their own deceased kin. But with that association, the basic premise of support from the spirit realm was now in jeopardy. The symbolic ground had shifted. Success became associated not only with producing goods, but also with acquiring Western goods on the order of those seen to be in the hands of those few Europeans in the area. The inevitable failure to acquire those goods implied, in local Bumbita terms, a rejection—a personal rejection, in fact—by the spirits of one's parents and close relatives. In view of these symbolic links, not receiving cargo implies some amount of ill will on the part of spirits of the dead. In psychological terms, then, Bumbita individuals experience not receiving the cargo as a kind of emotional abandonment, as a failure on the part of the dead to exhibit the generous care giving understood to prevail in relations among close kin. There is a tendency to blame oneself for alienating the dead. In this emotional environment, believing that the cargo *will* come, believing that the dead *are* communicating, can provide immeasurable solace.

At their core, the religious convictions about cargo, as Clark and Lattas have argued, must be understood as persistent attempts to domesticate the alienating experience of colonialism (Clark 1992; Lattas 1992d). The rhetoric offers a way of seeing bewildering changes in familiar terms. But beyond that, by casting modernization issues in the context of local relations, it offers some promise of control over one's destiny in a world that otherwise defies understanding. Lattas describes Kaliai narrative fictions as creating fields of "intersubjective action" where "the pain and suffering of colonialism is that of being alienated from one's double, the white man being the ultimate double, the ultimate second skin" (Lattas 1992d: 51). In Bumbita, with their emphasis more on casting Europeans as intimates, the dream of cargo is the dream that ancestors might affirm their ties by bestowing the requisite gifts.

Although the difference between Lattas' account of Kaliai and my own of Bumbita might at first appear insignificant, in fact Bumbita emphasis on relations with ancestral spirits argues against their having been wholly subjugated by a discourse framed by colonial rule. According to Lattas, the Kaliai "personalized" the structural inequalities between colonists and themselves, creating a moral frame to explain them, so they themselves became "morally responsible for the conditions of [their] own subjugation" (Lattas 1992d: 32). This response cohered well with colonial ambitions to define the locals as "primitive," "heathen," and otherwise morally inferior. Kaliai efforts to imitate Europeans imply, according to Lattas, that initially they accepted the colonial definitions of themselves as wholly different and morally inferior. This view suggests that, initially at least, colonial categories defined the conditions for the Kaliai response to colonialism. Jebens (2002) has argued, though, that Lattas likely overstates the extent to which the bush Kaliai embraced colonial definitions. In any case, the Bumbita focus on relations with ancestral spirits suggests a somewhat different position. Domesticating colonial presence under the umbrella of relations with the spirits implies not so much an acceptance of colonial categories as a transformation of them into terms that speak to very personal concerns. Abstract notions of being a "sinner" or "backward" are replaced by specific preoccupations with one's behavior toward one's own parents. It is a process that negates any effort by colonials to codify rigid moral distinctions between European and "native." Instead, they construct a much more personal discourse. The Bumbita personalization of European presence fits with what Errington and Gewertz have argued for Karavarans: "[A]lthough Karavarans did blame themselves as inadequate orderers, they did not internalize as fundamental to themselves that which marked them as different from Europeans. Though Karavarans clearly regarded themselves as in some way deficient, they never regarded their deficiency as a product of inherent nature" (Errington and Gewertz 1995: 32; emphasis omitted).

The Bumbita interest in Europeans' relations with the dead presupposes that we all live in the *same* moral universe, not that Europeans are somehow fundamentally superior. Errington and Gewertz go on to argue that for Karavar the cargoistic response was "a particularly Melanesian form of resistance, one by which local groups attempted to maintain or enhance their own worth" (1995: 22). In the Bumbita case, the focus on relations with spirits redefines the situation to such an extent that terms such as "resistance" can be applied only in a highly derivative sense. They have refused to accept the conditions of colonial discourse, but in a way that diverts their attention away from the political terms of their subjugation.

Space permits only a brief illustration of these points from the cases of specific individuals. What follows are brief summaries of case material, all published elsewhere. One of my closest friends was a young man in his late teens, whom I call "Aminguh." Aminguh's father was an important leader, and he died when Aminguh was in his early teens. Aminguh told me that he felt some responsibility for his father's death because he had been charged with looking after him when he was ill and had, as he tells it, briefly left him alone, enabling sorcerers to come in and finish him off. He describes himself as still preoccupied with his father. He says, "Sometimes I lie in the house and I think, I want to lie there and he must come to me. While I'm alone this man must come up and stand there and say [whispering], 'Hey! You look at me!' I must see him just once so I could feel the pain. I think like that." When I asked him to tell me how he imagines seeing him, he says, "I would [come up to him and] ask him, 'If you have something, you can help me. But if you don't have anything, it's all right, I can just see your face. Or whatever thinking you have, you must tell me.' I think of it that way.... 'Ach, I need some money,' and then, 'Or give me something, whatever, love magic, give me some rice, or some clothes, with a suitcase. Shorts.'"

What bothers Aminguh most is that in reality, his father seems not to hear his requests, for he has gotten no sign from him. He says, "Sometimes I lie there turning over and thinking, 'Ach, my father didn't want to—he sees me like this and he doesn't want to help me with some money.'" Toward the end of my stay in Bumbita, Aminguh became more preoccupied with getting some sign from me that I was communicating with his father's spirit or that I could give him some cargo secrets. He described a dream he had in which he happened upon me in the process of extracting cargo from a graveyard, and I promised him some of the wealth as long as he kept my secret. The story of the dream follows the pattern of his stories of spying on his friends as a child, where he managed to share their food by promising to keep their activities a secret. By this time, he had come to associate me with his father as well, so his cargo dream conveys some of his continuing anxieties over communication from his father.

In a second case, "Matthew" was a man known in the area for his zealous interest in cargo ideas, and he had a particular preoccupation with local missionaries and other Europeans. Everywhere he went, he carried a large bag of mementos of Christian literature, calendars of years past, photographs of favorite missionaries, and even some letters sent by them from abroad. Every item was tattered, stained, or frayed. I interviewed Matthew over a period of three months, and toward the end he told me a story about the time he discovered that one of the local European missionaries was in fact his own father, returned from the dead. This missionary was leaving Papua New Guinea for home, and Matthew went to see him to give him some yams and greens as a gift. According to his story, Matthew then realized the missionary was his father: "[The missionary] went and got a funnel and ... got some salt and filled up a bottle of it for me, and then I asked him. I said, 'I think you are my father. I think you have the face of my father, Turingi, and your wife is like my mother, Tinga'wen. I can see the resemblance.' And there was no answer. He did not answer me because he was ashamed. He said, 'Just take the salt and go. You shouldn't come and blabber too much.' [Laughs] And now you see here, I have written their names in my book." He then went on to tell me that if this man were only a missionary, he certainly would not have had to take all sorts of cargo and personal belongings *back* with him to his own country. It must be that the white people's cargo really comes from the ground at the local mission station.

Matthew told me this story to convince me of the authenticity of his religious ideas, much the way one would recount a miracle or an encounter with God. He was saying, in effect, that it was important to his religious worldview that this missionary be his own father. The story conveys an aura of unspoken communication, as if the gift were all that need be said. He has the missionary telling him to hush up. Seeing the local missionary as his father comes in a situation where Matthew was in fact alienated from his father for most of his adult life. As he tells the story, his father tried to seduce Matthew's intended bride when she moved to their compound. When Matthew found out about this, he attacked his father with a spear, trying to kill him. After that incident, the father was banished from the village and lived in an adjacent area until he was an old man. At that point, Matthew decided to accept his father back. He says, "[When my father] became sick, he came [to me] and said, 'I think that you my son should take me back.'... He called out to me and I felt sorry for him, thinking, 'Before, when I was little, he looked after me.' I felt sorry like that so I brought him back." Matthew's father lived for a few more years and eventually converted to Christianity. Matthew says, "He converted and was strong in his belief and died a believer and I think that now he is with God. [Whispers] I have already told you, he is with God here, he has become Jesus, later you, too, and I, too, will become Jesus like my father." It was in this context that Matthew came to see the missionary's gift of salt as a silent statement of goodwill after a painful and long-term rift.

In a final example, "John" was another older man who had been a village leader in his youth. After his conversion to Christianity, John began to have ambitions that he would be like "a king" in the new age. He saw God as his own father, as an ally in his crusade to convert others. He described to me dreams in which he asked his father to help him and his father responded by showing him visions of cargo. He says, "[One night] I took the Bible inside and made a fire and just lay down. I said, 'God'—I prayed—'God, I want you to show me my present now, where is it? I want to see it.'... All right, When I went to sleep, I went straight to it. Man, I went inside and they ... —Sorry! Huge huge cases, more and more of them, going up to the clouds." At this point he woke up abruptly and found himself lying on his bed. "Then what did I do? I cried and cried over the present that God had shown me." He later confirmed to me that the "God" of his dream was in fact his own father, "a short man, but now that he's gone, a big man.... Now he has shown me everything. Who is he? God the father." In John's case, there is euphoria in the vision of cargo that comes to him in dreams. For John, this is the gift (with its promise of more to come) that assures him that his father continues to care for him.

These stories point up in various ways the personal significance of seeing cargo as the gift from a cherished family member. They show that the heart of Bumbita postcolonial eschatology lies the hope that the world is to be transformed by renewed relationships with spirits of the dead. While people may disagree about which is the best "road" to follow in bringing this about—business development, revival Christianity, and cargo movements have all been considered—there is an insistence that *relations* with ancestral spirits are key to effecting any dramatic change. What this means is that when the Bumbita think about their futures, whether it is their own personal destinies or their larger place on the world stage, they tend to do so in terms of a familial scenario involving parental figures (spirits) sharing or withholding gifts and, in so doing, engaging or ignoring the affairs of their children. By thinking this way, they insist that general existential problems associated with the arrival of the Europeans be refracted through a particular set of ideas about getting nurturing and sustenance from the sharing of gifts.

Imagining a Self through Religious Consensus

The material presented thus far conveys how individual personal narratives, drawing on cargo themes, can serve to reframe colonial experience into an intimately personal context. The desire to acquire cargo becomes a foil for reestablishing good relations with deceased relatives. Behind all of this, though, I believe, is a broader effort to reimagine a basic sense of Self in relation to the local community. This larger effort speaks directly to the appeal not only of cargo ideas but to the hope for a new kind of community based on an adherence to a social movement, in the Bumbita case a Christian revival movement active during the time of my stay. Specifically, the religious movement provided the kind of unanimity that would allow villagers to imagine a new, relatively autonomous vision of themselves.

The argument runs as follows. As with many Melanesians, Bumbita Self schemas, emerging out of a deeply sociocentric view of social interaction, set up a tension between a desire for personal autonomy and an overwhelming sense that one is in fact defined by one's relations with others. Although one may yearn to act on one's own, without regard for others, the reality is that for each action one must consider a myriad of factors relating to one's relatives and associates. Social conditions like these prevail in face-to-face societies everywhere. In Melanesia, though, researchers have sought to establish the "sociocentric" bases of self understandings without asking much about what this means for individuals trying to live their lives on a day-to-day basis. The sociocentric Self is, for many Bumbita, a severe burden.

As the recent sociological research has pointed out, it is the overlay of specific local cultural understandings that gives each case its distinctive shape, and in Melanesia notions of Self and society emphasize the interconnected quality of human action to a striking degree. Consider some common examples: personal interactions are defined by exchange relations, so even personal slights may be avenged by offering a gift to the offender; deaths are often explained in terms of human agents acting either through sorcery or outright murders; and religion takes its power explicitly from the spiritual efficacy of collective action. In a society so defined, day-to-day living can seem oppressive to individual actors. In a sense, one is continually being invoked by others into acting a certain way. Each individual faces a contradiction—one longs to be free of these social encumbrances while nonetheless maintaining a deep sense that one's social relations define who one is. The idea of consensus promised by widespread adherence to a religious movement thus becomes immensely appealing because it neutralizes the contradiction—everyone, including oneself, is working toward the same goal while at the same time preserving a sense of personal autonomy. Thus, when the Bumbita revival sought to transform the society, there was an underlying promise that with consensus would come a release from the problems imposed by their definitions of who they are. When the prospects for consensus faltered, the movement lost its appeal.

Perhaps the most important feature of the proposed Christian society was the maintenance or attainment of a state of *wan bel,* a Tok Pisin term translated roughly as "collective harmony." Achieving a state of collective harmony could, the Christians believed, do more than anything else to set the stage for the arrival of Jesus. *Wan bel* refers not only to a lack of open conflict and dispute, but also to a united purpose of mind directed toward the apocalyptic goal. During the course of the revival movement, *wan bel* became a rallying cry for Christians. Whenever enticed into arguments, revivalists would call out to their adversaries with "*Wan bel! Wan bel!*" rather than continue the argument. It was their equivalent to turning the other cheek. In addition, *wan bel* replaced "good morning" or "good day" as the standard salutation when greeting someone or shaking hands. It was a theme stressed continually in church sermons. If the people were to get right with God, they had to be, more than anything else, united. Some people began to talk of *wan bel* as an important ingredient to miraculous events. In one sermon, a local pastor talked about *wan bel* in this way: "The revival is being *wan bel.* This is the core [*as*] of the revival. If there is unity [*wan bel*], then everything in the revival will happen [i.e., the new age will arrive]. If there is no unity, then the revival will stop like a cut tree which is stuck against the others as it tries to fall." He then went on to emphasize that Christians must seek to avoid all conflict in an attempt to remain pure. He pointed out that for three years he had personally avoided all contact with local magistrates because they dealt with disputes on a regular basis. Another man, in a revealing statement about the efficacy of miraculous "discoveries" of hidden sorcery implements, pointed out that discovery attempts by women filled with the Holy Spirit *(glas meri)* were only successful when the sorcerer himself had already been *wan bel,* had already agreed that they should be discovered. As he put it, "God will not allow her to see where the objects are hidden unless the owner is *wan bel.*" These examples show how local views link the achievement of collective harmony to the efficacy of magical activities and to the success of the revival as a whole.

The emphasis on collective harmony clearly intends to redress what is viewed as a fundamental local failing. If asked to describe the primary difference between themselves and Europeans, the Bumbita inevitably point to the perception that they can never get along with one another (see also M. Smith 1994: 161). Europeans possess an almost miraculous ability to coordinate their actions, and they have demonstrated a capacity to put aside petty personal aspirations in favor of collective goals. The Bumbita themselves never seem to be able to accomplish that. In this context, the idea of consensus emerges as something that has miraculous potential to heal body and soul. Any residue of the contention and dispute that characterized traditional Bumbita society now appears to be inimical to Christian action, to the point that individuals may react viscerally, even falling into seizures, if they do not wholeheartedly embrace the new vision. And residual disagreements also threaten the power of the movement as a whole. Thus, the ideas underlying the drive for consensus in the revival movement contained new visions for how one presents oneself to society, and the appeal of this completely new way of living had an overwhelming appeal.

Conclusion

I have hoped to show with these examples the value of a continued attention to the religious convictions displayed through cargo ideologies and manifested in local religious movements. The critics of the cargo cult literature have pointed out the failings of rubrics designed primarily to classify religious movements into this or that category. Their call for a renewed interest in the very specific, local understandings built out of the colonial context, shows promise of gaining a better understanding of the religious basis upon which cargo ideas are based. But it is my view that an even more enhanced understanding can emerge from the more intimate features of cargo ideology as revealed in the personal narratives of individual actors. In their specific stories lie the potential for having a better grasp of cargo ideology as a product of personal experience. Each person has his own story to tell, of grappling with the potential humiliations of the postcolonial world, of striving to create a new sense of identity out of what are at their heart deeply religious convictions. Such ideas do not lend themselves to global generalizations across cultural areas, a project inherent in the whole "cargo cult" enterprise. But they do offer the promise of our achieving a more empathic appreciation for the trials of cargo adherents.

COMPARISON AND CRITIQUE

CHAPTER 11 Cargo and Cult

The Mimetic Critique of Capitalist Culture

Doug Dalton

Knowing Ourselves

We owe Lamont Lindstrom (1993) a debt of gratitude for having looked into the history of "cargo cult" thinking in anthropology, traced its trajectory, and shifted the locus of discussion away from indigenous cultures and toward Western preoccupations. This sort of intellectual move was initiated at least by Roy Wagner when he suggested that "cargo" is the indigenous Papua New Guinea term for Western pursuits. Though Lindstrom does not follow the implications of Wagner's insight, he nevertheless shows that the basic trend in anthropological thinking about so-called cargo cult has been to nativize and normalize it by accounting for it as an expression of normal, rational, and logical processes and functions of indigenous Melanesian cultures.

There are good reasons for this theoretical course. Cargo cult was originally thought of in evolutionary terms as an indication of the irrational backwardness of native Melanesians, who were thereby deemed not yet capable of fully entering a rational capitalist economy. Stories in *Life* and *National Geographic* made this view acceptable to the middle-class American public. The term was therefore used politically to delegitimize cargo cult activities. "Cargo cult" functioned as a tool of political repression and as a justification for exploitation by colonial capitalist powers. It did so by fitting Melanesians into the Western ideological "savage slot" with the assumption that "man" is the animal endowed with the capacity to reason, and the non-Western Other is less so (Trouillot 1991).

Against this denigrating colonialist and racist view, anthropologists have long sought to make Western Europeans aware of the essential humanity of Melanesian peoples and the fundamental functional and logical symbolic rationality of their cultures. Yet most anthropological writings nevertheless recognize that there is something truly strange about these behaviors. Most recent cargo writings are therefore quite willing to attribute at least some of the odd mimetic behavior characteristic of these cults to the harsh struggles and stresses of grossly exploitive colonial apartheid situations. Cargo cults are thus also often thought of as what used to be called "syncretic" phenomena—combining characteristics of indigenous and European cultures. Yet anthropologists typically emphasize the local coherence and functioning of the native elements of cargo cults while attributing their more conceptually troublesome aspects to Western imperialism.

Anthropologists are the defenders of the "primitive" in the Western imagination. They strive to eliminate any suggestion that Melanesians might be in any way weird or suffer pathology except at the hands of outsiders. Because anthropologists are experts in interpreting and understanding human behavior in terms of the logic and function of "culture," it is inevitable that they account for and make sense out of the most curious features of cargo cults as normal, culturally organized native behavior. Yet, in the case of cargo cults, it may be necessary to question the anthropological idea of "culture."

Critically evaluating Western anthropological thought is always a necessary part of any anthropological study. It is logically an equal part of forging intercultural understandings. Anthropologists "defamiliarize" European assumptions and deploy native concepts to critique Western culture. The very method of intensive fieldwork entails putting at risk one's preconceptions, for anthropologists exert the least amount of control over the people they study of any social scientists. The critical evaluation of Western thought is even more necessary with cargo cults, for the behaviors thus designated are Papua New Guinea peoples' physical enactment of European capitalist culture. These behaviors therefore cannot be understood without a thorough interrogation of the most basic premises of modern Western culture.

Cargo Trouble

Cargo cults defy definition. They are inherently troublesome and problematic. Contemporary debates over the meanings of the term precipitate a sense of trouble, as if their indeterminacy may end up in the failure of anthropology's culture concept or Western science's ability to rationally comprehend everything. Rather than approach this cargo trouble in the mode of social science—as a problem to be resolved—I believe that it should be approached in the mode of an intellectual activist—as the sign of a political ruse. Trouble is something that one should not make precisely because it is something one can thereby get in. The prevailing law threatens one with trouble supposedly to keep one out of trouble. Trouble is therefore an inevitable condition and tautological ruse of power. The question is therefore not how to avoid it but how to best be in it—how to maximally deploy it.[1]

Because cargo cult has proven to be such a troublesome concept, it should be assumed that this is a characteristic feature of what it designates rather than something to be reduced or overcome in any way. The fact that we are publishing a set of conference papers on the concept after at least seventy-six years of attempting to explain it is indicative of its inherently unruly nature.[2] Many have recently recognized cargo cult's recalcitrance to naming, definition, and explanation to advocate doing away with the concept. Nancy McDowell has pointed out the parallel between cargo cult and totemism in arguing that, because the latter does not exist, being "merely an example of how people classify the world around them, cargo cults, too, do not exist, being merely an example of how people conceptualize and experience change in the world" (McDowell 1988: 122). Many others have also recognized that cargo cult phenomena seem ubiquitous, leading to the adoption of the idea of widespread "cargo cult thinking."[3]

Besides pointing out how the concept was used as a tool of colonialism, it has been argued that cargo cults do not exist because native peoples are not so fixated on obtaining Western manufactured goods as they are imaged to be.[4] Indeed, the announcement for the workshop for which the chapters contained in this volume were originally produced suggested that, "If ... economic metaphors have played a major role in describing and analysing cargo cults, this may not be caused by any innate materialism on the part of the Melanesians themselves, but by the fact, that for Westerners the economy has become the primary locus of cultural innovation." The classic Western cargo cult stereotype emphasizes the disparity between indigenous magical, religious, cultural symbolic means, on the one hand, and European rational economic or political ends, on the other. The hallmarks of cargo cult include fits of hysterical shaking and frenzied activity involving the mimicking of European behaviors in ways that are quite apparently ineffectual in obtaining the goals attributed to them. Thus, "cargo cult" stands for an intercultural misunderstanding. Although I believe that cargo cults are the precise opposite of a misunderstanding, at least on the part of native Papua New Guineans, I do not advocate that we necessarily drop the term—although I do not suppose the precise words matter very much, as long as they preserve the unruly nature of cargo cults. I do not believe that we should keep the term because it is adequate, which it is not. Rather, I advocate that "cargo cult" should be kept precisely because of its inadequacy—because the term preserves something of the troublesome nature, which is an essential characteristic of the behavior, it designates.

Roy Wagner writes that cargo cults are "strangely impervious to the kind of 'argument through dependency' that our rationalistic outlook fosters" (1979: 164). This strange imperviousness is captured in the paradoxical tension between the two terms "cargo" and "cult."[5] "Cargo" has been taken to mean the desire that Melanesians have for Western manufactured goods, which is often expressed in "cargo cult" concerns to be like Whitemen and obtain money and material wealth. "Cult" then stands for the indigenous cultural-symbolic or magical religious means that indigenous Melanesians employ to obtain those ends. It is this purported desire that anthropologists have most thoroughly shown to be erroneous, for the individualistic materialistic motives that are so central to Western bourgeois culture are simply not present in Papua New Guinea, where rural people maximize social relations and prestige by giving things away and employ wealth only to the degree that it is needed for ritual social benefit (Sahlins 1992).

At the same time, anthropologists have shown that the cult element of cargo cult actually consists of logically organized symbolic religious systems with their own functional rationality. The basic direction of the anthropological critique of the cargo cult concept has thus been to erase or cross-out the term "cargo" while culturally legitimizing the idea underlying the term "cult" by showing it to follow the functional logic of indigenous "culture." It should be noted that, although critical efforts directed toward the term "cargo cult" have specifically challenged "cargo" for falsely imputing materialism and such, they have less often interrogated the term "cult." When "cult" has been questioned, it has been to undermine the idea that the activities thus designated have no legitimate authority (i.e., to substitute for it indigenous "culture").

In other words, even if cult beliefs failed to bring cargo or make their followers impervious to Western bullets, they have the right to maintain a sovereign culture. After cargo cult, indigenous people are left with culture. We should remember, however, that there are at least two "savage slots" in Western ideology (Trouillot 1991). One is that of the relatively less rational (and therefore by implication less fully human) denigrated Other. The other is that of the nevertheless more "natural" or vitally social, relatively unfettered by the ills of Western civilization, romanticized Other. In displacing the "cult," the "culture" construct has tended to find the romanticized Other, displacing one savage slot with another.

Besides indigenous material desire, "cargo" has also been taken to stand for the Western rational industrial material economic political order, whereas cult indicates the indigenous religious cultural conceptual system. The former is generally assumed to be real and true, and the latter is symbolic and all too often sadly mistaken about the capitalist world economy. The disparity between cargo and cult is then seen as the engine of historic change among Melanesian people. The operative idea of history here would seem to be that the world is going in the direction of increasing Western rationality. The problem with this view of historic change is that not only does cargo cult thinking continue to be ubiquitous, but even specific cargo cult movements have never gone away.

Wagner has also suggested that, whereas "culture" is the word that anthropologists use to interpret and understand Melanesians, "kago" is the term that Papua New Guineans use to interpret and understand Western Europeans:

> If we call such phenomena "cargo cults," then anthropology should perhaps be called a "culture cult," for the Melanesian "kago" is very much the interpretive counterpart of our word "culture." The words are to some extent "mirror images" of each other, in the sense that we look at the natives' cargo, their techniques and artifacts, and call it "culture," whereas they look at our culture and call it "cargo." These are analogic usages, and they betray as much about the interpreters themselves as about the thing interpreted. "Cargo" is practically a parody, a reduction of Western notions like profit, wage-labor, and production for its own sake to the terms of tribal society. ... Cargo is really an antisymbol to "culture": it metaphorizes the sterile orders of technique and self-fulfilling production as life and human relation, just as "culture" does the reverse. (R. Wagner 1981: 31–32)

From this perspective, it is even more telling that the term "cargo" has come to be interrogated more than "cult," much less the concept that has come to replaced it, "culture." If "kago" is actually the Papua New Guinean word for Western culture—one that supplies critical insight into Western assumptions underlying the idea of "culture" from a Papua New Guinean perspective—then eliminating it effectively undermines an indigenous critical perspective and replaces it with a Western normalizing notion. Not only is this indigenous idea thereby erased, the critical and troublesome nature of "cargo cults," and the entire uneasy relation that continues between what Marshall Sahlins called the "West and the rest," tends to be eliminated: when what used to be called "cargo cult" is considered to be the expression of normal native "culture," the unruly troublesome nature of cargo cults is reduced (Sahlins 1976). "Cargo cultists" become indigenous "culture bearers," albeit victims of Western colonialism, and are thereby saved.

In other words, as the word "cargo" is eliminated and the explanatory emphasis is shifted from native "cults" to native "culture," what I call "cargo trouble"—the critical force of the term "kago"—is thus reduced and removed. And power is restored to the center. It should be recognized that this is happening in the context of increasing concentrations of power and wealth in the burgeoning global economy, and a great deal of social political retrenchment. Jean-François Lyotard calls this "a period of slackening," saying, "From every direction we are being urged to put an end to experimentation, in the arts and elsewhere," and adding, "In the diverse invitations to suspend artistic experimentation, there is an identical call for order, a desire for unity, for identity, for security, or popularity" (Lyotard 1984: 71, 73). In some spheres of higher education in the United States, for example, faculty are no longer rewarded for scholarship that goes beyond pedagogy, which leaves critical intellectuals, in Gayatri Chakravorty Spivak's phrase, "outside in the teaching machine" (1993). I suspect that my colleagues at more elite institutions are relatively unaware of this situation, which exemplifies just the sort of increasing concentration and division I am talking about. I wish not so much to chide my colleagues or complain as to impart a strong sense that things everywhere are in no way "normal," that they are other than they seem, and that the deceptive operation of power in language in practice is practically inescapable. What Lyotard is speaking to is the bourgeois desire to put an end to critical practice by subordinating it to a useful purpose in the way Hegel did with his dialectic, as though one could sustain a critical cargo cult careerism without contradiction.

In my view, it is hard to ignore the fact that, as cargo cult is being normalized and nativized, underdevelopment and the inability to pay back loans to the World Bank has led the Papua New Guinean Kina to lose well over two-thirds of its value. Eliminating the term is not so unlike making the activity it denotes illegal. The call for a solidly referential transparent language to replace the troublesome cargo cult can only sustain if not amplify the current world order even as it decries it. From my perspective, it is better not to lose the ambiguity and trouble of the term by replacing it with a term or set of terms that we consider to be transparent, regardless of whether the label itself remains. This does not mean, however, that we cannot know the truth empirically, only that the truth is not what we have generally thought it to be.

A Thesis: Corporeal Enactments of Context

My argument is that, in cargo cult discourse, anthropologists have underdifferentiated Western European and Melanesian cultures and mislocated the phenomenon of cargo cult. Part of the problem lies with the anthropological notion of culture, which tends to presume self-regulating functionally integrated wholes and logically organized socially functioning symbolic belief systems. There is much merit in McDowell's idea that cargo cults are simply instances of Melanesians managing change and the observation that the phenomenon is ubiquitous. Cargo cults, however, should not be described as a way of doing anything in particular. They do not exist to make things better in an ultimate or utopian sense, for they are in fact enactments in the present of such illusions. It is by assigning to cargo cults various purposes or ends for which they thereby become the more or less inadequate or adequate cultural symbolic means that anthropologists have gotten caught in the logical traps of what Wagner called "the kind of 'argument through dependency' that our rationalistic outlook fosters" (R. Wagner 1979: 164). These sorts of arguments tend to assume an unacknowledged *telos* of history implicit in a Western worldview, which presumes that man is primarily the animal endowed with reason who will make things better in the future.

Peter Worsley's (1968) theoretical consideration of cargo cult from this perspective is exemplary for its rigor, determination, and critical insight. Three separate times in his account Worsley runs through, in various orders, at least seven or eight different, somewhat inconsistent, explanations of what he alternately or simultaneously considers to be the unsound yet reasonable behavior found in Melanesian "cargo cults." They include the irrational irregularities of European economics and politics; the illogical fragmentation, capriciousness, and hypocrisy of European political hierarchies and missionaries; the sheer harshness of the colonial situation; the psychological ambivalence of natives engendered by this harshness and the ineluctable attraction of Western commodities; native emotional desperation resulting from a combination of this ambivalence and Melanesians' ignorance of, and consequent irrational magical beliefs about, the source of European wealth; the reinforcement of these beliefs by missionary teachings; and low levels of political integration.

At the end of these deliberations, Worsley finally infers that the odder—most difficult to explain—elements of cargo cults, particularly the hysterical mimesis of European behaviors, are an "emotional outlet" found in "imaginary projection" (1968: 247). That is to say, he ultimately deduces (correctly, in my view) that archetypal cargo cult behavior is its own end and goal—its own creative enactment. Having arrived at this astonishing insight, however, Worsley immediately reassumes his previous rationalistic "argument through dependency" by finally functionally explaining the entire phenomenon as incipient nationalism. This is consistent with his view of history as evolving reason.[6]

My thesis is that cargo cults are much like Worsley's self-fulfilling enactments. They are an aspect of, for lack of a better term, existence. They are simply what people do—that is, the physical or corporeal enactment of context. This enactment is by definition historically conditioned. It is also the condition of history. As such, far from being mistaken, particularly about Western culture, people of Papua New Guinea enjoining even the most archetypally bizarre cargo cult behaviors are absolutely realistic and truthful. This is because they accurately physically enact the illusionary imagination of modern bourgeois European society. Although cargo cult behavior is thus ubiquitous and general, the central element of it for Western thinkers—the defining feature of archetypal cargo cult behavior that most urgently requires reduction or explanation—is the odd apparently irrational behavior—the magical pursuit of rational ends—which I take to be hysterical mimicking of Europeans.[7]

As an instance of the bodily enactment of context, cargo cult can thereby be understood as both general and unusual. It is general because physical enactment of context is the normal comportment of Melanesians and, as Ton Otto (present volume) shows, a widespread technique of knowledge. It is unusual because what Europeans have fixed upon with fascination as so urgently requiring explanation and reduction is its strangeness. The former undermines the idea of "cargo cult" as a discrete phenomenon, whereas the latter provides a useful definition, albeit one that locates the term and its meaning and explanation in the European imagination and Western culture.

I do not wish to claim that cargo cults are bizarre for Westerners but not for Melanesians. Holger Jebens and Nils Bubandt (both in the present volume) provide examples of Melanesians experiencing "cults" as abnormal in their own right. Elfriede Hermann (present volume) also properly points out how a reified emphasis on the oddness of "cargo cults" can thwart an understanding of others' experience and, along with Martha Kaplan (present volume), shows how such views can be used politically to harm others. I wish, however, to emphasize the relativity of the experience of "normality." The sort of violence that Bubandt (present volume) discusses is for many people around the globe today a part of their normal everyday lives and has been for numerous people a lifelong reality. Part of my argument is that what passes for "normal" reality in modern middle-class Western culture is deceptive and unusual in the extreme and that Melanesians fathom this by enacting a version of it out of its "normal" context. So what counts as "bizarre" depends at least as much upon the positionality of the subject as it does on the "reality" in question, and that position can and does change. Indeed, cargo cult can be seen as a play on and transformation of the positionality of subjects, both Western and Melanesian, in such a way that normal and unusual become difficult to distinguish.

It is tempting to adopt Michael Taussig's analysis of mimesis, because he is perhaps the only anthropologist who deals precisely with the native mimicry of Europeans in colonial contact situations as primary; however, besides the fact that he tends to view mimesis as a technique of knowledge, Michael Taussig also tends to romanticize the notion by supposing that it overcomes alterity and difference.[8] "The fundamental move of the mimetic faculty," he supposes, "is to take us bodily into alterity" (Taussig 1993: 40). He supposes that this mimetic faculty is perverted by Western capitalist production as it is taken over and controlled through mechanical reproduction, which apparently robs people of this faculty by imitating it, creating the artificial alienating "mimesis of mimesis" and "mimetic excess" (Taussig 1993: 245–246). Native peoples are thus situated in the romantic savage slot.

Andrew Lattas uniquely appreciates the centrality of mimesis in New Britain cargo cults and avoids the romantic savage slot by viewing mimesis as "how people internalise the conditions of their colonial domination"—as instances of native people having assumed a negative Western view of themselves, which leads them to want to change their skins to be white (Lattas 1992c: 74; 1998). This, however, does not quite get at the ineffective peculiarity of the behavior in the way that I would like—that is, by viewing it as the wholly insightful mimesis of Western capitalist bourgeois cultural precepts and illusions. I see the strangeness of the behavior as less the outcome of the stress of exploitative colonial apartheid situations and more the product of the bizarre irrationality of the Western cultural precepts that Melanesians accurately enact, thus shifting the analysis away from indigenous "culture" and toward Western delusions.

Melanesianist anthropologists have clearly recognized the importance of the body in Melanesian cultures, where it is widely recognized to be a essential in the public, oftentimes competitive celebratory enactments of beauty, sexuality, and vitality and to be "intricately tied to cycles of fertility, depletion and regeneration," which are critical in those cultures (Knauft 1989: 252, 254). In his recent book on the matter, Andrew Strathern (1996) not only underscores and substantiates the importance of bodily enactments in a wide range of Papua New Guinea cultures, but also emphasizes the need to rethink the person against the Cartesian mind-body dichotomy. And although he emphasizes the anti-Cartesian, holistic, healthy, and vital "becoming body" in relation to fertility, the life cycle, and the expression of core cultural values, he also recognizes the more problematic "threatened body" subject to all sorts of physical and social illness and disturbances.

Wagner shows a general characteristic of a great many Melanesian cultures among the New Ireland Usen Barok, when he elucidates their notion that knowledge is obtained only through physical enactment rather than verbal instruction because it centrally concerns unglossable power (cf. Otto, present volume). Power can be known only as it is manifest through its physical enactment and embodiment. Cultural images work to elicit this physical enactment, although, if I understand Wagner correctly, the bodily performance of power is both its achievement and stimulus. In her expansion of analytic metaphoric possibilities, Marilyn Strathern (1988) shows that at the core of the physical embodiment of power in Melanesian cultures is gender difference, which is both culturally elicited and generative. Gender difference is not only summoned through ritual imagery but also elicits the difference it manifests. She shows that gender difference is the condition for agency: "Where the agent is defined by gender, then it is the one sex that 'causes' the other to act" (M. Strathern 1988: 332). Therefore "every act is an act of domination" albeit a momentary one, for "the acts of men and women do not in themselves evince permanent domination" (M. Strathern 1988: 332). The point I wish to emphasize here is that Melanesians in general engage in bodily performances and physical enactments as means of obtaining or, more accurately, being power, for I believe this to be crucial to understanding cargo cult behavior. As physical enactments of context, cargo cults are fundamentally enactments of power in colonial contexts.

What Is Really Wrong with Western Culture

Cargo cult discourse is a realm replete with cultural critique. First invented as a term of derision applied to native cultures, even the most sympathetic ethnographers often accepted the notion that "cults" were unable to comprehend a rational Western system even as they blamed the more troublesome aspects of "cults" on harsh Western colonial practices. Now criticized as a colonial racist stereotype, "cargo cult" also lends itself to the argument that Melanesian cultures were meaningful functioning wholes before the imposition of a foreign alienating exploitative regime. As Lindstrom (present volume) points out, so critical has cargo cult discourse become that it appears there is no potential redemption left in either Western or Melanesian cultures. The problem, as I see it, is that ethnographers have imagined cultures as meaningful wholes and so, when the absurdity of existence shows itself in cargo trouble, the critiques begin to fly.

Joel Robbins (present volume) argues that, as with others, these critiques are predicated on utopian, apocalyptic visions, in this case the vision of holistic cultures. This suggests the need for a nonmillenarian, nonapocalyptic type of criticism. We can borrow a lesson from the history of European phenomenology, which, in the reading I give it, began as an apocalyptic narrative that quickly developed an intellectual genealogy that attempted to break out of the utopian trap with which it began.

In the early 1900s, Edmund Husserl thought that European science and culture were in a crisis because they had forgotten the original insights into nature that had made Europeans superior. He invented his phenomenological method in order to return to those original insights by clearing away the sedimentations of culture that in his view had obscured them. His closest student, Martin Heidegger, adopted Husserl's method but had a very different vision of the purpose of philosophy that he took to be the comprehension of being or existence. For Heidegger, the entire history of European philosophy, including Husserl's phenomenology, is mired in Western metaphysical thinking (or roughly the quest for abstract universal Platonic essences, absolute nomothetic laws of nature, and transcendental ideals), for which he substitutes an existential analysis of being, and the ontico-ontological difference between Being and beings.

Heidegger thus moved away from millennial visions and apocalyptic narratives. One of his most astute readers, Jacques Derrida, takes Heidegger's critique of Western metaphysics but finds fault with Heidegger for having named Being, which falls into the trap of Western metaphysical thinking. Derrida instead offers an analysis of *différance*—the unnamable equivocal historical relationship between signifying images and concepts, which he says calls for an analysis of "where we are today" in "the real history of the world" (Derrida 1977). Derrida's understanding of the signifying process brings with it an appreciation of levels of consciousness and perceptual awareness without a primordial origin or ground to which one can return. He sees people as caught in their own cultures, so to speak, and relatively unaware of their predicament. His understanding can therefore be deployed in a nonapocalyptic critique. Yet this is the sort of critique anthropologists have had difficulty adopting.

Anthropology is a discipline that represents human origins for the Western imagination. In this way, it is also very close to Husserl's phenomenology, which sought to arrive at the original primordial experiences through which humans know things. When anthropologists read phenomenologists, they nearly inevitably employ a Husserlian perspective and miss the critical departure from Husserl's doctrines made by Heidegger and Derrida. For both of these thinkers, Husserl's quest for primordial origins represents the culmination of Western illusory metaphysical thinking. Anthropologists therefore often ignore a fundamental critique of Western culture. From Derrida's and Heidegger's standpoints, it is Western metaphysical thinking that tends to view Melanesians in terms of ahistorical, self-regulating, functionally integrated symbolic belief systems and find among Melanesians uncontaminated primordial perceptual experiences of fundamental concepts. Yet it is this view the strange imperviousness of "cargo cults" challenges.

Melanesianist anthropologists sometimes draw upon European phenomenologists to analyze the fundamental bodily enactments and experiences of Melanesians. Maurice Merleau-Ponty's (1962, 1964) investigation of primary perceptual physical experiences seems particularly apt for this purpose. In my reading, however, when anthropologists draw upon phenomenology to analyze Melanesian cultures, they often fail to recognize the critical transformations that area of thinking has undergone and, as a result, continue to place the Melanesian Other in the Western romantic savage slot. Despite his modifications of Husserl's phenomenological reduction, Merleau-Ponty stays very close to Husserl's original intention of arriving at the absolute primordial knowledge of things in human experience. When it is assumed that Melanesians represent this primordial knowledge, which Husserl thought could address the crisis in European society, Melanesians end up as a romanticized Other rather than one predicated on difference—one for whom every gendered corporeal enactment is an act of domination (Dalton, n.d.). In my reading of the development of phenomenology, even when his name is invoked, the critical possibilities offered by Derrida are therefore often missed by Melanesianist anthropologists. The levels of awareness appreciated by Derrida are therefore often ignored for the sake of a utopian vision of holistic culture. I argue that we particularly need to come to terms with our own awareness in comprehending cargo cult and that cargo trouble precisely challenges that awareness.

Otto writes, "The very word 'cargo cult' has provided us with a mirror in which we have failed to recognise ourselves" (1992a: 5). I would add that cargo cults are themselves mirrors of Western bourgeois culture in which we have failed to recognize ourselves. It is not so much that we are individualistic and materialistic and have projected that on to native cultures, although that has been done. Rather, Melanesians accurately physically enact European bourgeois illusions, and, failing to recognize ourselves in their strange behaviors, we explain them in terms of native "culture." To recognize ourselves in cargo cult behaviors, it is not adequate to critique European culture as alienated by contrasting it with the social relationality of Melanesians, as is often done and as Taussig did for South America (which is not to say that such a contrast is even wholly inaccurate). The problem with this mode of critique is that it so easily and often puts Melanesians in the romantic savage slot by characterizing them as free of such ills of Western civilization as individualism and materialism.

Instead, to comprehend cargo cult one needs a critique of the Western metaphysical thinking that produces savage slots and one needs to adopt a view of Melanesian "cultures" that does not see them as separate from the European global capitalist domination and sees them as neither its victims nor its resistance. Bubandt (present volume) provides a striking instance where millennial expectations feed ethnic violence and so can hardly be romanticized as a form of resistance, and he questions the degree to which Western modernity does not come to inhabit the consciousness of colonized peoples. To my mind, degrees of conscious awareness are indeed the issue, but cargo cult leaders vary in their perception of cultural ruses (as, for example, Yali did over the course of his life) and anthropologists have a most difficult time seeing themselves in cargo critiques.

Derrida offered the type of critique needed to bring an awareness of awareness to anthropology when he deployed a reading of Charles Baudelaire's "Counterfeit Money" against a critical reading of Marcel Mauss and the anthropological analysis of the gift and exchange (Baudelaire 1975; Derrida 1992). Baudelaire describes a type of exchange in which an ambiguous character (a "friend") attempts "to win paradise economically" by aiming "to do a good deed while at the same time making a good deal"—by giving counterfeit money to a beggar. He concludes that "to be mean is never excusable, but there is some merit in knowing that one is: the most irreparable of vices is to do evil out of stupidity" (quoted in Derrida 1992: 32).

This critique of capitalist society is not original with Derrida or Baudelaire, for others have noted the proclivity of Western colonists and missionaries to supposedly do good while actually doing well for themselves. I submit that this is a far more profound critique of bourgeois culture than the ideas that, unlike Melanesians, Westerners are materialistic or socially alienated.[9] It claims that Westerners (1) take more than they give (2) while thinking or supposing that they are doing otherwise. This is the bourgeois illusion—the white mythology—that Europeans have been cultivating for well over a century. It is the basis of the evolutionary theories developed last century during the period studied in Eric Hobsbawm's *Age of Capital* (1975). These ideas still largely govern the Western imagination about the Melanesian Other. One need not outwardly believe in cultural evolution or Western superiority to benefit from the global economy while supposing one is helping others. In fact it helps to maintain this illusion if one does not consciously or overtly denigrate the Other—and perhaps even romanticizes them.

Hobsbawm shows that, during the age of capital, European cultures experienced an economic industrial revolution that, unlike that experienced in the prior age of revolution, was not accompanied by a social revolution of the working classes (Hobsbawm 1962, 1975). He demonstrates that the reason for this was the enormous amount of wealth that came into European cultures, largely through the growth and exploitation of the resources of their colonial empires. The concentration of wealth and power in European cultures supported a growing bourgeois middle class and thereby undercut whatever revolutionary tendencies they might otherwise have had. Some mixture of happiness with what they had and fear of what they had to lose prevented them from bettering their conditions through political action. The triumph of the petite bourgeoisie brought calls to quell a truly critical practice. By this I mean a nonmillenarian critique that is not aimed only at others in order to bring about a normalizing practice and that does not indulge in self-justifying utopian narratives, which always end with happy hopeful conclusions. Yet this unfettered critical practice has been truncated in the Western world at least since the Greeks made Socrates drink hemlock and has certainly continued to the present.

Nevertheless, today a significant trait of the middle classes is their great anxiety about losing their status and wealth to become one among the poor working classes (Ortner 1991). Gilles Deleuze and Félix Guattari draw upon Spinoza and Reich in identifying "the fundamental question of political philosophy" to be how the middle classes come to will their own subordination.[10] Peter Gay details how the bourgeoisie became grossly self-absorbed at the same time as they cultivated what he calls "alibis for aggression," enabling them to exploit the world to fuel the cultural fantasies in which they imagined themselves to be involved, which included the evolutionary metanarratives about the triumph of human reason for the common good that spawned notions like manifest destiny and the white man's burden (Gay 1993, 1995). It also created a kind of middle-class bureaucratic conformism, which Hannah Arendt (1964) identified as the "banality of evil" and, further, spawned the sort of heroic self-narratives that Ernest Becker (1973) associated with its denial. It is, however, only by opening oneself to critical enquiry that one can open oneself to an understanding of others, and only by comprehending cargo trouble instead of trying to do away with it that cargo cult can be comprehended.

My point here is to underscore how widespread, deep, pervasive, and exceptionally historically peculiar is Western bourgeois culture. Only by underdeveloping and exploiting the planet could middle-class Europeans support and maintain their fantasies of being at the vanguard of human rational evolution or culture, which supposedly accounts for their enormous wealth, and the illusion of doing good for "mankind" while actually doing well for themselves. In the United States, 4 percent of the world's population consumes about 40 percent of the world's resources. In spite of this disproportionate consumption, a mass public believes that their government's military interventions are to bring peace, democracy, and progress to the ineffectual and therefore underdeveloped cultures of the world, and, as a distinct sign of these sorts of culture, "cargo cults" entered the Western imagination.

The Context of Cargo Cults

Melanesians who do not engage in cargo cults can be seen as enacting something like the notion George Foster (1965) calls "the image of limited good"—that is, the supposition that there is a finite amount of power or good in the universe and that one therefore necessarily does inordinately well only at the expense of others. This is the source of many conflicts between in-laws and of the sorcery divinations and vengeance raids following many deaths. Trade stores often fail as business enterprises precisely because people recognize them as taking and profiting from others in communities where giving freely is the norm and source of prestige. Therefore, Melanesians might be viewed as willing to recognize exploitation when they see it and to do something about it, understanding the economic principle that "there is no such thing as a free lunch." Western Europeans might therefore be characterized as enacting a notion like "the image of unlimited good"—namely, the supposition that, with the rational capacity endowed them by their creator, they have very nearly achieved a perfect technical mastery of nature. This mastery, in turn, accounts for the incredible wealth they enjoy and that they bring to less fortunate others by developing and then taking and consuming their capital and resources.

In Melanesian cargo cults, villagers typically act as though they had already directly grasped the primordial limitless origins of the power that they themselves can only manifest through physical enactments of difference. One finds them giving and sharing profusely and enjoying unlimited goods and returns, free from social conflict by virtue of having somehow tapped into the infinite source of life and fecundity and so having arrived at the end of time and history. Cargo cultists typically kill all their pigs and abandon their gardens, forego exchange, and abdicate in-law, gender, and sexual taboos perceived to have divided and so caused conflict, sometimes also handling sexual substances thought to embody powers of growth and fecundity. On the other hand, many cultists also institute new regimentations, labors, taboos, and sexual regulations as though, instead of having arrived at the origin of power that overcomes all strife and difference, absolutely everything is rendered countable and is enumerated, accounted for, and perfectly regulated. Either way, conflict and difference are supposedly overcome, infinite productive capacities liberated, and interminable returns realized.

Many of the enactments of these ideas are overtly of European behaviors involving flagpoles, uniforms, rifles, taxes, political offices, wireless radios, telephones, cameras, binoculars, and so forth. Melanesians also have a proclivity to view the Europeans who live among them for a time as the capricious ghosts of their dead ancestors—those who have reached the infinitely removed origin of life and power, who they have to cajole to give them things, and who by all rights should not be there unless they are willing to provide wealth and power (cf. Leavitt, present volume). In cargo cults, Melanesians thus not only mimic Europeans, but also act in the way that Europeans imagine themselves to be, that is, according to the image of unlimited good.

Gerrit Huizer (1992) argues that the millenarian character of Judeo-Christian bourgeois capitalist expansion created situations in which local millenarian cargo cults movements emerged. This is a view with which I have obvious sympathy, although I stress the illusionary and deceptive character of bourgeois capitalist colonial culture rather than its millenarian dreams because I suppose that Western Europe could probably actually relieve world poverty and hunger and achieve similar millennial-like aspirations were it not so deluded and deceitful. Anthropologists, however, have more frequently argued that many cargo cult activities actually consist of perfectly rational economic and political action. For example, George Morren reports that an airstrip constructed by the East Miyanmin in the mid-1960s, unbeknownst to government or missionary officials in what must have been a cargo cult–like enterprise, was subsequently "discovered" by an Australian patrol officer, who found it perfectly serviceable and reported it to missionaries. The missions employed it to deliver medical and store supplies along with money for its upkeep and later opened two more landing strips in the area. All that kept its building from being classified as a cargo cult was that fact that it was successful (Morren 1981).

McDowell has pointed out that millenarian "cargo cult" movements may follow economic disappointments of failed rational large-scale business enterprises (1988: 128–129). Worsley, though, sees a general historical progression of movements from millennialism to rational political activity. There seems to be some disagreement, because, whereas Worsley describes Paliau's movement in Manus as a primarily practical one, downplaying his unusual biblical themes and followers' millennial expectations associated with the break with past tradition, others focus on just these sorts of beliefs and desires and categorize it as "cargoistic" or "millennial."[11] Worsley points out how Paliau's more pragmatic albeit oppositional movement became mixed up in the more radical "the

Noise." By 1947, however, Paliau "attacked Cargo fantasies, and vigorously set about organising communal agriculture in which once-hostile communities cooperated" (Worsley 1968: 188). Worsley describes the movement as "not millenarian, though millenarian ideas were in the air concurrently." Theodore Schwartz and Otto, however, describe in detail the dream-inspired biblical millennial message with which Paliau began his movement.[12]

Yali's famous Rai Coast movement, at least in its last phases, can also be described as a pragmatic political economic program with its fringe cargo cult elements (Morauta 1972; Worsley 1968). What may have begun as a relatively conformist practical enterprise also met with millennial expectations which Yali himself seems to have fermented after having discovered, through his participation in Western culture, that Europeans had deceived him and his people—that Europeans do not believe in Christianity so much as they do in human evolution. Once he became aware of this, Yali began an anti-European nativistic revivalistic movement with millennial expectations, which he maintained with political legerdemain. Through those tricks he became the self-indulgent, relatively well-to-do leader of a large Western-style political organization. But with government suppression and millennial disappointment, Yali's movement faded away (Lawrence 1964; see Hermann, present volume).

These cases point to the fact that it is not always easy to separate pragmatic activities from millennial expectations or cargo cult thinking.[13] More important, they show that these movements require an analysis of the symbolic obviation of cargo cult beliefs, for they clearly go through phases based on the masking or unveiling of understandings and illusions. This is why cargo cults are so often based on secrecy. One economic activity that is widely accepted as practical rather than cargoistic was the Tommy Kabu movement (Oram 1992; Worsley 1968). Kabu initiated a European-style social-political organization and started business cooperatives in the Purari Delta bordering Gulf Province without any millennial "cargo" expectations. The enterprise failed, however, because "those involved failed to understand simple economic principles": their expenditures outstripped their incomes or, in other terms, not unlike Yali's "cargo" phase, or bourgeois Europeans, they tried to take more than they gave (Oram 1992: 95). A similar enterprise, albeit with suspected "cargo" beliefs, was begun as a copra plantation cooperative on Manam Island by a man named Irakau but failed when he discovered that, without capital, the only way he could afford to get his product to market was to steal from the missionaries who were trying to aid him (Burridge 1960). When the missions found him out, they subverted his supposed cargo movement.

It seems to me that Irakau understood better than Kabu that the trick of getting more than one gives is based on an illusion that is difficult to maintain. Rather, I should say that it is impossible to maintain when a dominant global colonial power is willing to deploy force to quell it and so thereby foster its own grand illusions. Moreover, it is impossible to maintain without power over a colonial subject from whom one can take more than one gives while pretending to do otherwise. Cargo cults cannot be separated from pragmatic economic and political movements on the basis that they do not succeed, for all too often these also collapsed. Like Yali and Paliau, Kabu and Irakau simply did not have the capital or power to maintain their illusions.

There is no reason to believe that this sort of situation will change any time soon, so one can still take heart in the fact that Melanesians continue to question bourgeois capitalist contradictions. Melanesians, however, do not usually get away with such illusions in their own communities, which is why cargo cults are so dynamic. Although the concealing and revealing of illusions are at the heart of Melanesian culture, these illusions enable partible gendered persons to give life energies to one another and sustain their communities. Melanesians do not generally allow anyone to take extravagantly in their own communities for very long, no matter the pretense, but have little choice when it comes to Whitemen.

Conclusion

In this chapter I have argued that the analysis of cargo cult as a phenomenon of native culture is a mistake because the culture concept tends to fit Melanesians into a romanticized Western savage slot. I assume instead that cargo cult is the Melanesian physical enactment of historical context, which is provided by Western colonial culture. Cargo cult therefore requires a thorough interrogation Western culture's most basic premises.

I have questioned the term "cargo cult" but contend that it expresses an essential critical nature through the tension between the terms "cargo" and "cult." I maintained that the tendency to eliminate "cargo" and substitute "culture" for "cult" effectively eliminates the critical force of a Melanesian idiom regarding European colonial culture by replacing it with a Western normalizing notion. In this view, "cargo cult" means this troubling critical force, which is both general and manifest in what appears to Western intellects as the strange disconcerting "irrational" behavior that has spawned many years of cargo cult explanation. The attempt to "explain" cargo cult in terms of the function and logic of culture denies and masks its extraordinary troubling character, but viewed as a phenomenon of the corporeal enactment of historical context, cargo cult is an accurate mirror of the exploitative self-contradictory ideology of modern Western bourgeois culture that desires to deflect and normalize critical practice—and to accomplish yet another political ruse by removing cargo trouble.

In this view, the real problem with Western capitalist culture is not merely that it is alienated, individualistic, and materialistic. Rather, the problem with bourgeois culture is the idea that Westerners help the people they take from by bringing the world historical progress, which is deeply rooted in ideas that Europeans are at the vanguard of human history, which many presume to be the unfolding of technology and God-given reason. Western bourgeois culture assumes this endowment accounts for its enormous wealth, rather than attributing the windfall to the exploitation of its colonies, even though it has actually systematically underdeveloped them.

I found that classic cargo cult movements and pragmatic political and economic activities are difficult to differentiate, not because cults achieve practical ends or colonial culture is millennial, but because both share the cultural illusions that are necessary to maintain power. Cargo cults must therefore be understood in terms of a historical process of masking and unmasking illusions that mime those of Western bourgeois culture. But most cargo cults and practical economic political activities fail because they do not have the capital or power to maintain the illusions that sustain them.

I came to know a group of "cargo cultists" among Rawa-speaking people in the mountains of northeast Papua New Guinea while I was there from 1982 to 1984. They had participated in a large-scale local movement in about 1980 and had not apparently changed their views when I visited the area again in 1999. Perhaps the most telling statement ever made to me by some of them on one occasion during my first visit was, "Some of us don't believe that Whitemen are telling us everything." Although they sometimes participate in church activities, they also understand that they are being deceived. As of 1999, the local culture appeared to me to be divided between skeptical, doubtful intellectuals—the cargo cultists—on the one hand, and Christian believers, on the other. Nevertheless, many good cultists go to church, just as many good Christians also engage in so-called cargo cult thinking. One time, in the early 1980s, a church leader sat me down alone and asked me a question that must have been on many others' minds: "How is it that Whitemen ever thought to make machines?" How does one answer that question? Jean Gimple (1976) points out that the architects of medieval cathedrals who were also responsible for making the first mechanical clocks were worshiped right alongside the saints and the Holy Trinity. Like others after them, they presumed that they were modeling the mechanical laws of God's universe—peering into God's mind. (One persistent effort of these architects was to construct perpetual motion machines.) I take the questioner to have been asking me, "Are you Whitemen really the gods you pretend to be or not?"—the corollary to the question being, "Since you have so much stuff that you claim is the product of your technology, why can't you share it?"

This question points toward the very heart of the contradiction in bourgeois colonial culture. Some Melanesians seem to challenge it while trying to adopt it for their own. Others seem to accept it along with the view of Western superiority it assumes. Many, like my friend, are apparently of two minds, questioning the contradiction but choosing not to challenge it outwardly. Faced with an insurmountably powerful culture founded upon that striking contradiction, what would you do? What, in fact, do you do?

Notes

I wish to thank the organizers and participants of the "Cargo, Cult, and Critique" workshop at Aarhus for which this chapter was originally written.

1. I am paraphrasing Judith Butler (1990: ix).

2. Since at least F. E. Williams 1923 article (1976a).

3. Michael Young, for example, reports, "Ideas usually associated with cargo doctrine ... are pervasive and universal on Goodenough" (1971: 55).

4. See Kaplan (1995b), Sahlins (1972), and Thomas (1991).

5. Otto (1992a: 5) perceives the importance of the tension between these two terms when he writes, "The fascination with cargo cults derives from their dual classification as mind (millenarian movement) and matter (cargo)" (cf. "Introduction," present volume).

6. Dalton (1996). Worsley writes, "The essential rationality of Melanesian thought and action is shown on a larger scale by the directional tendency of the movements, the transition from magical to political action" (1968: 269). This is not dissimilar to Williams's conclusion that the "Vailala Madness" was the result of "certain effects of contact with and subjugation by a superior people" (F. E. Williams 1976b: 393).

7. Two of the most insightful theorists of "cargo cult," Worsley and Williams, find this to be the most interesting and curious, if not also entertaining, element of this behavior (F. E. Williams 1976a: 350–351; Worsley 1968: 247).

8. Taussig relies on Walter Benjamin for this view when he writes that "Benjamin wants to acknowledge a barely conscious mode of apperception and a type of 'physiological knowledge' built from habit" (Benjamin 1968; Taussig 1993: 26). I do not want to underestimate the brilliant technical achievements that this sort of physical enactment has accomplished in human history, which Lévi-Strauss has called the "neo-lithic paradox" (Lévi-Strauss 1966). I do, however, want to avoid the rationalistic or functionalist "argument through dependency" that would reduce its explanation to this mission.

9. These are nevertheless certainly Western maladies.

10. Deleuze and Guattari (1983: 29). They write that the question is "not that some people steal or that others occasionally go out on strike, but rather that all those who are starving do not steal as a regular practice, and all those who are exploited are not continually out on strike: after centuries of exploitation, why do people still tolerate being humiliated and enslaved, to such a point, indeed, that they actually want humiliation and slavery not only for others but for themselves?" (Deleuze and Guattari 1983: 29).

11. See Oram (1992), Otto (1992b), Schwartz (1962), and Worsley (1968).

12. See Otto (1992b), Schwartz (1962), and Worsley (1968: 192).

13. See Jebens and Leavitt (both in present volume).

CHAPTER 12 Work, Wealth, and Knowledge

Enigmas of Cargoist Identifications

Ton Otto

In its relatively short history, recently explored by Monty Lindstrom (1993) and others (Jaarsma 1997; Worsley 1999), anthropological cargo cult literature has served a number of different functions: from an interest in colonial control and policy advice, via the study of acculturation and cultural change, to the comparative study of Melanesian cultures and religious movements. In the wake of postmodernist criticism, anthropologists have turned to a critical deconstruction of the concepts and explanatory models of the cargo literature. The analytical usefulness of the term "cargo cult" has come under strong doubt. In addition, even though somewhat hesitantly, the archive of cargo literature is being explored for its potentiality for developing a Western culture critique (Lindstrom 1993; see also Kohl, present volume).

In this chapter I will take up such a cultural critical perspective. I will do so not only because the continuing popularity of cargo literature in general points to some Western preoccupation or a Western metanarrative, as Lindstrom has suggested, but also because I believe that a culture critical perspective is an intrinsic part of the anthropological method of comparative-ethnographic research as well as a raison d'être of the discipline as such (cf. Marcus and Fischer 1986). The comparative dimension of all anthropological analysis should perhaps be made more explicit in order to improve the empirical quality of our interpretations. I would argue that it is not sufficient for an anthropological culture critique to focus only on Western discourses about cargo cults, without being concerned about the ethnographic reality to which these discourses refer (cf. Lindstrom 1993: 12–13). The way in which these discourses construct and deal with empirical data should also be part of the critical analysis, because it is in the field of arguments about local "realities" that we can perceive and criticize the inadequacy of our concepts and the biases of our theoretical approach. The basis for anthropological culture critique should therefore lie in sustained comparative analysis in which the researcher uses Western and Melanesian concepts, values, and practices to mutually illuminate each other (cf. Robbins, present volume).

In the comparison of Melanesian and Western cultures, the semantic field indicated by the concept of "cargo" or "cargoism" appears to point to a discursive space of mutual fascination and interpretation. I think it is important to be aware of this geographical location of the cargo discourse in view of attempts to generalize this particular field of comparison to include the whole world. In a recent volume intended to compare cargo cults and millenarian movements around the world (Trompf 1990), the case studies that were included clearly suggest that the cargoist part of the comparison only applies to the Western and Melanesian movements described, and not to the examples of millenarian movements in Timor, Jamaica, and Africa.

Western and Melanesian cultures appear to have a common cultural orientation, indicated by the notion of cargo. Among other things, this common interest has facilitated the common Western caricature of cargo cultists as primitive and confused people who use irrational means to pursue rational ends. Whether the goal of striving for an infinite increase of material wealth is rational or irrational is a question that is rarely posed. By inventing the notion of cargo cults, Westerners have celebrated their material accomplishments and visions, the "secret" of which was impenetrable to "less developed" people. On the other hand, for Melanesians the cults, with their undeniable component of cargoism, were a means to understand and come to terms with the Western world (R. Wagner 1981). The cultists integrated some mimicry of Western goods and practices into their local performances and cosmologies in order to "crack the code" of the dominant Others. The overlap in the semantic loading of mutual attempts to understand (and parody) each other points to a resonance of cultural values. For a proper understanding of this resonance, however, it is necessary to investigate in more detail the various semantic domains that appear to be similar.

A considerable number of cargo cult researchers have argued that in Melanesia, the term cargo does not really mean "cargo" (in the restricted sense of material wealth) but "Cargo" (in the larger, abstract sense of redemption, emancipation, and spiritual freedom). This is undoubtedly true, but it must be remembered that the signifier of these different connotations is "cargo," which also and primarily refers to material goods. This is should come as no surprise. Also in the West, material goods carry meanings that transcend the materiality of the things themselves: cars and clothing can express status and lifestyle, houses can express wealth and power, and ecological food can express political choice. The interesting thing is that in both Melanesian cargo cults and Western consumerism, material goods are a privileged idiom for expressing identity, status, opposition, and power.

Once we thus accept a convergence of interest in material wealth, we have to compare the various notions of value represented by this wealth in Melanesia and the West. In this chapter, I will investigate an important axis of cultural comparison in relation to cargo that anthropologists generally have neglected to explore, namely, "work." Work is one of the central Western categories and values and is intimately linked with the creation of economic value through the production of goods, as well as with personal and social identity and moral obligation. In Melanesian societies, notions of work carve out different semantic domains and are not linked with concepts of personal identity with the same prominence as in the West. To illustrate this point, I will rely mainly on my material about Manus, in Papua New Guinea. An analysis of work in relation to cargo reveals different theories about the origin of material goods and illuminates common misunderstanding in the mutual cargoist interpretations of Melanesians and Westerners. The analysis of work and wealth will necessitate the investigation of a third term, namely, "knowledge," which takes a central place in Melanesian conceptions of the origin of cargo. This double axis of comparison allows me to develop a culture critical perspective of Western and Melanesians notions of cargo and value.

Work and Worth in the West

Work has not always been a central concern of Western peoples. The Western work-ethos is a relatively modern invention, which the Dutch historian Jan Romein characterized as a deviation from the "general human pattern" (1971). The development of work as a central category and value can be seen as part of an ideological shift connected with the rise of the market as a central economic institution and, later, with the emergence of the industrial organization of production. Louis Dumont (1977) has introduced the term "economic ideology" to refer to this new worldview. In his analysis, this ideology is characterized by individualism—as opposed to holism—and an emphasis ("primacy") on the relations between human beings and things—as opposed to relationships between human beings (Dumont 1977: 4–5). Dumont, surprisingly, fails to identify work or labor as a central value of the new economic ideology, even though the category figures on many pages of his interesting book. By adding work to the two values identified by Dumont, I believe we have a good characterization of the central ingredients of this ideology (Otto 1984). Building on the efforts of Dumont and others, I will outline the specific character of the Western economic ideology by sketching a brief history of its genesis.

Aristotle was one of the first Western philosophers to develop thoughts about what later became known as "the economy." For him economic activities were part of a whole characterized by a hierarchy of values. The highest value for human beings was contemplation. Next came the value of living a virtuous life as a citizen. A necessary condition for pursuing these two main values was economic independence (*autarkia*). To achieve *autarkia* a man needed a certain amount of wealth, which depended on the wise management of his household (*oikonomia*). Aristotle emphasized that *autarkia* could be achieved only if the material needs remained limited. Economic activities should not be considered as an aim in themselves; they should be subordinated to the pursuit of the higher values.

A similar type of ideology concerning economic enterprise dominated the Christian Middle Ages. In the late Middle Ages there was a substantial increase of trade, but the Christian doctrine opposed the pursuit of economic gain as a goal in itself. An important representative of the medieval philosophy was Thomas Aquinas. In his *Summa Theologiae*, he described human society as a totality directed toward one goal, the attainment of eternal happiness. Society was conceived as an organism, consisting of different levels performing hierarchically ordered functions. Economic activities had a subordinate place in the system; they provided the necessary basis for striving for higher values. People were prohibited from pursuing more wealth than was strictly necessary for living a life in accordance with their rank or class. The church explicitly forbade one from demanding interest on lent money (this was called usury). Trade was accepted because it was necessary to provide for local needs, but the price had to be just and reasonable.

At the end of the fifteenth century, great economic changes swept Western Europe. In Robert Heilbroner's description (1962), a "market society" was in the process of being born. At the same time, profound changes took place in the organization and interpretation of religion, namely, the Protestant Reformation. These transformations had their impact on Western philosophy, which I take here as an indicator of developments in the ideological outlook of the time. According to Dumont (1977: 47–60), it was John Locke who, in the seventeenth century, separated an economic theory from the contemporary practice of viewing society predominantly in political terms—the separation of politics and religion had occurred earlier (e.g., in the work of Machiavelli). Locke (1988) made the property-owning individual the cornerstone of his philosophy. This represented a major shift from the medieval focus on the society as a whole. The individual's right to property was based on his work, which, according to Locke, was not only completely his own but also the main source of economic value.

A further development of economic ideology can be traced in the work of Bernard Mandeville. In his famous *Fable of the Bees*, he argued that it was acceptable for individuals to pursue their economic self-interest, because this would lead to the greatest wealth for the society as a whole (Mandeville 1988). The subtitle of his essay is telling: *Private Vices, Public Benefits*. With this separation of public morality and individual economic activity, Mandeville made a crucial step. Individual self-interest, or "self-love," was redefined as a virtue, at least in the economic domain. And the main motivation for this lay in the field of relations between humans and things, namely, the growth of material wealth. Dumont argues that, with Mandeville, the second value of the economic ideology received clear expression—the primacy of human-thing relations. As a result, ethical considerations no longer inhibited the ruthless pursuit of wealth, as was the case in classical Greece and the European Middle Ages.

Later on, in the late eighteenth and the nineteenth century the concept of work was firmly established as the central source of economic value. This process can be followed in the work of such economic philosophers as Adam Smith, David Ricardo, and Karl Marx. Smith's *An Inquiry into the Nature and Causes of the Wealth of Nations* (1976) further developed the idea that the working of the "invisible hand" of the market should not be inhibited by moral and political interventions. In addition, the book postulated that labor (and the division of labor) was the only source of wealth. Labor was considered as both the origin and the measure of (exchange) value. In Smith's work there was still some ambiguity concerning the establishment of value (through exchange or through labor), but with Ricardo and Marx the labor theory of value found its full elaboration.

The development of labor as a central category of economic analysis corresponded with the emergence of work as a central virtue in Protestant morality. In Max Weber's *Die protestantische Ethik und der Geist des Kapitalismus* (1979), this process was analyzed in an exemplary way. In the new Protestant worldview, a person's work or profession was considered as a divine vocation. To work hard was therefore a divine duty, and the resulting increase of one's individual wealth was not interpreted as unethical but, to the contrary, as a sign of being among God's chosen ones. At the same time the Protestant ethic preached an ascetic attitude toward consumption and pleasure. This interesting mix of virtues, conceived as serving God's will and contributing to His glory, in fact facilitated the merciless pursuit of self-interest and even avarice. It thus accorded well with the developing industrial capitalism in which capital became an important factor of production (Tawney 1938).

Even though modern Western economists have long rejected the labor theory of value and extreme forms of Puritan asceticism and work-ethos have long withered away, it stands beyond doubt that work remains a central structuring category of modern capitalist society. In daily life, work provides an important focus and source for personal and social identification, and, for most Westerners, work is the main means of acquiring wealth and related social status. In the decades after World War II, work was so much a part of the natural way of understanding the world—of Western *doxa*, so to speak—that it did not need to be problematized. Only the large-scale unemployment of the late 1970s and early 1980s caused cracks in this self-understanding and led to a spate of books on work-ethos and work identity.[1]

For the patrol officers and anthropologists confronting the upsurge of cargo cult movements after World War II, a belief in the value of work was a natural and nonreflected part of their ideological luggage. Before I discuss how this ideological stance informed their interpretation of cargo cults, I first investigate the meaning of work in a Melanesian context.

Work and Knowledge in Melanesia

In order to convey a sense of the place of work in a Melanesian worldview, I will follow a different strategy from the one pursued in the previous section. For obvious reasons I am not able to present a genealogical sketch of Melanesian notions of work and value as I have attempted for the Western case. Historical sources are simply lacking, but also contemporary ethnographic sources are relatively scarce and approach the concept of work from quite varied perspectives. For example, Maurice Godelier (1977) is interested in the relationship between price and value and puts the Marxist labor theory of value to the test in a Melanesian context. Erik Schwimmer (1979) attempts a semiotic comparative approach, but his conceptual frame of reference is very Western (and Marxist), consisting of two sets of oppositions, namely, use value/exchange value and identification/alienation. I am more interested in a less ambitious semantic analysis that stays closer to the local concepts (see also Panoff 1977). Therefore, I will follow the common anthropological strategy of discussing one ethnographic example and use this to draw some more general conclusions. The case is Baluan, an island in Manus Province, Papua New Guinea, where I have conducted fieldwork intermittently from 1986 to the present.

A first observation has to be that Baluan terms carve out different semantic fields for activities that Westerners call work. The Baluan word *mangat* refers to effort, work, and task. One of the most important forms of *mangat* is the organization of traditional feasts during which food and wealth are distributed *(puron)*. In Tok Pisin this is expressed as *kastamwok* (work of custom/tradition). Not only is *kastamwok* one of the most valued forms of work, it is also one of the hardest, in Tok Pisin called *hatwok*. Work in the gardens is sometimes also considered as hard work, but fishing and hunting never are. Theodore Schwartz, who worked in other parts of Manus, remarks that sexual intercourse is also a form of work leading to aging and decline (Schwartz 1976: 197). Hard work is not a virtue in itself; to the contrary, it is something to be avoided if possible, because it wears one down. I heard people often complain about the heaviness of their tasks. Molat Aumbou, at the time the main political leader of Baluan Island, once told me: "Sometimes I think that this world of ours is a hell. Everything is hard work, food, house, transport. Nothing comes about without effort."[2]

Nevertheless, the terms *mangat* and *wok* can also be used in a positive way—for example, to praise an enterprising man as a *man bilong wok* (a man who is able to work a lot). Laziness is certainly not a virtue and people who carry out their tasks are respected, but work in itself is not seen a source of social status. One's status depends on the extent to which one successfully transforms work into wealth that can be distributed. It is common anthropological wisdom to emphasize that a Melanesian person develops his or her self in and through exchange. If one is able to amass a lot of food and wealth for distribution at a feast, one will acquire high status. It is crucial that the collected wealth is distributed and consumed; one does not gain status by just possessing it. Melanesian persons have correctly been depicted as nodes in networks of exchange (e.g., M. Strathern 1988), and their relative status is linked to the degree to which they function as nodes where wealth temporarily gathers before it disperses again. Therefore, Dumont's second value of the economic ideology—the primacy of human-thing relationships—appears to have relevance for Melanesians as well. Their social relationships are to a large extent constituted through the exchange of things.

Even though the value of individualism, the first Dumontian value of the economic ideology, is not irrelevant in this context, I will leave this aside for the present discussion.[3] Let me only repeat my conclusion that individualism as an explicit ideological value does not seem to have great importance in Melanesia, even though a strong focus on individuality and self-expression may be seen as informing social practice. Returning to work, it should be concluded that this concept does not have a central ideological position either, not as a moral duty, not as social status, and not as a source of wealth. From a Melanesian perspective, work can be seen as contributing to wealth and thus to status, and in some contexts it could be even constructed as a duty (especially in exchange relationships). Nevertheless, work does not have the same explanatory and moral weight as it has in Western economic ideology.

With regard to the production of food and wealth, one can argue that work may be considered as one of the production factors, also in a Melanesian understanding. I would suggest, however, that work is not seen as the crucial factor in the creation of wealth. The crucial production factor, I would venture, is knowledge. It is not sufficient to work hard in the garden for produce to be bountiful. One has to know the proper procedures, the proper magic, and the proper herbs that facilitate the growth of garden food. If someone comes back from a fishing trip without any catch, his lack of knowledge is blamed—knowledge of places, the habits of the fish, and the proper procedures and magic. The same applies to construction work: whether one makes canoes, houses, traditional artifacts, or modern outboard motors, knowledge is the crucial difference between success and failure. Therefore, it is no wonder that knowledge was a focal point in Melanesian interpretations of Western wealth and power.

Before I turn to the mutual interpretations of Manusian cargo cultists and Western colonial agents, I have to say something about the concept of knowledge. On Baluan the word for knowledge is *mapai*. There are basically two ways of obtaining knowledge. One way is to observe someone with a certain skill doing something. The latter person's knowledge is thus transferred to the keen observer. Related to this is carefully listening to what a knowledgeable person says. Hearing knowledge, however, has not the same status as seeing knowledge executed in practice. There is always a danger that one is told only stories (*pwapwa*). The ultimate test is seeing the effect of knowledge with one's own eyes. A second basic way of obtaining knowledge is through revelation from deities, for example, via a dream or in a trance. Such revelation often concerns important knowledge, for example, concerning the cause of illness or concerning significant rituals.

From a Baluan perspective, it is not possible to create or invent knowledge. All knowledge is present somewhere from the beginning of time, even though it may be concealed from human beings. This appears to be a common Melanesian conception.[4] As a limited good, knowledge (including the knowledge of rituals) can enter into exchange relationships, just like material things.[5] As mentioned above, competitive exchange of valuables is a central Melanesian mechanism for obtaining status. In such exchange, knowledge is a particularly valued valuable as it is directly linked to the production of wealth. True knowledge is effective.

By contrast, Western notions of knowledge connect it with creativity and invention. The authorship of knowledge is a crucial aspect in securing ownership through patents or copyright, whereas in Melanesia legitimate ownership of knowledge is achieved through proper exchange relationships. As a factor of production, knowledge has been much less foregrounded in Western economic understanding than it is in Melanesia. A quick check of a number of introductory textbooks to economics reveals that knowledge is not generally included in the subject index and, therefore, is presumably not considered as a key economic term.[6] The concept is, of course, not completely absent, because it is normally implied as an aspect of one of the four main factors of production: labor, land, capital, and entrepreneurship (Parkin 2000: 36). Knowledge and skill are considered as an aspect of capital, namely, human capital, that enhances the productivity of labor. In modern economics the concept of work is still at the center of the discipline (Elkan 1979: 25).

Paliau Movement and Western Reactions

As an example of mutual attempts at interpretation between Melanesians and Westerners, I will present the well-known Paliau movement in Manus. Even though this movement is quite unique in a number of ways—not the least because of its longevity—the central tendencies in mutual misunderstanding can be considered as typical for colonial interactions regarding a large number of cargo cults and indigenous reform movements. Melanesians frequently assumed the existence of secret knowledge that was stolen or hidden from them, whereas Western administrators and particularly entrepreneurs did not stop complaining about a perceived Melanesian contempt for hard work.

Paliau Maloat was born on Baluan Island around 1915, and, after a career in the native police, he returned to Manus in 1946 to start a reform movement that was later named after him.[7] Even though ideas about change had been around since the late 1930s, it appeared that the presence of large numbers of American soldiers during World War II had functioned as a catalyst for Manusian reflections about the colonial situation and had greatly intensified their wishes for change. Coinciding with the beginning of the Paliau movement were a number of cargo cults in a restricted sense: strongly emotional episodes in villages in which people destroyed their own property and waited for their ancestors to come with Western goods. Paliau was able to canalize the energy unleashed in these local movements to build up an unparalleled program for reform of indigenous society. This brought him under the suspicion of the colonial authorities, which first tried to stop him by arresting him. A more enlightened policy followed, which introduced limited political reform through native representations and allowed Paliau to take the lead as a representative of native society.

From the beginning of the movement, the glaring inequality between Westerners and Melanesians had posed a critical problem for Manus self-respect and the conviction that Westerners had kept the relevant core of their knowledge to themselves was deeply rooted. A common belief was that Westerners used metaphors to conceal the true meaning of things. In Tok Pisin, the movement's communicative vehicle, this kind of metaphor was referred to as *tok piksa* (Schwartz 1962: 251–252, 327) and also as *tok bokis,* which even more explicitly denotes the hidden nature of an image's true meaning. In the 1930s the new knowledge of the missions had been embraced as a way to healthier, wealthier, and longer lives (Otto 1991, 1998a), but after a decade and a half many felt that conversion had not lived up to their expectations. When the American army appeared with its enormous material wealth, the idea that the white people had been hiding something all along impressed itself with added force. This is very clearly expressed in a text, which was written down in the early years of the movement by a Catholic catechist:[8] "The reason for this [the movement and especially "the Noise," the local name for various cargo cults] was the sight of all the things of the white people. During the war this was already in everyone's mind. When Paliau wanted to begin, they went ahead with him. Their thoughts were as follows, they said: when the white people first arrived at our place, they lied to us, and now we have seen something real with our own eyes, and at present we cannot listen to the stories of white people anymore, they are liars."

When J. H. Wootten, a staff member of the Australian School of

Pacific Administration, spent five months in Kawaliap, a village in central Manus, in early 1947, he was confronted with similar ideas after the initial mistrust toward him had subsided. An old man confided to him, "If only you would not hide your tingting [thoughts, ideas] from us, we could be brothers. ...You and I and my children would sit down at one table, sleep in one house. We would not have to go away while you eat. ... If the white man would only open his hand, we would be brothers. But he keeps it tightly shut. He has locked all his knowledge in a box, and where are we to find the key?" (Rowley 1965: 166–167).

It was assumed that the missionaries had been able to conceal the core of Western knowledge by using *tok piksa.* Therefore, a lively speculation developed concerning the true meaning of the images used by the mission. As an example of such an explanation, I quote from an account collected by Schwartz. It concerns the image that the door of heaven is closed and Petrus is holding the key. It gives a wonderful synopsis of some central tenets of the movement and emphasizes the importance of knowledge:

> What kind of key is this that the missionary speaks of? It is not a key. It is the minds of men. As long as men cling to the ways of the past and follow all of the fashion no good of their fathers, their minds are closed, this key remains unturned in the lock. But now we have found the meaning of the key. Our minds must be cleared of the ways of Lucifer, we must think of God, then our minds will open. We will be all right. Now this key is in the hand of Paliau. It is just like the key that God gave to Petrus, but it is not a real key, it is knowledge. Paliau has gone ahead in finding knowledge. He holds the key that will open the door for us. (Schwartz 1962: 260)

Let me now turn to the way in which Western colonial agents tried to make sense of these indigenous reactions and attempts to create wealth. In 1957, district commissioner J. Preston White wrote in the concluding paragraph of his section on education: "It seems that ultimate success in our work in Manus has chiefly to do with the mind. If through our sound and consistent guidance we can foster in the people the growth of a sure belief in themselves and in their own capacity to face and overcome their problems, we will finally defeat the cult tendency to discard the philosophy of practical work and effort as a means of progress; thus we may hope to avoid the unrewarding reversion to reliance on the supernatural powers of their ancestors as the providers of material benefits" (*Manus District Annual Report* 1956/1957: 35).

Preston White's successor, E. G. Hicks, largely copied this paragraph in his 1958 report making but a few additions: one of these was to characterize as "peculiarly Manus" the "tendency to discard the philosophy of practical work and individual effort as means of progress" (*Manus District Annual Report* 1957/1958: 46). L. J. O'Malley, who succeeded Hicks, expressed almost identical views. He stressed that "the biggest problem of all is the one of getting the people to realize that improvement to their standard of living can only be obtained by their acceptance of the principle that nothing is gained without continuous personal effort in all spheres of human activity" (*Manus District Annual Report* 1958/1959: 20).

These quotations may suffice to indicate the drift of the mutual interpretations. Melanesians were very eager to get access to Western knowledge, which was in their eyes the very basis of Western wealth and power. Conversion to Christianity, the Noise (cargo cult), and the Paliau movement were all means to achieve this aim of becoming equals to the white people through the appropriation of their true knowledge. The colonial officers saw these attempts as evidence of a fundamental misunderstanding on the side of the natives. Only if the latter would accept that work was the basis of all wealth could they start with making progress toward their desired goal. Which position can be regarded as more rational is a moot question. Melanesians had been working on plantations and other Western workplaces for many decades without making much progress toward their goal of material equality with Westerners. On the other hand, the particular religious knowledge they pursued could not provide the desired goods either.

There is a fine irony in this example of cultural contact and mutual interpretation. The colonial officers' quotes are taken from sections in *District Annual Reports* dealing with education. Western education was seen as the key to enlighten the natives and cure them from "cult thinking" and "semi–religious mystic practices." The followers of the Paliau movement, after initial mistrust, responded with an "almost fanatical thirst for education" (*Manus District Annual Reports* 1956/1957: 34; 1959/1960: 30) to the introduction of government primary schooling. Manus villages showed an almost 100 percent school attendance. Both Melanesians and Westerners appeared to agree on the crucial importance of education. They had, however, their own reasons for this. For Melanesians this was another attempt to appropriate the truly efficacious Western knowledge, whereas the Westerners considered it as a medicine for the uncultivated mind, as an antidote for a kind of mental disease. Ironically again, history has proven both of them right, at least partly so, even though their assumptions may have been wrong. Through their high level of education Manus Islanders were able to gain a large number of well-paid jobs in the public administration and in the expanding school system. This led to a stream of remittances in the direction of Manus

Province. Thus, the pursuit of true knowledge had indeed created native wealth and, in a Western sense, at least a number of Manus people were working to earn a living.

Cargo, Knowledge, and Freedom

In this section I will further discuss Manus concepts of wealth and cargo. In particular I want to show that the values of these concepts have changed over time and that it is important for the analyst to be attentive towards continuity as well as change. Nowadays, the term "cargo cult" has become part of the Manus vocabulary, just as in many other places in Melanesia (cf. Hermann and Jebens, both in the present volume). It is mostly used in discussions about the Paliau movement, which continues to exist up to the present day, recently under the name *Win Neisen* (Gustafsson 1995). Followers of this movement are eager to point out that they are not cargo cultists and that this mistaken label was invented by anthropologists and other foreigners to disparage Paliau and his plans for reform. In a kind of counterattack, they use the term to criticize contemporary politicians for their handout election politics and empty promises and for not delivering real development to the villages. Outsiders to the movement, mostly have no inhibitions about using the label "cargo cult" to describe certain aspects or phases of the movement.

There is, however, general consensus about certain events that took place soon after the end of World War II and became known as "the Noise": intense expectations swept Manus. In several villages, people became seized with convulsions and had visions of nearing airplanes and cargo boats. In a number of villages, property was destroyed and traditional wealth (dogs' teeth and shell beads) was thrown into the sea. In one village, a local prophet was killed, at his own request it is told (this is also documented in the contemporary patrol reports). In contrast to this consensus about what happened, interpretations of the events vary widely. Some people maintain that the millennium was near but did not eventuate only because not all villagers were in the right mind. Others admit that they made a mistake and now regret the loss of traditional wealth. Others again did not join at the time. Two villages on Baluan had earlier converted to the Seventh-day Adventist Church and proved quite resistant to the Noise. This is not to say that they were in any way less millenarian at the time, but they had been warned for false prophets. Others again privately doubted the wisdom of the Noise and hid their own valuables, while participating in the meetings and prayers.

Paliau Maloat had returned to Manus after the war and was in the process of establishing himself as an influential political leader and reformer. His role in the Noise appears to have been ambivalent. He is not considered as the source of the cargo belief, but apparently he did not oppose it either. Only when the goods failed to arrive, did he intervene, by saying that the villagers should now follow another way, his way. Before turning to Paliau's ideas, I will try to interpret the meaning of the cargo belief in the first cultist movements on Manus. Following Schwartz I would like to stress, that, whatever psychological and political-economic explanations we may want to put forward, it is important to realize that notions of cargo played a central role in these original cults. As Schwartz noted, "I repeat, it's the cargo. For Melanesia, the primary issue was not, 'Are you a man or a woman, a white man or a black man?' The issue was 'Are you a man with a name, a man who commands wealth, or are you rubbish?'" (Schwartz 1976: 177).

If the characterization of Melanesian cultures as having a strong emphasis on exchange and status competition is correct it should not come as a surprise that any reactions to Western colonial dominance would also, and even primarily, find expression in the field of human-thing relations. This is not the same as claiming that Melanesian cultures were naturally cargoist. Notions of cargo developed in a context where Melanesians tried to interpret Western culture and unveil its secrets. The Melanesian notion of cargo may thus be considered as the equivalent of the Western notion of culture, as R. Wagner has argued (1981: 31; cf. Dalton, present volume). But cargo was more than cultural interpretation. It was also an attempt to reappropriate the sources of wealth, to regain local autonomy, and to reestablish a sense of selfhood that was very much affected and diminished by the unequal access to wealth.[9]

There is a second aspect to this cultural reinterpretation and revaluation that occurred in cargo cults, one that has received less attention in the anthropological literature. Cargo cults can also be interpreted as internal revolutions, as social movements aiming to put an end to the dominance of big men. If there is abundance of everything no one will be able to gain status by controlling the flow of wealth. The cargo millennium makes everyone equal. There is no longer a need to harangue followers into action in order to meet a challenge. Competitive distribution is meaningless. This interpretation is corroborated by the absence of any apparent concern among Melanesians about the distribution of the cargo (cf. Stanner 1958 and Schwartz 1976). Whereas anticipations and calculations concerning the amount of gifts and counter-gifts are very much part of Melanesian exchange practices, this appears to be absent in cargo cults. Cargo is an image of endless abundance and consumption that resolves both colonial and local social inequality. Cargo is a resolution of the network structure of exchange, creating an infinite field of humans and things. Cargo is in fact the transcendence of the Melanesian Self (cf. Crapanzano, present volume). It is a vision of absolute freedom.

Whereas the initial cargo cults in Manus had an evidently millenarian character without elaborate programs for change, Paliau and his followers designed a new structure for society based on a new historical cosmology (Otto 1992b). Like the Noise, the movement arose from strong sentiments of dissatisfaction with the colonial situation, which were clearly spelled out in a charter myth, the "Long Story of God." Paliau was presented as the conduit for knowledge that originated directly from God and that would effectuate the emancipation of the natives from colonial inequality. The movement thus had strong political undertones but first of all aimed at building up wealth. To this end, Paliau forbade the traditional funeral feasts during which large amounts of food and wealth were distributed. He considered them wasteful of goods and human energy, just like the bride-price payments, which he transformed into a single payment of a small amount of money. Paliau discouraged the villagers from working for white people and told them to save up the money they had gained through the sale of produce. The building up and securing of native wealth was thus a crucial element in Paliau plans for reform to help the natives regain their lost autonomy. Other elements concerned the communal organization of productive practices and the establishment of new villages with houses built in straight rows.

The Paliau movement can be considered a great success for native development, because it forced the colonial government to take native wishes seriously. Baluan and Manus became privileged places for the introduction of new administrative systems, such as native councils, primary schools, health centers, and cooperative societies. These developments are still celebrated as achievements of the movement by its members.[10] Paliau became a respected politician and the first Manus representative in the newly established House of Assembly in 1964 (he was reelected in 1968). In the 1970s his political career declined, but his leadership received a new impulse in the 1980s through a revival of his movement under a new name, "Makasol," and with the help of a number of young and well-educated helpers.

The ideological basis of the invigorated movement was still Paliau's knowledge. It was claimed that he had not been able to communicate all the knowledge he had received from God under the repressive colonial regime. Because Papua New Guinea had become an independent country, Paliau was finally able to share also the remaining part of his original knowledge. This was called *las sape* (the last knowledge), and Paliau began to present himself as the last prophet of the world. As soon as his followers would heed words and accept this last knowledge, they would enter a condition of "freedom" *(fridom)*.[11] This situation was characterized by

- Absence of aging,
- Absence of illness,
- Absence of death,
- Absence of hunger, and
- Absence of work (*hatwok*).

This is an image of a blissful, millenarian situation, but it is interesting that the concept of material wealth is downplayed. In the movement's new doctrine, the basis of Western wealth is rejected as the work of the fallen angel Lucifer, who created factories and money. In this later phase, the movement was considerably smaller than in its high days after the World War II. It acted in opposition to the local indigenous government, which controlled the state subsidies for local development projects. It may well be that the conspicuous absence of material success at that time had an impact on the ideological content of the movement's belief. But it is nevertheless significant that the millenarian vision of this phase of the Paliau movement had turned Western cargo into a negative value. Freedom was not defined as an abundance of goods, but as the absence of negative bodily conditions, including hard work. The way to achieve this freedom was to follow the true knowledge as revealed by Paliau Maloat.

Work, Wealth, and Consumption

Also in the West conceptions of work and wealth have changed during the past decades. In his influential book *The Corrosion of Character* (1998), Richard Sennett argues that the flexibility required in modern work conditions affects the moral dimension that was formerly attached to work. Personal character, endurance, and loyalty are being replaced by short-term profit-seeking alliances and continual reinvention of the Self. The stability and long-term time horizon that previously defined labor relations allowed strong identification and the building of "character": a sense of sustained purpose, integrity of Self, and trust in others. This possibility is corroded by the demands of the new capitalism, which lacks the longer time horizon and requires continual adaptation and redefinition of identities.

Another aspect of changing labor conditions is analyzed by Paul Du Gay (1996). He points out that the domains of consumption and work have become blurred, whereas formerly sharp distinctions existed. Focusing on forms of identification, Du Gay argues that consumers and employees are represented in equal terms, namely, as autonomous, responsible, and calculating individuals. The enterprise discourse about the requirements of workers and the consumption discourse about the characteristics of consumers greatly overlap, both defining persons as entrepreneurs of the Self, whether at work or at play. Work could be claimed to be a form of consumption (leading to individual expression and development) and consumption could be considered as a form of work (to develop and realize the Self).

These two books refer to major changes in modern Western conceptions and valuations of work. The economic ideology sketched above is possibly in a fundamental transition leading to a relative redefinition of the values of work, wealth, and consumption. This change in reflective awareness is no doubt connected with changes in capitalist work practices. Is it too far-fetched to assume that this ideological change heightens the culture critical potential of the cargo archive? In this chapter, I have attempted to make a contribution to such culture critique by comparing Western and Manus (Melanesian) notions of work, wealth, and knowledge. Among other points, I have shown that the cargo dimension of the millenarian dream has diminished in the Paliau movement. The identification of the Western concept of wealth with money and property is a relatively modern development (particularly from the seventeenth and eighteenth centuries onward). The term originally referred to happiness and prosperity more generally (R. Williams 1983: 331–332). It is well possible that new conceptions of work, knowledge, and consumption will lead to a new understanding of wealth, deemphasizing again its materialistic bias.[12]

Notes

Dedicated to the memory of the late professor Gerrit Huizer, who as no other has opened my eyes to the cargoistic dimension of modern Western society.

1. Compare Gorz (1980), Achterhuis (1984), and Leadbeater and Lloyd (1987).
2. "I nogat samting i kamap nating" (Fieldnotes 201237).
3. I have taken this point up elsewhere (Otto 1990, 1997).
4. See Lawrence (1964: 30), M. Strathern (1988: 322–324), and Lindstrom (1990a: 74; 1990b).
5. See Otto (1991, 1998a) and Harrison (1993, 2000).
6. I found only one exception—namely, Parkin (2000: 440–446)—but compare n. 12.
7. See Schwartz (1962) and Otto (1992b, 1992c, 1998b).
8. The catechist was M. Tapo, according to a typed account found at Bundralis mission and presumably recorded by Father Dahmen.

9. Compare MacLean (1994). Schwartz remarks the following about the confrontation of Western and Melanesian cultural interpretations: "The [Melanesian] value system was not replaced or undermined so much as it was overwhelmed on its own terms. By their own previous standards Melanesians were suddenly impoverished, dominated, overpowered. I call this kind of situation 'value dominance'—being overcome by others in terms of one's own values. Under value dominance there is no chance of telling oneself that the wealth of the other is of no importance compared to one's own values. The two cultures, broadly speaking, met on the common ground of materialistic, competitive striving for prestige through entrepreneurial achievement of wealth" (Schwartz 1976: 174).

10. Compare the following text from a leaflet distributed by the movement (Maloat 1985):

The Last Knowledge:

This knowledge arose from the 1945–1946 movement on the 9th of October 1947. The school of knowledge was then established on the 19th March 1984 at Baluan and continuing to the present.

1. 1950—Local Government Council was established at Baluan.
2. 1951—Education (schools) was established at Baluan.
3. 1952—Aid post (hospital) was established at Baluan.
4. 1953—Cooperative society (business development) was established at Baluan.
5. Local Government Council brought independence to Papua New Guinea on the 16th September 1975.

11. This situation of freedom was described in various leaflets. Here follows a quote from an English version found on the same leaflet as quoted in n. 10 (Maloat 1985):

The Six Orders Wing the Creator Gave Adam and Eve:

1. Adam and Eve, you shall not grow *old*.
2. Adam and Eve, you shall not become *sick*.
3. Adam and Eve, you shall not *die*.
4. Adam and Eve, you shall not become *hungry*.
5. Adam and Eve, you shall not *labor*.
6. Adam and Eve, you shall live in everlasting happiness, laughter, play and sing joyously and in freedom.

12. Since I completed this chapter, several years ago, I have become aware that knowledge has truly become a key concept in contemporary political debates about social and economic change. Recently knowledge has been increasingly presented as a key factor in economic growth and international competitiveness. As an early academic precursor to this discursive trend, one could point to Daniel Bell's *The Coming of the Post-Industrial Society* (1973), in which he argues that a new type of economy is emerging with a much greater emphasis on the production of knowledge and information. In recent years policy papers from national governments and international organizations often make reference to the new conditions and special requirements posed by the "knowledge society." My own preliminary inroads into this new field of study suggest that the concepts of knowledge involved in this discourse predominantly connect knowledge with measurable economic results, even though one also finds references to human development in a more general sense. If this impression holds water, it belies my rather optimistic conclusion in the chapter that changes in concepts of work, knowledge, and consumption could possibly lead to a deemphasis of the belief in monetary value and limitless economic growth. The millenarian drive in Western society (Huizer 1992) is perhaps unbroken, but this observation would at least underscore another assumption of my chapter: the usefulness of intercultural comparison and cultural critique, in this case in particular concerning the role of knowledge both in the Paliau Movement and in our modern "knowledge society."

CHAPTER 13 Thoughts on Hope and Cargo

Vincent Crapanzano

It is indeed beautiful to see a person put out to sea with the fair wind of hope; one may utilize the chance to let oneself be towed away, but one ought never have it on board one's craft, least of all as pilot, for it is an untrustworthy shipmaster. For this reason, too, hope was one of Prometheus's dubious gifts; instead of giving human beings the foreknowledge of the immortals, he gave them hope.

—*Søren Kierkegaard*

I BEGIN with a fear—the fear of the field anthropologist who discusses an area of the world to which he has never been and has, therefore, to depend on written sources with which he can never have the confidence he has in his own findings. He is a stranger to both the area and the modes of discourse—the styles, theoretical concerns, and substantive preoccupations—through which that area, its peoples, cultures, and societies, are constructed by those ethnographers who have worked there. He lacks, in other words, the "comfort" of these—repeated and conventional—constructions. Doubly a stranger, he has, though, a certain privilege: his outsider's view allows him new ways of seeing what has been seen and perhaps even ways of seeing what has not been seen. He is also free of certain epistemological conundra that, though affecting anthropology generally, can become at times illuminating, at time crippling, area-specific preoccupations. I will not enter into a discussion of the political, ethical, and epistemological legitimacy of the use of "cargo" and "cargo cults," which have been amply discussed in this volume and elsewhere, other than to observe, as Elfriede Hermann (present volume) does, that they should be written under erasure, for they reflect European philosophical presuppositions that are not necessarily shared by the "cargoists" themselves.[1] I should note further that in many hyperreflective discussions of ethnological categories of description, even—perhaps particularly—

those that are concerned with preserving the subjectivity of the people studied from the researcher's hegemonic representations, there is a risk of what can be called metaorientalism, in case in point, metacargoism. In attempting to preserve the subjectivity and agency of those one represents through critical commentary on those representations, one risks sidestepping, if not altogether ignoring, precisely that subjectivity and agency, as Edward Said (1978) often does in *Orientalism*.

I begin, too, with a hope that what I have to say will ring true to those who have worked in Melanesia—or at least alert them to a blindness in the way in which cargo cults have been described and explained. I begin then with a provocation, and a plea: to consider the role of hope in cargoism.[2] I should note that, though hope has received considerable attention in theological and phenomenological circles, it has received scant attention in anthropology and the other social and psychological sciences. Ernst Bloch's *Das Prinzip Hoffnung* (1959) is of course an exception. Desire, on the other hand, is the central focus of social, psychological, and literary theory. As Lamont Lindstrom (1993) has demonstrated, it figures mightily and perversely in studies of cargoism. We must ask why hope is not a category of understanding and analysis in the social sciences. It is certainly no more difficult to define than desire. It should, however, like "cargo" and "cargo cult," be written under erasure, for "hope" is deeply embedded in philosophical, indeed the psychological, presuppositions of "our" constituted world.[3]

I

"We need some imaginative stimulus, some not impossible ideal, such as may shape vague hope, and transform it into effective desire, to carry us year after year, without disgust, through the routine work which is so large a part of life" (Pater 1911: 19). I quote, improbably, from the Victorian aesthete and critic, Walter Pater because in these few words from his novel he reveals several significant features of hope (at least as we construe it): "imaginative stimulus" (presumably from the real world), "some not impossible ideal," "vague hope" (I stress "vague"), "effective desire" (I stress "effective"), and the carrying us through the "routine work" of life—curiously—"without disgust."[4] Pater's words are as important for what they do not include but are often associated with hope: namely, dreams, waking dreams, daydreams (remember Aristotle said somewhere that "hope is a waking dream"); illusions and shadows, as of hope; waiting; future; fear (as an opposite of hope, as Bloch emphasizes); utopia; and, of course, a quantity of theological terms like redemption and salvation. To these I would also add realism and resignation.

Is hope an emotion, as Bloch (1959) thought it to be? He referred to it as an "expectant emotion." Or is it better described, as I think it is, as an emotionally and morally toned descriptor of an existential stance or attitude? Is it—in linguistic terminology—a stative or a performative? If it—"I hope"—is a performative, like "I promise," it is very weak. If it is a stative, it postulates a mental condition that is rather illusive. Certainly, if Bloch is right, hope is historically conditioned.[5] It is transitive insofar as "one hopes for..." or "one hopes that. ..." That is, one speaks of the object of hope the way one speaks of the object of desire. Its object may be concrete—as in "I hope that I will find gold"—or abstract—as in "I hope it will all work out in the end." As a noun, "hope" tends to be abstract or, as Pater would say, "vague." It may even appear to be without an object. There are, I believe, in American English at least two distinct uses of "hope" and "to hope": one in which the object of hope is specific and concrete, like cargo with a small c, and the other in which it is vague and abstract, like Cargo with a capital C. I suggest that the rhetorical force of "hope" rests largely on the potential and real play between its concrete and abstract objects. When its object is concrete, *hope* resembles—in usage at least—desire and may be confused with it. When its object is abstract, it suggests a philosophical perspective on life, a sort of positive resignation, for example. Such a perspective is often masked by hope's concrete object, which "transforms" resigned hope into active desire. This conversion activates, as it were, our more abstract hopes and conceals the resignation that lies, inevitably, behind them. I would of course like to know the "grammar" of hope in the languages of Melanesia where cargo has figured.

Remember Pater's words "to transform vague hope into effective desire." Desire is effective. It presupposes human agency. One acts on desire—even if that act is not to act on desire because one has judged it impossible or prefers the desire to its fulfillment. Except where hope is used as an equivalent to desire—and even then it is usually ambiguous—hope depends upon some other agency—a god, fate, chance, an other—for its fulfillment. You can do all you can to realize your hopes, but ultimately they depend on the fates—on someone else. I desire her. I hope she will desire me. I do everything in my capacity to bring about her desire, but ultimately there is a limit to what I can do. I can only hope. We might be able to say, simplistically but revealingly, that whereas desire presupposes a psychology, hope presupposes a metaphysics. Both require an ethics—of expectation, constraint, and resignation. And this ethics is founded on one notion or another of the real—on a realism.

In *Le temps vécu,* published in 1933, the psychiatrist Eugène Minkowski examines hope and desire phenomenologically, from within the structure of lived time.[6] For Minkowski, hope and desire are characteristic of that zone of experienced time that he calls the "mediate future." It lies between the zone of immediate future, characterized by expectation and activity, and the zone of remote future, characterized by prayer and ethical action. As opposed to activity and expectation, associated respectively with joy and terror, Minkowski finds desire and hope to be positive because we are always aspiring to more than we have and envisaging the future hopefully. "We are charmed by hope because it opens the future broadly before us."[7] Both desire and hope have to be understood in terms of the "further" as an essential characteristic of human life.[8]

For Minkowski, desire surpasses as it contains activity; it is fuller; it looks further into the future than activity to the beyond. It is more intimately connected with the ego than mere activity. "In desire there is a withdrawal in relation to activity, a withdrawal to the intimate me, toward the interior, toward the inside of the active ego."[9] Unlike activity, which can only go from object to object, desire enables us to settle on something. It is more episodic than activity. Hope shares the same direction as expectation—toward the future-present. It penetrates further into the future than expectation. It is more ample, full of promise. "It separates us from immediate contact with ambient becoming; it suppresses the embrace of expectation and permits me to look freely, far into lived space which now opens up before me." "I have an intimation of all that could be in the world beyond the immediate contact which expectation achieves between becoming and the ego." I am put into contact with a becoming that is unfolding at a distance. There is—in my terms—a transcending quality about hope. Hope allows me to take refuge in myself in order to see life unfold around me.[10] Minkowski puts it this way: "Desire contains activity within itself, while hope liberates us from anxious expectation. And yet, it holds us breathless. Unlike desire, which is continuous, hope assumes a moment of arrest."

For Minkowski, prayer and ethical action are, as I have said, characteristic of the zone of the remote future.[11] Prayer here is a life structure—a temporal attitude. It requires neither a man nor a god. It is a movement inward—"a totally lived interiorization"—and an exteriorisation—"a totally lived extrospection." For, "in springing up from the depths of my being, it goes beyond the universe. In prayer, we lift ourselves up above ourselves and all that surrounds us and turn our eyes to the distance, toward an infinite horizon, toward a sphere beyond time and beyond space, a sphere full of grandeur and clarity but also mystery." Minkowski adds, importantly, "we can then replace this mystery with the idea of an active divinity. But this idea is not in any way originally included in the phenomenon of prayer, which, far from affirming whatever it may be from this point of view, above all puts a problem before us." In other words, as Minkowski works out or at least conceives of, his phenomenology, the postulation of a god would be an "empirical question"—a culturally or historically determined symbolization for mystery.

Is prayer wholly different from hope? Can a line be drawn between mediate and remote time? Or do they fade into each other. I would argue that prayer, as Minkowski understands it, as a life structure, is a necessary horizon of all hope. Hope, particularly in its abstract form, always invokes a final horizon—a beyond, a mystery, a metaphysics. It may be idealized in Minkowski's "remote future" but all future presupposes and proclaims a horizon—something beyond, unreachable. It is the object of hope in its concreteness that diminishes the horizon, that directs attention away from the horizon to itself—in its specificity. This is why Minkowski distinguishes between ordinary prayer—to a god, with appropriate ritual, for an object—from prayer as attitude toward the future. It may well be possible to understand the focus on an object as a way of defending oneself from consideration of the beyond—the awe, the dread, the joy, it may well inspire, the sublime. I note that when anthropologists have considered prayer and magic they have focused on the object and the instrumentality that arises from such a focus rather than on the horizon and the metaphysics it presupposes, the mystery it calls forth.

II

I want to suggest here—in a preliminary and provocative way—that the between of desire and hope, of effective desire and vague hope, is the "space," the "space-time," of magic and ritual manipulation—of the fantasmatic conversion of a fantasized object into reality. Or, in other words, of the fantasmatic realization of desired possibility. I want to stress hope with respect to magic, however, rather than desire with which magic has been traditionally understood. Magic is an attempt—we are told—to bring about the object of unfulfilled and realistically unfulfillable desire. It is an instrumentality that operates between desire and its object. This approach to magic, as has often been remarked, gives to magic an instrumental quality that may well reflect the utilitarianism of the observer.[12] It also stresses the individual quality of magic and risks placing it, our understanding of it, in the "psychological." Now, without denying the instrumentality of magic, without denying its individual orientation, I want yet to emphasize the fact that magic operates within a set of specific metaphysical assumptions about the world and its actors. Among them is the temporal frontier—the moment beyond: the space of hope that resists definition but contains our aspirations, the object of our desires. It is, I believe, the way that hope is constructed—Minkowski would probably say "empirically constructed"—that has to be determined. It is here that magic is given its metaphysical slant. It is hope, rather more than desire, that calls forth in an act of situating desire or at least its object, in the hoped for, which evokes this metaphysically presupposed world.

The two—desire and hope—cannot easily be separated. Our ignoring hope seems to reflect our own particular assumptions about the individual, motivation, and agency and the agent's situation in the world. It is the object of desire that comes then to play a world-situating role. It is always more than itself; it is also a symbol. It evokes the world, the moral order, society. Cargo, we are told, refers at once to the actual objects the cultists long for—say, the proverbial refrigerator (see Lindstrom, present volume)—and to a new moral, social, and cultural order in which these objects figure. In such an analysis, the object of desire comes to bear enormous pragmatic weight, for it alone casts—constitutes—the world of its assumption just it denies its symbolic-evocative, its pragmatic, dimension by emphasizing its real, concrete quality. After all, it is not the universe that is desired. It is the object—the refrigerator, the love that has until then been unrequited.

Jacques Lacan (1966) speaks of the ultimate impossibility of fulfilling desire, for its object, having passed through the defiles—*les défilés*—of the signifier, is always a substitute for an unrealizable and inadmissible desire, which he understands from within the *mythoi* of psychoanalysis. In so doing, he situates that object in the linguistically constituted world—in the *symbolique*. He also evokes a world, a metaphysics, in which lack, absence, a *manque-à-être* predominates. Desire has always to trick itself. *Il devait toujours se tricher*. Can we say the same for the object of hope? By Lacan's standards, it too would also have to pass through the defiles of the signifier. But, unlike the object of desire, it gives recognition to its own impossibility—at least to the limits of human intervention. It requires a kind of passivity, which gives recognition, surrenders even, to the resistance posed by an Other. Can we say that, unlike desire, hope does not trick. I hardly think so. We play with hope as we do with desire. Though we recognize through hope the limits of our powers—that we are living in a world we can never fully master—we, nevertheless, defy those limits not only through what we take to be rational, practical activity (preparation) but through "magical" activities and prayer.

III

"Ideally, comprehension [of the new order introduced by the colonists] would have required of Tangu a knowledge of the new environment in terms of a language that could describe and analyze all its aspects and relations. Pidgin English on Tangu tongues is largely a vocabulary syntactically ordered as in the Tangu language. Economical in simple directives and closely related to traditional life, even at its most verbose straining at the meaning in English, it is not a language with the contextual referents necessary to a full understanding of the new world that is forming. It is a language adapted to relations between superior and inferior. The attempt to use the Tangu language to explain the parts of the new environment, on the other hand, puts a European into a situation of complete *rapport* with Tangu themselves. Conceptions of space, time, number, causation, and relationship cannot be reduced to Tangu terms. Then, as the Tangu remark, one is either a liar, speaking of marvels beyond the imaginative grasp, or implying the existence of a 'secret' which white men possess and are withholding from the black man" (Burridge 1969b: 33). One could, of course, reverse the terms of the argument, replacing Tangu with English.

My description of hope is, certainly, inevitably ethnocentric. It assumes a set of metaphysical, anthropological, and psychological assumptions that are by no means universal. It is, in this respect, like our understanding of desire, which plays so fundamental a role in our world that we naturalize it and take it for granted. Where we glimpse difference, we attribute it to differences in expression, personality, and the articulation of desire's object. There are those, the pragmatic, whose desire is straightforward, and those, the quixotic, the bovarian, as René Girard (1961) noted, whose desire is the desire they take to be the desire of the character to which they aspire. Or there are those, so beautifully described by fin-de-siècle writers, especially in France, who desire desire rather than its object. We can restate all of this in terms of hope.

But we must recognize that, like desire, hope is grounded on a set of assumptions about the nature of man, agency, fate, time, space, the possible and impossible (call it "realism"), and the power, be it transcendent or not otherwise, of whoever—the Other—is deemed to control the object of hope. It rests as well on prevailing ethical and aesthetic stances we call activism, passivism, resignation, aestheticism, stoicism, hedonism, and still others no doubt elaborated in other cultures. (Note how seldom any of these terms—so important in our own personal understanding—occur in ethnography!) Hope—its articulation, if one can draw the distinction—may well be influenced by the "grammar" of the language in which it is expressed. It can certainly be related to indigenous social understanding, indeed to structural and normative features of a society, as well as to the myths and legends that give expression to that understanding.[13] Obviously, I cannot do justice to any of these—and still other—assumptions here. Let me simply pose a few suggestive questions at three, never fully independent levels of consideration: the linguistic (or grammatical), the cultural (or ideological), and the social structural.

IV

Hope, as Minkowski has described it, presupposes a system of tense—past, present, or future—that spatializes time and divides and measures it chronologically. How would a Melanesian articulate (if not experience) "hope" if his language, like so many Papuan languages, has more than one future "tense," which are distinguished not only by temporal "distance" but by status. The Fore, for example, distinguish between a definite future, in which events are expected to occur, and a dubitative future, in which the occurrence of events is doubtful. As Foley notes, the Fore future "tense" also categorizes status, ontological status we might say (1986: 160). For the Yimas speakers, who also have two future tenses (one for tomorrow; one for beyond tomorrow), the entire tense system can be detemporalized by substituting for tense- ("time-") indicating suffixes an irrealis one. "The irrealis suffix indicates either that the occurrence of the event in the future cannot be fixed or that it occurred in the legendary past, so that again it is beyond real time."[14] And in Angaatha, verbs mark status ("real" and "unreal"), and those that mark the real also indicate past or present; the future is always expressed by the irrealis—and not by tense (Foley 1986: 162). Without necessarily committing oneself to a Whorfian position, it would still seem of interest to consider tense and other grammatical features in the way in which cargo prophets and others, even retrospectively, articulate their expectation of cargo. Kenelm Burridge notes that, although traditional narratives refer to the past in the present tense (beginning with *arin*, "once upon a time"), new narratives, those dealing with cargo, refer to the future in the present tense.[15] (According to Burridge, the Tangu language has no past tense. He considers it to be an Austronesian language, though it belongs, in fact, to the Sepik-Ramu family.) "When Tangu say that the newer tales are 'more true' than the traditional narratives," Burridge observes, "they seem to intimate that realisation of being in the terms of these stories is more possible or relevant or desirable than realisation of being in terms of the traditional narratives. Since that which is past is now irrevocably past, the alternative is to fill out the future" (Burridge 1969b: 426). Certainly rhetorical analysis of "cargo talk"—one that would have to take into consideration tense, status, aspect, and so on—would be a prerequisite for theorizing cargo cults.

V

When we speak of collective hopes (and desires), we do so by (metaphorical) extension. We locate hope in the individual—in an individualized and relatively autonomous space we call inner. But, if there is any truth in the postulation of relational, dividuated, or sociocentric selves—selves that seem somehow to flow beyond what we would call the individual or what we take to be the body—or if the boundaries between the inner and the outer are not as fixed as we see them, as, say, in those societies in which spirit possession occurs or where the "soul" is said to wander in dreams or shamanistic trances, would hope (and indeed desire and agency) be experienced, at least articulated, in the same fashion? The issue is ticklish, because the evidence for such differences is often questionable; nevertheless, the case has often been made. Elfriede Hermann has observed,

> Next to the spirit being [*Geistwesen*]-characteristic of men and women, by which the Self defines itself, the social web is vitally necessary for their existence as a person. Typically the Yasaburing speak of a single person embedded in an extensive network of kin and in different friendship relations. ... Often a man or woman speaks in Yasaburing of his or her own

> thoughts, feelings, knowledge, and behavior in the plural form *ning*, "we," seldom in the singular *na*, "I." ... This mode of expression suggests that a man or woman conceives of him or herself less as individual in the Western sense and far more as a person in an intimate relationship to the social structure. At the same time, this mode of expression also suggests that thoughts, feelings, and actions do not have their source, mono-causally, in the individual, but develop through contact with others. (Hermann 1995: 59–60; translated by V.C.)

Included in these others would be the ancestral spirits. How would hope be articulated among the Yasaburing-as-described-by-Elfriede-Hermann?

VI

However conceptualizations of time and history are embedded in language, they are givens or at least derivable from discursive practices. Ever since Frederick Errington (1974) made use of Ernest Gellner's (in my view oversimplified) distinction between evolutionary and episodic views of history and social transition, it has been noted by many Melanesianists that the Papuans have an episodic view of history. Errington puts it this way, "History is a series of discrete and static states: human customs and institutions have either always been as they currently are or they instantaneously acquired their present form. The transition between states and the creation of social form is not seen as a gradual and cumulative process: it occurs when some decisive event transforms one state into another" (Errington 1974: 257).

The cargo prophet Yali's inability to understand evolutionary thought, reported by Peter Lawrence, has become a sort of iconic representation of this view (Lawrence 1971: 173–178). The Karavarans, whom Errington studied, believe that with the arrival of the Methodist missionary George Brown, in 1876, transformed "in a decisive leap" (Errington's words, one supposes) their existing society into what it is today. (Prior to Brown's arrival, the Karavarans characterized theirs as a sort of antisociety, wild and bestial.) More recently, Wolfgang Kempf has shown with considerable finesse the way in which the preaching of the Second Coming fits this episodic notion of change. Kempf writes,

> What I am arguing is that the (neo-)episodic concept of change appears to have structured Sibog behavior patterns, their perceptions and expecta-

> tions of Christianity during the time of the first encounters with the mission some 60 years ago. By adopting Christianity, the Sibog hoped to bring about a rapid and deep-seated change. According to Lawrence's enquiries, these hopes found an outlet in the conviction that the "Second Coming of the Lord" and the return of the ancestors with "cargo" were at hand and would be accompanied by cataclysmic events: if change were to occur it would be dramatic, comprehensive, total. (Kempf 1992: 80)

But, as Kempf shows, at least in the retrospective accounts he collected of the Yali movement—the one he has been restudying—there appears to be a tension in the neoepisodic notion of change between discontinuity and continuity—the former resonating with colonial power structures, the latter with, among other things, the maintenance of male dominance.

This is not the place to critique the episodic notion of change other than to note that insofar as it insists on a single and singular notion of time/history/change it risks becoming, like the cargo cults themselves, yet another emblem of the imposition of colonial/postcolonial hegemonic discourse. Though Lawrence attributes Yali's surprise at the contradiction between creationist and evolutionary theories in European thought to the fact that the natives of Madang District "always possessed ... an essentially homogeneous intellectual system" (Lawrence 1971: 174), we might hypothesize that, like other "intellectual systems" the Madang's was in fact rife with contradiction. Certainly, studies such as Janet Hoskin's *The Play of Time* (1993) suggest that in even relatively simple societies more than one notion of time (and by extension of history and change) coexist. This would certainly be the case for Kempf's and Errington's informants. How these multiple temporalities are reflected in informants' accounts not just at the substantive, at but the rhetorical level, would seem to be revealing of their inevitably contorted understanding of cargoism. For our purposes, however, I wish simply to ask how the articulation (if not the experience) of hope would be articulated in a putative (if not real) episodic understanding of time, in one at least in which abrupt change was accented.

VII

"Equivalence in communication is a moral imperative; the actual or potential capacity to participate in reciprocities indicates the range and nature of moral relationships; and the explicit agreement not to communicate the parts, usually entered into after a series of formal exchanges and known as *mngwotngwotiki*—enough, sufficient, equivalent—points to a plateau of achievement, an approximate but mutually acknowledged moral equivalence" (Burridge 1969b: 60). Burridge stresses the role in the Tangu response to the colonizer of the gap between their expectations of "moral equivalence" and the Europeans' notion of social, if not moral, hierarchy. According to Burridge, Tangu society is based on siblingship rather than descent and descent-groups. "The term 'siblingship' connotes reciprocal relations, is defined by the element of reciprocity in relationships, and thus, in the most general context, refers to any relationship (among friends, for example) within which there exist mutual expectations of reciprocal obligation" (Burridge 1969b: 62–64). Relations of filiation, however, are not of reciprocal obligation but of nonreciprocal normativity. They provide for continuity over generations. Unlike sibling relations, they are not mutually enforceable and may be abused. They require self-restraint and self-will. Sibling reciprocity, apparently the dominant and effectual metaphor for social relationships, is reciprocally enforceable and subject to resolution, if abused, in formal, public assemblies (*br'ngun'guni*). Those who do not reciprocate are *ranguma*, odd or singular persons, prone to sorcery and other antisocial acts.

This is not the place to elaborate on Tangu social relations, other than to observe that because Europeans did not participate in the reciprocity of moral equivalence, they were identified, if implicitly, with the *ranguma* and by extension with nonreciprocating supernatural beings *(puoker)* (Burridge 1969b: 150, 271). Were the relations with the European understood then in terms of normative filiation? Burridge notes that the linking of black and white in reciprocal relations was one of the cargo prophet Mambu's principal themes (1969b: 31, 459). Unlike earlier movements, where white and black were taken as wholes or personalized as brothers, however, Mambu contrasted moral and immoral Europeans. The "moral European," was one who engaged, at least ideally, in fantasy perhaps, in a sibling sort of reciprocity. In a parallel fashion, at least according to Burridge, "the model of a new man, an individual, a black man with primary Christian virtues and characteristics" evolved (1969b: 31; 1995: 254). Burridge is of course anxious to situate the Tangu in what I see as an allegory of moral regeneration—in what he calls the "numinous translation of one order of being into another." The cargoists tried to create a new social and moral order, which would offer them both "cargo" and the possibility of redemption, that is, ultimate freedom from obligation (Burridge 1969a: 6).

Whether by fostering individuation, by distressing traditional social and cultural assumptions, or by rendering the Tangu's world incomprehensibly more complex, the European brought new and great uncertainties in his wake. These could be neither understood in, nor managed through, the traditional kin idiom (Burridge 1969b: 63). Burridge writes, "Traditionally, one may suppose, the dynamic of social relations as between living persons and their categories could be seen and understood in terms of the interaction between moral and divine or wild. Changing particulars within a relationship could be explained as the interplay of unchanging general principles. When *br'ngun'guni* failed to maintain reciprocities, a variety of particulars described as *imbatekas* might be invoked: a ghost might deceive, a dream could be misinterpreted, narrative misunderstood; a storm might destroy.... But Europeans have brought with them an ambience in which relations are existential, uncertain, and not always predictable" (Burridge 1969b: 184). And manageable, one might add.

However if we evaluate Burridge's allegory of individuation and the uncertainties, the *crisi di presenza*, to use Ernesto di Martino's expression (1975), it postulates, we have to recognize that it signals possible changes in the articulation and experience of hope—to a less secure, less shared, more individualized, lonely sense of hope. But, as Burridge sees it, it also heralds a move from apprehension to comprehension, from what he calls the myth-dream to aspiration. His is also an allegory of intellectualization.

VIII

"[A] myth-dream is a body of notions derived from a variety of sources such as rumours, personal experiences, desires, conflicts, and ideas about the total environment which find expression in myths, dreams, popular stories, and anecdotes" (Burridge 1992: 27). All people participate, Burridge tells us, in these myth-dreams (1995: 148). They are a sort of "community day-dream." They "are not intellectually articulate, for they exist in an area of emotionalized mental activity which is not private to any particular individual but which is shared by many" (1995: 148). We might refer to them today as collective paradigms. (Burridge was writing in 1960.) They provide a store of knowledge and express a set of desires and hopes. The items of knowledge become instrumental in the optative domain. They are practical, but within the "space" defined by desire and hope. Burridge himself notes: "If those involved in a myth-dream were capable of fully comprehending and intellectualising its content and meaning then 'aspiration' might have been a better word [for it]" (1995: 27).

The status of the myth-dream is unclear. Is it an analytic concept characteristic of all people in the same way? Does it reflect specific attitudes toward myth and dream? Does it reflect potentially different psychological, or experiential, structures that lie behind—or are a product of—these attitudes toward myth and dream? Restricting ourselves to the Tangu, I would argue that to understand how the "myth-dream" works for them, one would have to know how they understand and evaluate dream and myth.

For the Tangu, myths bear truth.[16] They are about—and originate with—*puoker*, self-willed divine beings who resemble men but are, as I noted, not subject to the rules of reciprocity. Like the firefly, the *puoker* are normally invisible but make their presence known in flashes of luminosity (Burridge 1969b: 159). Myths, their truths, have, like the *puoker*, an independent existence. They are enigmatic, "unobliged to men in community" (Burridge 1969b: 63). "They are essentially oblivious, oracular: it is up to men and women to extract such truths as are contained in them and to accept the consequences of doing so" (Burridge 1969b: 161). Their truths are, if I understand Burridge correctly, imperative but mediated less through interpretation than immediate application. "[In] the course of regarding their narratives in relation to their own particular circumstances and awarenesses, individuals among Tangu may either confirm, or perceive alternatives to, current beliefs and activities. And, in causing such a flux—albeit momentary—or questioning in relation to current moralities, narratives bear the same kind of relation to Tangu themselves as does the *ranguma*, a violent storm, or an earthquake" (Burridge 1969b: 163–164).

The Tangu, Burridge insists, do not comprehend, but apprehend, their narratives, the traditional ones at least (1969b: 199). When they are asked to say what a tale is about, they give a long précis, repeat the last few sentences, or describe the events recounted in it. They do not interpret, perceive inner meaning, or correlate it with other experiences, these being for Burridge criteria of comprehension. It is only the "new" narratives about cargo and the European challenge that are comprehended, Burridge tells us. He is never clear whether they demand comprehension—interpretation—or are simply comprehended.

Like myths and narratives, dreams bear truth. They "are not simple fantasies woven from sleep. They are a normal technique for solving a problem or finding a way out of a dilemma." They are not weak reflections of truth; they are its source (Burridge 1995: 219). The dream, Burridge remarks, is "the chosen vehicle for expressing the desires and hopes of the cult leaders" (1995: 219).

Further, when expressed through a dream, hope merges into positive expectancy. Any man may wish or hope for something at any time. But when in association with a dream the hope comes near to realization. Dreams tend to pull a future into current sensible reality; they give definity to hope, adding faith, thereby putting the dreamer in touch with a verity shortly to be manifest.

The dream is then instrumental, but, like hope, it cannot be forced. Once it has occurred, once cult leaders like Mambu, announce their dreams, they become imperatives for action—and presumably sources of comprehension. In light of the gap—the puzzlement, the challenge—that inspires and is inspired by comprehension—taken here, not in some allegory of intellectual development, but as marking a change in response to narrative—one presumes that hope is rearticulated, however painfully and with whatever uncertainty, in an expansive fashion.

IX

By way of conclusion, I want simply to quote the passage, from Aeschylus' *Prometheus Bound* (1959), to which Kierkegaard referred in the quotation from *Either/Or* with which I began this chapter:

> Prometheus: I caused mortals to cease foreseeing doom.
> Chorus: What cure did you provide them with against that sickness?
> Prometheus: I placed them in blind hope.
> Chorus: That was a great gift you gave to men.
> Prometheus: Besides this I gave them fire. (Aeschylus 1959: 250–254)

Fire must be taken here, I believe, in full symbolic dress.

Notes

Portions of this chapter have been developed in Crapanzano (2003b).

1. At this point in history, as "cargo" and "cargo cult" have been so incorporated into Melanesian discourse, we might also reverse the argument, noting that they reflect Melanesian presuppositions not shared by the Europeans!

2. Gesch (1990) does recognize the role of hope in cargoism. He does not elaborate on it, though.

3. See Crapanzano (1990a), and Hermann (present volume).

4. My discussion of hope relies heavily on a much longer discussion in Crapanzano (2003a).

5. This is obviously also true of desire. See Robbins (1998a) for an interesting study of the rearticulation of desire in the western Sepik among the Urapmin people.

6. My summation of Minkowski's position and all quotations in this and the next paragraph are taken from Minkowski's *Lived Time* (1970: 92–102). However illuminating, Minkowski's work, like that of all phenomenologists, has to be treated with caution, for it takes into consideration neither the cultural nor the linguistic determination of the experience being described—of the description itself.

7. Minkowski, however, refuses to be called an optimist. Optimism and pessimism are secondary—empirical—attitudes that have to be distinguished from the general structures of time. "Pessimism and optimism always have to be substantiated with supporting proofs, while we never have to ask ourselves whether we desire or hope."

8. Heidegger writes, "... im Dasein immer noch etwas aussteht, was als Seinkönnen seiner selbst noch nicht 'wirklich' geworden ist. Im Wesen der Grundverfassung des Daseins liegt demnach eine ständige Unabgeschlossenheit. Die Unganzheit bedeutet einen Ausstand an Seinkönnen" (1993: 236).

9. Minkowski is referring to the phenomenological ego—and not the ego of psychoanalysis.

10. For a discussion of the openness, as well as the closure, brought about by hope see Mittendorf (1985: 75ff.), which is far more technically phenomenological than Minkowski's treatise.

11. All quotations that follow are from Minkowski (1970: 103–111).

12. I do not want to deny the instrumentalism, indeed the utilitarianism, of the people anthropologists study. Rather I want to emphasize our paradoxical projections of rationality and pragmatism in our interpretations of what we regard as irrational. I should note that Melanesians are insistently characterized as pragmatic in the literature and in conversations I have had with Melanesianists, including the participants in the Aarhus conference. They have found my emphasis on "hope" surprising and not especially relevant for such a "practical" people.

13. See Lacey for a discussion of the ways in which traditional culture hero tales served as—and to—model the life stories of cargo prophets (1990).

14. Foley (1986: 161). I should note that the Yimas system is in fact far more complicated, because Yimas also has a series of status markers (real, likely, potential but unlikely, and unreal) that are independent of tense.

15. "So that although the word *arin* specifically places the action as having occurred in the past, the use of the present tense cannot but bring the narrative into significant relations with the present: as in the past, so now; as now, so in the past" (Burridge 1969b: 425). Are the newer narratives, recited in the present but referring to the future, oracular, prophetic, effectively so?

16. In *Tangu Traditions*, Burridge refers to narratives and not myths, as he does in *Mambu*.

CHAPTER 14 On the Critique in Cargo and the Cargo in Critique

Toward a Comparative Anthropology of Critical Practice

Joel Robbins

As MANY of the chapters in this volume attest, the concept of cargo cult has recently come in for some extremely vigorous critique at the hands of Melanesianist anthropologists. The notion of cargo cult has been tarred not only as a misrepresentation of what actually happens in Melanesia, but also as a misrepresentation that is self-interested and ideologically suspect. In thinking about these criticisms and what they might mean for future uses of the archive of material that has been and in some quarters continues to be published about cargo cults, it is worth recalling that the upsurge of critical energy currently aimed at the concept of the cargo cult is not unprecedented in the history of anthropology. I begin this chapter by comparing the critique of cargo cult to other important critiques of key anthropological categories. This effort at comparison ultimately leads to the claim that the anthropology of cargo cults and other forms of millenarianism might well be reconfigured as part of a comparative anthropology of critical practice. It is with this idea in mind that I finally turn to the cargo cult archive and attempt to substantiate the claim that millenarianism is a form of critique that we can study empirically in ways that will allow us to situate our own critical work more satisfactorily.

On Millenarianism and the Critique of Anthropological Ideas

Nancy McDowell begins the article that can claim to have been first among the recent critiques of the notion of cargo cult by announcing that her own efforts to dissolve the concept of cargo cult are analogous to those Claude Lévi-Strauss (1963) undertook to do away with the idea of totemism (McDowell 1988: 121). This analogy has been appreciated by later critics,[1] and thus the critique of cargo cult has been outfitted with a respectable anthropological lineage. Left out of this lineage, however, is an important critique of a key anthropological category that appeared between Lévi-Strauss' initial invocation of this form of argument and its recent deployment in the cargo cult literature: no one, to my knowledge, has attempted to recruit David Schneider's (1984) critique of notions of kinship into the lineage of cargo critique. In pondering the critique of cargo cult and its import for future uses of the cargo cult archive, my argument is not that Schneider any more than Lévi-Strauss should serve as our model, but rather that by looking at both of these earlier cases of critique we can pinpoint what may be unique about the current arguments surrounding cargo cult and can consider what they might offer to the genre of anthropological critique itself that neither of these other two cases were able to provide.

When one places the critique of cargo cult in the company of those of totemism and kinship, there is one sense in which it is clearly distinct from them. This distinctiveness is grounded in the success of the latter two critiques as compared with the relative failure of the critique of cargo cult. Let me quickly specify what I mean by success or failure, lest I be misunderstood as saying that there is nothing of value in recent critiques of the cargo cult concept. After Lévi-Strauss, totemism essentially disappeared as an object of anthropological study. After Schneider, kinship too largely faded from view, at least in the Anglophone anthropological world.[2] In contrast to these two cases, the critique of the notion of cargo cult has presided over a return of this subject to the center of Melanesianist anthropology after a lengthy hiatus in which is was very much marginalized. There is more careful writing about cargo cults in general and there are more detailed ethnographic accounts of specific movements now than there were throughout the 1970s and 1980s. If we count the sort of demolition of the object of study Lévi-Strauss and Schneider achieved as the mark of success in the realm of critique, then how can we account for this failure of the critique of cargo? Why has a method that has worked well in other domains had such perverse effects in the case of cargo cult?

One might of course simply answer these questions with the claim that the critique of cargo cult has been less well argued than those earlier ones and is thus less convincing than they have been. But this line of argument is not particularly promising, for any serious reading of the literature of cargo critique has to admit that it has managed to present in compelling terms critical analyses similar in form to those that made both of the prior critiques effective. One type of critical analysis, practiced by both Lévi-Strauss and Schneider, takes the form of a "defetishizing" critique in which a reified object of study is dissolved into parts and reconstituted (cf. Benhabib 1986). In her influential article, McDowell (1988) takes this tack in arguing that the concept of cargo cult does not cut the world at its joints, that it groups things (in this case, different kinds of movements for and images of change) that in reality are separate and separates things that in reality are linked. Some scholars, and Schneider is again a good example here, add to this defetishizing critique a genealogical one aimed at explaining how scholars and others come to reify their object of study in inappropriate ways.[3] Though McDowell did not go in for such genealogical critique in her discussion of the concept of cargo cult, those who have come after her have added this strand, showing how the exigencies of the colonial situation or the engrossing tropes that are central to Western models of desire have decisively shaped the construction of reified notions of cargo cult.[4] So, even if cargo cult critique has yet to find a figure as influential as Lévi-Strauss or Schneider to argue its case, the pieces are there in various works to assemble a critique as well rounded as those that served to make real trouble for totemism and kinship. We cannot say, then, that cargo cult critique has failed simply for the lack of a good argument.

Having ruled out explanations of failure due to shoddy or incomplete argument, one could also approach the question of the failure of the critique of cargo cult as a matter of intellectual or world history. From this vantage point, the success of the critiques of totemism and kinship would appear to be largely matters of timing. Perhaps Lévi-Strauss and Schneider simply launched their critiques at a time when anthropologists were already losing interest in these domains because of intellectual shifts within the discipline or because the lives of the people they studied were changing in such a way that totemism and kinship no longer satisfied those people as ways of organizing their relations with the natural and social worlds. Things that resemble cargo cults and related religious movements, by contrast, have clearly continued to be important to Melanesians themselves and at the same time they raise issues of power, change, colonialism, globalization, and so forth that interest anthropologists today (cf. Lindstrom 1999; Augé 1999). If these arguments are correct, it should come as no surprise that the already battered notions of totemism and kinship emerged limping from the rigors of critique, whereas the robust one of cargo cult only gained in strength while undergoing similar treatment.

Sketched in the very broad terms I have just used, these historical factors surely play some role in the differential success of the cargo cult critique and those that have come before it. Of more importance for an attempt to think through the future of the cargo cult literature as an archive under critique, however, is an argument that explains the failure of the critique of cargo cult by relating critique itself to the object of cargo cult in a way that it cannot be related either to kinship or to totemism. The claim here is that the very practice of critique is formally similar to that of cargo cultism and to millenarianism more generally. "Apocalypse" is etymologically rooted in notions of revealing, uncovering, unveiling. These verbs apply as fittingly to the activity of critique as they do to the search for the cargo secret. In both cases, a new world of truth and fulfillment is just over the horizon. Jacques Derrida (1993) has argued this point for Enlightenment critique with welcome clarity; even the most "rational" of our critical arguments find their motivations in the rhetoric of apocalypse. All of these arguments promise to unveil a previously hidden truth and allow us to live without error in the domain that they enlighten. Viewed from the perspective of this reading of the nature of critique promises to uncover the truth of cargo cult and in so doing to usher in an eschaton in which scholarship is free from conceptual error, the taint of colonialism, or mystifications that serve our own obsessions with unrequited love are no less millenarian than the cargo cult activity they claim to help us explain away.[5] Critique of cargo cult thus fails because it is mired in performative contradiction: it is a naturally occurring apocalyptic argument that asserts that people do not naturally think apocalyptically. It reproduces simply by being stated the very form of thought and action whose existence it questions. One can, in critical and millenarian tones, reveal the end of an old era of analyses confused by illusory notions of totemism or kinship and the dawn of a new one freed from the influence of these chimera, but one cannot similarly invoke the critical imagery of ends and new beginnings in the case of millenarianism without becoming caught up in ironies so dense that one's whole project begins to look untenable.

This performative contradiction is, I think, at the heart of the failure of the critique of cargo cults to do away with its object and accounts for the way these critiques lead scholars to go back to the millenarian data themselves rather than accept the claim that such data are simply a construction of scholarly or more narrowly colonial discourse (e.g., Otto 1999). The real remains stubbornly persistent in this case because the critique of the real here resembles the real too much to let anyone forget that it is out there.

What then should we do in the face of this performative contradiction? Should we abandon critique as simply another apocalyptic move? Derrida, for his part, answers no: "We cannot and we must not—this is a law and a destiny—forgo the *Aufklärung*, in other words, what imposes itself as the enigmatic desire for vigilance, for the lucid vigil, for elucidation, for critique and truth, but for a truth that at the same time keeps within itself some apocalyptic desire, this time a desire for clarity and revelation, in order to demystify or, if you prefer, to deconstruct apocalyptic discourse itself and with it everything that speculates on vision, the imminence of the end, theophany, parousia, the last judgement" (Derrida 1993: 148).

What is required is a willingness to apocalyptically critique (for there is no other kind of critique than one that holds out the promise of a truer or better future) apocalyptic critique itself. In this exercise, the kinship between non-Western millenarianism and Western forms of critique becomes a positive rather than negative fact. For if, as I argue here, just as all critique is millenarian, all millenarianism is also critical, then what the cross-cultural study of millenarianism, including that contained in the cargo cult archive, leads to is a comparative study of critique itself. Such a comparative study would aim to discover the social conditions in which critique arises, the cultural forms that it takes, and the effects that it has within societies in which it is practiced. A comparative anthropology of this sort could significantly enrich the Western tradition of critique. Aiming at a less lofty target, it is worth noting that it would also make the cargo cult archive relevant to cultural anthropology more generally in a way that it has not been since the 1960s.

I will return to sketching this wider comparative project in the conclusion, but before continuing in this general vein I want to pause to discuss two ethnographic cases that exemplify the way critique is embedded in millenarianism while also pointing out some of the critical traps that a comparative anthropology of critique can help to uncover. One example is drawn from the corner of the archive I know best, that formed by my own work among the Urapmin of Papua New Guinea. The other draws on Hélène Clastres' work on Tupí-Guaraní movements in search of the

Land-Without-Evil. Our understanding of these two cases requires that we recognize not only that critique is millenarian, but also that millenarianism is critical. It is to this second point that I turn in the next section.

Millenarianism as Critique

All millenarianism is in essence critical of everyday understandings in force in the societies in which it takes place. In the name of a future that will either be better or worse than the present, it subjects the givens of that present to the kind of distanced scrutiny that they do not usually suffer during the course of everyday life. The cargo archive is rich in such critical moments: everyday routines foregone, taboos suspended, gardens abandoned, etc. Every one of these moves away from daily life represents a critique of that life and its failures. So, too, do the reevaluations of myth that frequently provide cargo participants with ways of articulately condemning the lives they lead as the flawed results of poor choices and previous misreadings of the drift of history (e.g., Lawrence 1971; Lattas 1998).

Even with only these few examples in place, one may ask whether the conjunction of millenarianism and critique is a matter of analogy or actual identity. In favor of identity one could cite the equivalence of ends discussed in the last section: critics and millenarians alike want to penetrate the veils of illusion that obscure our empirical and moral vision of the present in order to create a better future (whether on earth or in heaven). A reading in terms of analogy, by contrast, would focus not on the ends so much as the means, for it is in relation to means that the differences between critique and millennial movement seem so striking. Critique, after all, draws deeply on the intellectual tradition of the West and particularly on the post-Enlightenment commitment to the use of reason as the means of discovering truth and grounding social life. Millenarianism finds its critical tools elsewhere, primarily in the very religious inspiration that the Enlightenment commitment to reason has led Westerners to eschew as an invalid source of knowledge (Connerton 1976). Thus, it is not surprising that, from a Western critical point of view, millenarian language often lacks what Jebens (present volume) calls, in his discussion of Koimumu, "specification" and "detailed definitions" of what it expects from the future and sometimes of what it condemns in the present. This difference in the means deployed in critical and millenarian practice renders difficult a claim for complete identity between the two, but does it disqualify an analysis in terms of analogy? This is a question best answered by considering the ways people actually take up critical ideas as part of their outlook on daily life.

Despite our Enlightenment prejudices, the ethnographic record plainly shows that whatever millenarianism as a means of reforming life lacks from the point of view of philosophical explicitness, it makes up for in its ability to establish what Fabian in another connection calls "critique ... as a pervasive practice" (1999: 242). "Critique may express itself," he adds, "in a pervasive mood rather than in pointed statements" (1999: 243). Critique may be lived out as well as thought out, emergent rather than systematically refined. Arguably, religious and other popular critical forms (such as the tradition of popular painting studied by Fabian), rather than philosophically sophisticated scholarly forms, are the primary ones in which critical thinking enters people's lives as a force for social transformation.[6] This suggests not only that there is a substantial analogic relation between critique and millennialism, but also that the analogy is one in which the similarities that connect the two are important. Indeed, these similarities are of some moment for those interested in the way philosophical critique might come to influence social life.

Turning back to cargo cults, anyone familiar with the literature on these millenarian movements recognizes how frequently they are built around the kinds of critical activities of taboo suspension, garden abandonment, and the like that I discussed in the opening paragraph of this section. As striking as these outbursts of critical energy are, what is equally striking is the extent to which they usually fail to change everyday life very much. Worsley's (1968) hope that millenarian movements might become full-fledged political movements resulting in radical social change, while still alive in some quarters, has not been realized with impressive frequency. Kenelm Burridge's argument that movements produce a "new man," a similarly compelling image of change, has also failed to hold a place at the center of cargo cult research—even as his ethnography and other aspects of his theoretical work have remained a crucial part of the archive (Burridge 1969a, 1995). In contradistinction to the general failure of these models of change, Peter Lawrence's claim that cargo cults leave basic structures and understandings intact has remained if not an orthodoxy, at least an influential position (Lawrence 1971). Indeed, most analysts of cargo cults either explicitly or implicitly follow Lawrence in claiming that they result in the reproduction of fundamental cultural ideas in the societies in which they take place (Robbins 1998b). As Lindstrom notes, perhaps the most powerful of these models of reproduction in Melanesia have been those that simply make "cargoism" constitutive of everyday life in the region (Lindstrom 1993). Models of this sort proclaim that cargo cults cannot change Melanesian everyday life no matter how strongly they seem to criticize it, for their very existence reproduces that everyday life in its traditional form. On the basis of the ethnographies such models of reproductive continuity have produced, we have to recognize that, for all of their critical bluster, cargo cults and other millenarian movements often seem to leave everyday life little changed.

At this point, one might take this argument in two different directions. One would involve a critique of the anthropological commitment to cultural continuity and would argue that perhaps millenarian movements do change daily lives in ways this commitment prevents us from seeing. I have tried elsewhere to make a related argument about the role of Christianity in cultural change (Robbins 1998b, 2003). Here, though, I want to accept in general terms the idea that the critiques embedded in millenarian movements often fail to produce the large-scale results they aim for: even if they do change everyday life, they do not transform it as thoroughly as their criticisms of it seem to demand.[7] In accepting this point, I move to take the argument in a second direction, one that explores the kinds of relations critique can contract with everyday life and asks what sorts of relations between critique and everyday life tend to leave the latter at least somewhat unchanged. How do cargo cults relate to everyday life such that they vigorously criticize it but fail to remake it along their own lines? In the broadest terms, this exploration takes up the question of the conditions under which critique fails to realize its transformative goals. In the next section, I explore answers to this question by taking up the cases of Urapmin Christian millenarianism and the traditional millenarian movements of the Tupí-Guaraní.

Millenarian Critique and the Conditions of Its Failure

The Urapmin are a group of 390 people living in the Sandaun province of Papua New Guinea. Never directly missionized, the Urapmin first encountered Christianity during the 1960s when they sent young men to several neighboring groups to study with local evangelists and expatriate Baptist missionaries living among them. Several cohorts of young men were sent to seek such instruction, and when they returned they carried the rudiments of the Christian doctrine back to Urapmin. A decade and a half of this Christian coming and going produced some Urapmin converts, especially among those who had traveled to receive instruction, but it was only in 1977 that the Urapmin in their own understanding came to form a completely Christian community. It was at that time that the Urapmin became caught up in a Christian revival (TP *rebaibal*)[8] movement that was sweeping many Baptist communities in the Highlands. In the course of this revival, everyone in the community either experienced directly or witnessed at first hand the power of the Holy Spirit to "shake" people and make them feel deeply the weight of their own sinfulness. They also experienced or saw the Spirit's power to heal. With these proofs of God's power in hand, all of the Urapmin converted, throwing out their traditional rituals and severing relations with indigenous spirits in the process.

The initial period of the revival was, the Urapmin remember, a time of intense millennial speculation. People were sure that Jesus' return was imminent, and they remade their religious life in the hopes that he would take them to heaven when he came. The same strongly held sense of millennial expectation has remained at the forefront of Urapmin life from the time of the revival into the ethnographic present of this study (1991–1993). This expectation sometimes fuels periods of activity we would see as constituting millenarian movements: periods when people leave their gardens and other daily routines and spend enormous amounts of time in church or in prayer in their houses. But even outside of such periods of heightened millenarianism, the Urapmin remain preoccupied with the possibility of Jesus' return and with their own need to be ready for this event. During these quieter periods, Urapmin millenarianism settles into the flow of Urapmin daily life as people constantly monitor and criticize their own feelings and behavior in an effort to be ready should the Second Coming transpire. Urapmin millenarianism thus becomes, I have suggested elsewhere, an everyday millenarianism (Robbins 2001). If, as I have argued here, millenarianism consists in part in the critique of everyday life, how can the two coexist side by side in Urapmin? My argument in what follows is that they do not coexist comfortably and that the Urapmin sense of themselves as profoundly sinful is a product of their failure to do so.

The millenarianism of Urapmin Christianity is tied to a harsh moralism that is its other most prominent feature. This moralism is focused on the evil nature of desire and of the emotions of anger, jealousy, and envy in which it finds expression. Desire in general and the anger *(aget atul)* that follows when it is frustrated are particular targets of Christian moral condemnation. For the Urapmin, a person's goal should be to live completely by the dictates of God's will *(san)* as conveyed to them by the Holy Spirit. The Spirit conveys God's will to people by giving them "good thoughts" *(aget fukunin tangbal)* that advise them not to act on desire and to avoid entering into situations that will make them angry. When he comes, Jesus will take to heaven only those who have heeded the promptings of the Spirit and lived in accord with God's will. Yet despite the importance of taking God's will as one's own, and despite the help the Spirit offers by teaching people the divine will, the Urapmin recognize that living by the light of God's will is difficult. This is so because human beings also have wills of their own and these often "push" them to act in sinful ways that contravene God's will.

Urapmin constantly remind themselves of the evil of the human will in a genre of speech called *weng kem bakamin*. Literally, this translates as "speaking clear talk," or, as people sometimes gloss it in Tok Pisin, as "giving advice" (TP *advisim*). *Weng kem* most often takes the form of impassioned harangues about human sinfulness—the human propensity to desire too much, to anger quickly, to think only of one's own will. These harangues are delivered in church, in the village plaza, or in more private settings, and their style also shapes the way people talk in less charged genres of speech such as sermons and everyday conversations. In the context of the argument of this essay, we can gloss *weng kem* as "critique," for it dwells on errors of the current human order and demands that people change their lives so as to leave that order behind. The critique of the human will and the promotion of God's will as substitute for it constitute the critical heart of Urapmin Christian millenarianism.

Most Urapmin try very earnestly to live in accord with God's will and to follow the dictates of *weng kem*. But they find this kind of life difficult to lead, for a life lived without desire is not one that succeeds very well in accomplishing the tasks of everyday Urapmin life. Daily life in Urapmin is governed, as the Urapmin see it, by people exercising their wills. There are no specific rules that draw on idioms of kinship or residence in order to tell people whom to live with, whom to work with, whom to share with, or whom to marry. None of these relations follow from an indigenous notion of a social structure that "automatically" positions people vis-à-vis one another. There are, especially outside the nuclear family, no "given" relationships in Urapmin. Instead, people must assert their wills, sometimes angrily, in efforts to bring others into relationship. Only such willful behavior produces villages, work groups, households, married couples, and so forth. In the absence of such willful behavior, Urapmin society would cease to exist.[9] Put otherwise, the Urapmin will has no social structural alibi: Urapmin have no language except that of the human will to use in talking about how their daily lives come to take the social shape that they have.

Yet, despite the centrality of willfulness to Urapmin social life, it is precisely the kind of willful behavior that everyday Urapmin life requires that their Christianity critiques. Thus, as people go about their everyday lives, they are inevitably led into sin. This paradox has led the Urapmin to create an elaborate ritual life aimed at "removing" sin from the body (Robbins 2004). It has also created within (a Urapmin metaphor) all Urapmin a never-ending dialogue of self-criticism, a dialogue that people regularly share with their pastors and deacons during the organized confessions that are held every two months or so in the church.[10] These inner dialogues are the personal analogues of the publicly pronounced *weng kem* harangues. They attest to a deeply seated drive for moral clarity that loses none of its force for being always unsuccessful.

Urapmin critique is driven within the person in this way because it makes no compromise with everyday life. With no suggestions for how one might live a successful life in Urapmin terms by following God's will alone, Urapmin critical discourse becomes strictly utopian. Finding itself without a place in which to realize itself, it moves inward. Borrowing some apt phrases from Soeffner's brilliant analysis of Lutheran Christianity, we can say that Urapmin Christian critique eschews practical reason in favor of an "impractical reason" that "is under no obligation to the logic of action" (Soeffner 1997: 41). It demands that one creates a life of inner order—a life free of desire, anger, envy, and the like—but provides no instructions for how to deploy that inner order as equipment for living in the world.

Because it condemns everyday life without offering a workable substitute for it, Urapmin millenarian critique manages to dominate the tone of everyday life through its rhetoric while at the same time changing very little of the way that life is lived in terms of action. People must still depend on their desires to keep daily life rolling, and must do so in ways that force them and others to use anger and other sinful emotions as prompts to action. Thus, most Urapmin at once continually criticize themselves and continually reproduce the behaviors they criticize. The Urapmin solution to this dilemma, if solution is the right phrase to apply to the output of this self-reproducing problematic, is to dwell on their own sinfulness and to work assiduously through ritual not to prevent sin (as their critical discourse would like them to) but to deal with its constant reoccurrence.

In producing not a new, better society but rather a society of sinners, Urapmin critique clearly fails in its mission of reforming daily life. Its failure is grounded in its utopianism. By treating daily life as the Urapmin live it as irredeemably evil, it leaves no room to reform that everyday life by building some new society from its parts. It is not, in the terms Jürgen Habermas (1983) applies to the work of Walter Benjamin, a "redemptive" critique.[11] A redemptive critique would be one that struggled to find some good in the object it critiques, some saving remnant from which to build a future. The Urapmin case suggests that critique that does not contain this element can be long-lived, as it has been in Urapmin, but must ultimately fail to transform the everyday life it essentially fails to engage. Such totally dismissive critique, then, is not a good starting point from which to initiate change.

There is one somewhat attractive strategy for dealing with dismissive critique—more attractive at least than the perpetual reproduction of the sense of failure (sinfulness) that comes from engaging everyday life and its dismissive critique simultaneously—that shows up on the edges of Urapmin life and that appears in more fully realized form elsewhere. This strategy involves using dismissive critique as a basis for withdrawal from the evil life revealed by that critique. Here one does not so much remake everyday life along new lines as withdraw from it into a world free of its problems. Some Urapmin attempt this, refusing to participate in the key social institutions that create Urapmin society—institutions like brideprice, death payments, and village dwelling—because such participation inevitably leads one to sin. I knew well two middle-aged men who were forgoing promising political careers for fear of the way political participation would wreck their "Christian lives" (TP *kristen laip*). In their quietism, these men managed at times to fulfill some of the demands of the critical message of Urapmin Christianity, but they were unable to work on the basis of the lives they built in its terms to create a new kind of society around themselves. Instead, to the extent that they did live more nearly perfect Christian lives, they did so by isolating themselves from their fellows and forgoing the rewards of Urapmin social life.

The Tupí and Guaraní of Brazil and Paraguay present a more spectacular case of what can occur when a completely dismissive critique leads to withdrawal from everyday life. These groups are well known among scholars of millenarianism for the migrations, led by prophets, that they formerly undertook to find the Land-Without-Evil. The land they expected to find was an earthly paradise in which humans would be immortal, crops would grow by themselves, and people would spend their time feasting and dancing. The migrations could last upward of a decade or longer, and many of those who undertook them died before returning home in failure.

In one of the most striking anthropological monographs on millenarianism that we have, a work that ranks with those of Lawrence and Burridge in Melanesia, Clastres (1995) argues that these migrations have been going on from before Tupí-Guaraní contact with the West. They are in the first instance, she argues, a response not to colonialism but to contradictions in the indigenous cultures of this region. At the heart of these cultural contradictions is a tension between the chiefs who build villages and the prophets (*karai*) who live outside of those villages and go from place to place singing and speechifying about the Land-Without-Evil. In Clastres' terms, the prophets' discourse on the Land-Without-Evil has always had a "critical vocation" (1995: 95). Its core message has from the beginning been a critique of the social world of structure, toil, and death built by the chiefs. When people accepted this critique in the fullest possible terms, they left their villages to follow a prophet in search of a radically different world.

What one takes away from Clastres' account is not just a deeper appreciation of the sense in which millenarianism is always founded in critique, but also a fuller sense of the extent to which dismissive critique tends to destroy society rather then rebuild it along better lines. The tragedy of Tupí-Guaraní society is that there is no possibility of compromise between the everyday order of the chiefs and the critical one of the prophets. Tupí-Guaraní society has gone so far as to push the critical function and the prophets who represent it outside of its boundaries, making them dwell apart from the villages in which people live and allowing them to visit those villages only as interlopers. As in the Urapmin case, among the Tupí-Guaraní there is no integration of critique and everyday life, and hence critique aims to eradicate everyday life rather than engage it constructively. The Tupí-Guaraní fail to keep critique and everyday life in dialogue and instead become self-imposed exiles from their own communities, doomed to wander in search of a better life they will never find because they have no map that tells them how to find it in the only way possible: by making it themselves. The Urapmin problem is in the end not so different: they keep the dialogue going after a fashion, but only at the cost of finding themselves in a state of self-imposed internal exile that makes the cost of social action in the world ruinously high. In both cases, critiques of everyday life that find no way to work with the structures that life provides lead not to the renewal of everyday life but to the adoption of responses to it that leave people vulnerable and unable to fully exploit the strengths of the social worlds in which they live.

Conclusion

Looking back at the preceding argument, it is clear that I arrive at this concluding point by way of the examination of two kinds of failed critique. I began with the critique of cargo cult and its failure to do away either with the anthropological perception that Melanesians participate in millenarian movements or with the anthropological interest in those movements. I then turned to the critique of everyday life embedded in cargo cults and other millenarian movements themselves and noted that when such critiques tend toward total dismissal of everyday life they often fail to change that life. Internal withdrawal, as in the Urapmin case, or external withdrawal, as in that of the Tupí-Guaraní, presented themselves as two "pathological" outcomes of critiques that fail to engage daily life constructively. In conclusion, I would like to begin to flesh out the possibilities for a comparative anthropology of critique by examining what the Urapmin and Tupí-Guaraní cases might teach us about critique more generally.

Starting close to home, we can turn to the outcome of these ethnographic explorations to draw some conclusions about the critique of cargo cult itself. What becomes evident when we do this is that the equivalent of the complete dismissal of everyday life in the critique of the anthropology of cargo cults is the complete dismissal of the possibility or value of the ethnographic study of the lives of Melanesians as a part of anthropological practice. Where critique aims for a kind of epistemological perfection by ignoring the lives of Melanesians and their role in anthropological practice, it is bound to fail to change very significantly the way anthropologists analyze those lives. Perfection in the form of a theory that cannot be applied to materials is, like the moral perfection the Urapmin aim for, not one that supports much in the way of practice, in this case ethnographic practice. Hence this practice is destined to go on in its own terms when faced with such critique. Inasmuch as anthropological critique aims to reform ethnographic practice, this outcome will have to count as a failure.

This analysis suggests that successful critiques of anthropology will have to settle on terms that criticize ethnography not simply by pointing out how it is more or less determined by our own Western presuppositions, but that also teach us how we might remedy this by finding new ways to open ourselves to the understanding of other cultures. Through those understandings, other cultures can critique our concepts in ways that allow us to continually develop them.[12] This point may sound prosaic, but if anthropology is to continue to take others seriously (and it is worth recalling that it is the only discipline bound to do this by definition), then it will have to be at the center of our critical horizon.

Glancing just briefly at the wider tradition of critique in and for the West, it is worth noting that the ethnographic remarks on critical failure that are at the heart of this chapter echo those made of the Enlightenment notion of critique by Koselleck (1988). For Koselleck, the notion of critique was born out of the separation of politics and morality that attended the founding of the European absolutist states. Formed in response to the wars of religion that preceded them, the absolutist states made peace by placing the sovereign and the realm of politics he controlled above the realm of morality (i.e., religious conviction). The latter realm was thus left to the citizens, who now found themselves and their moral convictions excluded from the realm of politics. In this context, there emerged a morality that in its own self-understanding was devoid of political import and it was on the basis of such a morality that the rising bourgeoisie developed the tradition of critique. Free from the need or possibility of political efficacy, critique developed in a "utopian" direction and became accustomed to setting politically impossible goals. As the absolutist state crumbled, this utopian tradition became a political force, but one that was most comfortable promoting its own brand of moral absolutism because it had no sense of the political efficacy of compromise.

Although Koselleck makes it clear that his argument in *Critique and Crisis* (first published in 1959) developed in response to the rise of the Third Reich and in the context of the cold war (1988: 1–12), he only alludes in the most general terms to its bearing on contemporary traditions of critique. But in an era where totalizing systems of all types have come under suspicion, it is not difficult to see how his critique of critique articulates with concerns that currently haunt the tradition of critical argument. His conclusion—that we must be wary of critiques that only condemn everyday life in the name of an unattainable ideal—also fits well with the conclusions that followed from our ethnographic examinations. In the West, too, just as in Papua New Guinea or among the Tupí-Guaraní, what is needed is a critique that deals in real possibilities and that has sufficient imagination to lay out for us how those possibilities might be brought together in a better life.

And finally, then, we can ask about the role of anthropology in this project. One role, already laid out, involves looking comparatively at the kinds of critiques people make of their own societies and studying the conditions in which such critiques become effective in transforming social life. A second role has to do with helping the critical tradition find out what real human possibilities might be; that is to say, with rescuing that tradition from a tendency to take shelter in utopian perfectionism.

In her influential analysis of the relationship between anthropology and feminism, Marilyn Strathern (1987) argues that the two fields "mock" each other because each of them achieves quite easily something that despite serious efforts often eludes the other. As she puts it, "Anthropologists mock feminists by almost effortlessly achieving that distance from their own society which feminists create with such anguish" (M. Strathern 1987: 291). Feminists, for their part, find it easy to create a real community of interests between themselves and their subjects, something that is extremely difficult for anthropologists to accomplish. Although the content of what is easy and what is difficult is different, I want to suggest that anthropologists and members of millenarian movements (of cargo cultic or other critical varieties) similarly have an awkward relationship. What millenarians achieve without undue difficulty is a deep commitment to a new picture of the world; they are ready for change and ready to work for it; they seem to find it easy to open themselves to the possibility of a different life. Most anthropologists in their everyday lives are not so open, even as the rhetoric of Enlightenment and critique makes such openness a goal for them. But in the course of their studies, anthropologists do find it easy to set different ways of living side by side and to explore which kinds of human arrangements seem to work and which kinds do not, which kinds of change bring much misery and which redeem at least a tiny part of the millenarian promise of a better life. Most millenarians do not have this kind of knowledge at their disposal—certainly cargo cultists have fashioned their views of the good life on the basis of very limited information about human possibilities, and many other critical utopians are not so much better informed as we might think. So an ethnographically grounded anthropology that continues to explore how human cultures are put together and how they become the medium out of which different kinds of human lives are made ought to have a crucial role to play in the formation of a workable critical theory: a theory with which it should continue to have an awkward rather than a subordinate relationship.

Notes

1. For example, Kaplan (1995b: xiii), and, more hesitantly, Lindstrom (1993: 1–12).

2. It is my experience that nostalgic wishful thinking of a variety that I sometimes share leads many people whose own anthropological education was steeped in the study of kinship to greet every conference or review article on the subject as a sign of its return to anthropological prominence. But a realistic appraisal, I think, has to acknowledge that the kind of kinship study that Schneider attacked is not likely to return to the center of the discipline any time soon. At the very least, one has to recognize that where kinship does remain an object of study today, it is most often treated in Schneiderian cultural terms, rather than in the structural-functionalist and structuralist formulations that Schneider attacked.

3. On genealogical critique see Lindstrom (1993: 11–13), after Foucault (1976). See also Guess on "genetic" and "functional" forms of critique (1981: 21).

4. See Lattas (1992b), Lindstrom (1993), Kaplan (1995b), and Hermann (present volume).

5. In a very stimulating analysis of four possible storylines that one might rely on in analyzing cargo cults, Lindstrom (present volume) notes that the prophetic storyline that renders both cargo and cult as good is one that is taken up by cultists but not by the scholars who purport to describe or analyze them. My analysis here suggests that, although ethnographers of cargo cults may not rely on the prophetic storyline, their critics very much do.

6. See Bowen (1993) and Fabian (1999) for examples of this process.

7. My point here is not of course the rather obvious one that the millennium generally fails to arrive, but is rather the more prosaic but also more socially powerful one that the kinds of reform millenarians attempt to introduce into daily life in order to prepare people for the coming of the millennium generally fail to stick.

8. In this chapter, Tok Pisin terms are marked with "TP." Urap terms are not.

9. This argument and that of the following paragraph are developed in more detail in Robbins (1998a, 2004).

10. I have presented elsewhere a translation of a confession that indicates the nature of the inner dialogues that produce them (Robbins 2004).

11. "Redemptive criticism" is Wolin's phrasing (Wolin 1994: xiii). The English translation of Habermas' essay employs the phrase "rescuing critique." Throughout his book, Wolin provides a good account of the messianism at the heart of Benjamin's notion of critique.

12. See Otto and Dalton (present volume).

References

Abu-Lughod, Lila. 1990. "The Romance of Resistance: Tracing Transformations of Power through Bedouin Women," *American Ethnologist* 17: 41–55

Achterhuis, Hans. 1984. *Arbeid, een eigenaardig medicijn*. Baarn: Amboboeken

Aeschylus. 1959. "Prometheus Bound." In *The Complete Greek Tragedies*. Vol. 1: *Aeschylus*. Trans. David Grene. Chicago: University of Chicago Press

Allan, C. H. 1951. "Marching Rule. A Nativistic Cult of the British Solomon Islands," *Corona* 3: 93–100

Amarshi, Azeem, Kenneth Good, and Rex Mortimer. 1979. *Development and Dependency: The Political Economy of Papua New Guinea*. Melbourne: Oxford University Press

Andaya, Leonard. 1993. *The World of Maluku: Eastern Indonesia in the Early Modern Period*. Honolulu: University of Hawai'i Press

Anderson, Benedict. 1990. "The Idea of Power in Javanese Culture." In Benedict Anderson, ed., *Language and Power: Exploring Political Culture in Indonesia*, 17–77. Ithaca, N.Y.: Cornell University Press

Anderson, Christopher. 1988. "A Case Study in Failure: Kuku-Yalanji and the Lutherans at Bloomfield River, 1887–1902." In Tony Swain and Deborah B. Rose, eds., *Aboriginal Australians and Christian Missions*, 321–337. Adelaide: Australian Association for the Study of Religions

Anthony, Dick, and Thomas Robbins. 1999. "Religious Totalism, Exemplary Dualism, and the Waco Tragedy." In Thomas Robbins and S. Palmer, eds., *Millennium, Messiahs, and Mayhem: Contemporary Apocalyptic Movements*, 261–284. New York: Routledge

Aquinas, Thomas. 1964. *Summa Theologiae*. Latin text and English translation, introductions, notes, appendices and glossaries. Edited by Thomas Gilby et al. London: Eyre and Spottiswoode

Arendt, Hannah. 1964. *Eichmann in Jerusalem: A Report on the Banality of Evil*. New York: Penguin Books

AsiaNow. 2000. "Aid Workers Bury Hundreds of Dead on Indonesian Island," *AsiaNow*, January 10, 2000 [http: //www.cnn.com/2000/AsiaNow/southeast/01/10/indonesia.killings]

Attenborough, David. 1960. *People of Paradise*. New York: Harper & Bros.

Augé, Marc. 1999. *An Anthropology for Contemporaneous Worlds*. Trans. Amy Jacobs. Stanford, Calif.: Stanford University Press

Ballard, Chris. 1999. "Blanks in the Writing: Possible Histories for West New Guinea," *Journal of Pacific History* 34: 149–155

Barnes, Robert H.. 1974. *Kédang: A Study of the Collective Thought of an Eastern Indonesian People*. Oxford: Clarendon Press

Barnett, Homer G. 1953. *Innovation: The Basis of Cultural Change*. New York: McGraw-Hill

Barth, Fredrik. 1987. *Cosmologies in the Making: A Generative Approach to Cultural Variation in Inner New Guinea*. Cambridge: Cambridge University Press

———. 1993. *Balinese Worlds*. Chicago: University of Chicago Press

Baudelaire, Charles. 1975. "Le Fausse Monnaie." In Claude Pichois, ed., *Charles Baudelaire, Oeuvres Complētes*, 323. Paris: Bibliothèque de la Pléäade

Baudrillard, Jean. 1988. *America*. London: Verso

Becker, Ernest. 1973. *The Denial of Death*. New York: Free Press

Bell, Daniel. 1973. *The Coming of the Post-Industrial Society: A Venture in Social Forecasting*. London: Heinemann

Benedict, Ruth. 1946. *The Chrysanthemum and the Sword: Patterns of Japanese Culture*. New York: Houghton Mifflin

Benhabib, Seyla. 1986. *Critique, Norm, and Utopia: A Study of the Foundations of Critical Theory*. New York: Columbia University Press

Benjamin, Walter. 1968. "The Work of Art in the Age of Mechanical Reproduction." In Hannah Arendt, ed., *Walter Benjamin, Illuminations*, 217–251. New York: Schocken

Bern, John. 1979. "Ideology and Domination: Toward a Reconstruction of Australian Aboriginal Social Formation," *Oceania* 50: 118–132

Berndt, Catherine H., and Ronald M. Berndt. 1971. *The Barbarians: An Anthropological View*. London: Watts

Berndt, Ronald M. 1951. "Influence of European Culture on Australian Aborigines," *Oceania* 21: 229–235

———. 1952/1953. "A Cargo Movement in the Eastern Central Highlands of New Guinea," *Oceania* 23 (1): 40–65; 23 (2): 137–158; 23(3): 202–234

———. 1954. "Reaction to Contact in the Eastern Highlands of New Guinea," *Oceania* 24: 190–228, 255–274

———. 1962. *An Adjustment Movement in Arnhem Land*. Paris/The Hague: Cahiers de L'Homme/Mouton

Berndt, Ronald M., and Catherine H. Berndt. 1954. *Arnhem Land: Its History and Its People*. Melbourne: Cheshire

———. 1988. *The World of the First Australians*. Canberra: Aboriginal Studies Press

Biersack, Aletta. 1990. "Money Magic: Paiela Perspective on the White World." Paper presented at the annual meeting of the American Anthropological Association, New Orleans, November 28–December 2

———. 1991a. "Introduction: History and Theory in Anthropology." In Aletta Biersack, ed., *Clio in Oceania: Toward a Historical Anthropology*, 1–36. Washington, D.C.: Smithsonian Institution Press

———. 1991b. "Prisoners of Time: Millenarian Praxis in a Melanesian Valley." In Aletta Biersack, ed., *Clio in Oceania: Toward a Historical Anthropology*, 231–296. Washington, D.C.: Smithsonian Institution Press

Billig, Michael. 1995. *Banal Nationalism*. London: Sage

Bird, Norris M. 1945. "Is There Danger of a Post-War Flare-Up among New Guinea Natives?" *Pacific Islands Monthly* 16: 69–70

———. 1946 "The 'Cargo Cult,'" *Pacific Islands Monthly* 16: 45

Bloch, Ernst. 1959. *Das Prinzip Hoffnung*. Frankfurt am Main: Suhrkamp

Bodrogi, Tibor. 1951. "Colonization and Religious Movements in Melanesia," *Acta Ethnographica Academiae Hungaricae* 3: 259–292

Borsboom, Ad. 1992. "Millenarianism, Australian Aborigines and the European Myth of Primitivism," *Canberra Anthropology* 15: 11–26

Bos, Robert. 1988. "The Dreaming and Social Change in Arnhem Land." In Tony Swain and Deborah B. Rose, eds., *Aboriginal Australians and Christian Missions*, 422–437. Adelaide: Australian Association for the Study of Religions

Bowen, John. 1993. "A Modernist Muslim Poetic: Irony and Social Critique in Gayo Islamic Verse," *Journal of Asian Studies* 52: 629–646

Brown, Michael. 1996. "On Resisting Resistance," *American Anthropologist* 98: 729–735

Bubandt, Nils. 1995. "Warriors of the Hornbill, Victims of the Mantis: History and Embodied Morality among the Buli of Central Halmahera. Canberra." Ph.D. thesis, Australian National University

———. 1998. "Imagined Globalities: Fetishism of the Global and the End of the World in Indonesia," *FOLK* 40: 99–122

———. 2000 "Conspiracy Theories, Apocalyptic Narratives and the Discursive Construction of 'the Violence in Maluku,'" *Antropologi Indonesia* 63: 15–31

———. Forthcoming. "Mobolising for Conflict: Rumours, Pamphlets, and the Politics of Paranoia." In Jon Goss and Kirk Lange, eds., *What Went Wrong? Explaining Communal Violence in Eastern Indonesia*. Stanford, Calif.: Stanford University Press

Buck, Pem Davidson. 1988. "Cargo-Cult Discourse: Myth and the Rationalization of Labor Relations in Papua New Guinea," *Dialectical Anthropology* 13: 157–171

Buck, Peter D. 1991. "Colonised Anthropology: Cargo-Cult Discourse." In F. V. Harrison, ed., *Decolonizing Anthropology: Moving Further Toward an Anthropology of Liberation*, 24–41. Washington, D.C.: American Anthropological Association

Burridge, Kenelm O. L. 1960. *Mambu: A Study of Melanesian Cargo Movements and Their Social and Ideological Background*. London: Methuen (1995: *Mambu: A Melanesian Millennium*. Princeton, N.J.: Princeton University Press)

———. 1965. Review of Peter Lawrence, *Road Belong Cargo*. *Man* 65: 96–97

———. 1969a. *New Heaven New Earth: A Study in Millenarian Activities*. New York: Schocken

———. 1969b. *Tangu Traditions: A Study of the Way of Life, Mythology, and Developing Experience of a New Guinea People*. Oxford: Clarendon

Burton-Bradley, Burton G. 1981. "Cargo Cult." In R. D. Craig and F. P. King, eds., *Historical Dictionary of Oceania*, 45–47. Westport, Conn.: Greenwood Press

Butler, Judith. 1990. *Gender Trouble: Feminism and the Subversion of Identity*. New York: Routledge

Calley, Malcolm. 1964. "Pentecostalism among the Bandjalang." In M. Reay, ed., *Aborigines Now: New Perspective in the Study of Aboriginal Communities*, 48–58. Sydney: Angus and Robertson

Cameron, Roderick. 1964. *The Golden Haze: With Captain Cook in the South Pacific*. Cleveland: World

Campbell, Colin. 1987. *The Romantic Ethic and the Spirit of Modern Consumerism*. Oxford: Basil Blackwell

Campion, Nicolas. 1994. *The Great Year: Astrology, Millenarianism and History in the Western Tradition*. London: Penguin Arkana

Chauvel, Richard. 1990. *Nationalists, Soldiers and Separatists: The Ambonese Islands from Colonialism to Revolt*. Leiden: KITLV Press

Chowning, Ann. 1977. *An Introduction to the People and Cultures of Melanesia*. Menlo Park, Calif.: Cummings

Clark, Jeffrey. 1992. "Madness and Colonisation: The Embodiment of Power in Pangia."

In Andrew Lattas, ed., *Alienating Mirrors: Christianity, Cargo Cults and Colonialism in Melanesia*, 15–26. Oceania 63

———. 1997 "Imagining the State, or Tribalism and the Arts of Memory in the Highlands of Papua New Guinea." In Ton Otto and Nicholas Thomas, eds., *Narratives of Nation in the South Pacific*, 65–90. Amsterdam: Harwood

Clastres, Hélène. 1995 [1975]. *The Land-Without-Evil: Tupí-Guaraní Prophetism*. Trans. J. G. Brovender. Urbana: University of Illinois Press

Coates, Austin. 1970. *Western Pacific Islands*. London: Her Majesty's Stationery Office

Cohn, Bernard S. 1987. *An Anthropologist among the Historians*. Delhi: Oxford University Press

———. 1996. *Colonialism and Its Forms of Knowledge: The British in India*. Princeton, N.J.: Princeton University Press

Cohn, Norman. 1970. *The Pursuit of the Millennium*. London: Paladin; New York: Oxford University Press

Comaroff, Jean. 1985. *Body of Body, Spirit of Resistance: The Culture and History of a South African People*. Chicago: University of Chicago Press

Comaroff, Jean, and John Comaroff. 1992. *Ethnography and the Historical Imagination*. Boulder, Colo.: Westview Press

———. 1993. *Modernity and Its Malcontents: Ritual and Power in Postcolonial Africa*. Chicago: University of Chicago Press

———. 1999. "Occult Economies and the Violence of Abstraction: Notes from the South African Postcolony," *American Ethnologist* 26: 279–303

Connerton, Paul. 1976. "Introduction." In Paul Connerton, ed., *Critical Sociology: Selected Readings*, 11–39. Middlesex: Penguin Books

Coronil, Fernando. 1996. "Beyond Occidentalism: Toward Nonimperial Geohistorical Categories," *Cultural Anthropology* 11: 51–87

Counts, Dorothy Ellen Ayers. 1971. "Cargo or Council: Two Approaches to Development in North-West New Britain," *Oceania* 41: 288–297

Crapanzano, Vincent. 1981. "Text, Transference, and Indexicality," *Ethos* 9: 122–148

———. 1990a. "Afterword." In Marc Manganaro, ed., *Modernist Anthropology: From Fieldwork to Text*, 300–308. Princeton, N.J.: Princeton University Press

———. 1990b. "On Self Characterization." In James W. Stigler, Richard A. Shweder, and Gilbert Herdt, eds., *Cultural Psychology: Essays on Comparative Human Development*, 401–423. Cambridge: Cambridge University Press

———. 2003. "Reflections on Hope as a Category of Social and Psychological Analysis," *Cultural Anthropology* 18: 1–32

Dalton, Doug. 1996."'Cargo Cult' and Discursive Madness." Paper presented at the annual meeting of the American Anthropological Association, San Francisco, November 20

———. 2000a. "Introduction." In Doug Dalton, ed., *A Critical Retrospective on "Cargo Cult": Western/Melanesian Intersections*, 285–293. Oceania 70

———. 2000b. "Cargo Cults and Discursive Madness." In Doug Dalton, ed., *A Critical Retrospective on "Cargo Cult": Western/Melanesian Intersections*, 345–361. Oceania 70

———, ed. 2000c. *A Critical Retrospective on "Cargo Cult": Western/Melanesian Intersections*. Oceania 70

———. n.d. "Phenomenology and Evolutionism in Melanesian Anthropology: The Spirit of Europe and Its Archaic Other." Unpublished manuscript

Deleuze, Gilles, and Félix Guattari. 1983. *Anti-Oedipus: Capitalism and Schizophrenia*. Trans. Mark Seem, Robert Hurley, and Helen R. Lane. Minneapolis: University of Minnesota Press

Department of Government Secretary. n.d. *Subject "Complaint re Native Yali."* CA 35/6/6. Waigani: National Archives of Papua New Guinea

Derrida, Jacques. 1977. "Afterword: Toward an Ethic of Discussion." Trans. Samuel Weber. In Limited Inc., ed., *Limited Inc.*, 111–160. Evanston, Ill.: Northwestern University Press

———. 1992. *Given Time. I. Counterfeit Money.* Trans. Peggy Kamuf. Chicago: University of Chicago Press

———. 1993. "On a Newly Arisen Apocalyptic Tone in Philosophy." In Peter Fenves, ed., *Raising the Tone of Philosophy: Late Essays by Immanuel Kant, Transformative Critique by Jacques Derrida,* 117–171. Baltimore: Johns Hopkins University Press

Destination Vanuatu. n.d. *John Frum and the Cargo Cult.* Port Vila [?]

Dietrich, Stefan. 1985. "'Religiöse' und 'säkulare' Reaktionen gegen die koloniale Verwaltung auf Flores." In Wolfgang Marschall, ed., *Der große Archipel.* Schweizer ethnologische Forschungen in Indonesien, 275–303. Bern

Di Martino, Ernesto. 1975. *Morte e pianto rituale: dal lamento funebre antico al pianto di Maria.* Torino: Boringhieri

Du Gay, Paul. 1996. *Consumption and Identity at Work.* London: Sage

Dumont, Louis. 1977. *From Mandeville to Marx: The Genesis and Triumph of Economic Ideology.* Chicago: University of Chicago Press

Eliade, Mircea. 1973. *Australian Religions: An Introduction.* Ithaca, N.Y.: Cornell University Press

Elkan, Walter. 1979. "Views from Three Other Disciplines: (i) Economics." In Sandra Wallman, ed., *Social Anthropology of Work,* 25–30. London: Academic Press

Englund, Harri, and James Leach. 2000. "Ethnography and the Meta-Narratives of Modernity," *Current Anthropology* 41: 225–248

Errington, Frederick. 1974. "Indigenous Ideas of Order, Time, and Transition in a New Guinea Cargo Movement," *American Ethnologist* 1: 255–267

Errington, Frederick, and Deborah Gewertz. 1995. *Articulating Change in the "Last Unknown."* Boulder, Co.: Westview Press

Evans, Julian. 1992. *Transit of Venus: Travels in the Pacific.* New York: Pantheon Books

Fabian, Johannes. 1999. "Culture and Critique." In Mieke Bal, ed., *The Practice of Cultural Analysis: Exposing Interdisciplinary Interpretation,* 235–254. Stanford: Stanford University Press

Finney, Ben R. 1973. *Big-Men and Business: Entrepreneurship and Economic Growth in the New Guinea Highlands.* Honolulu: University Press of Hawai'i

Foley, William A. 1986. *The Papuan Languages of New Guinea.* Cambridge: Cambridge University Press

Foster, George M. 1965. "Peasant Society and the Image of Limited Good," *American Anthropologist* 67: 293–315

Foster, Robert J. 1995. *Social Reproduction and History in Melanesia: Mortuary Ritual, Gift Exchange, and Custom in the Tanga Islands.* Cambridge: Cambridge University Press

Foucault, Michel. 1973. *Madness and Civilization: A History of Insanity in the Age of Reason.* New York: Vintage/Random House

———. 1976. *The Archaeology of Knowledge and the Discourse on Language.* Trans. A. M. Sheridan Smith. New York: Harper & Row.

———.1980 [1977]. "Truth and Power." In C. Gordon, ed., *Michel Foucault: Power/Knowledge. Selected Interviews and Other Writings, 1972–1977,* 109–133. New York: Pantheon Books

———. 1991 [1977]. *Die Ordnung des Diskurses.* Frankfurt am Main: Fischer

Franke, Richard. 1972. "Limited Good and Cargo Cult in Indonesian Economic Development," *Journal of Contemporary Asia* 2: 366–381
Friedman, Jonathan. 1994. *Cultural Identity and Global Process*. London: Sage
Gamson, William A. 1992. "The Social Psychology of Collective Action." In A. D. Morris and C. M. Mueller, eds., *Frontiers in Social Movement Theory*, 53–76. New Haven, Conn.: Yale University Press
Gay, Peter. 1993. *The Cultivation of Hatred*. New York: W. W. Norton
———. 1995. *The Naked Heart*. New York: W. W. Norton
Geertz, Hildred. 1968. "Latah in Java: A Theoretical Paradox," *Indonesia* 3: 93–104
Gesch, Patrick. 1990. "The Cultivation of Surprise and Excess; The Encounter of Cultures in the Sepik of Papua New Guinea." In Garry W. Trompf, ed., *Cargo Cults and Millenarian Movements: Transoceanic Comparisons of New Religious Movements*, 213–238. Berlin: Mouton de Gruyter
Geschiere, Peter. 1997. *The Modernity of Witchcraft: Politics and the Occult in Postcolonial Africa*. Charlottesville: University Press of Virginia
———. 1998. "Globalization and the Power of Indeterminate Meaning: Witchcraft and Spirit Cults in Africa and East Asia," *Development and Change* 29: 811–837
Gillion, Kenneth L. 1962. *Fiji's Indian Migrants: A History to the End of Indenture in 1920*. Melbourne: Oxford University Press
———. 1977. *The Fiji Indians: Challenge to European Dominance*, 1920–1946. Canberra: Australian National University Press
Gimple, Jean. 1976. *The Medieval Machine: The Industrial Revolution of the Middle Ages*. New York: Penguin Books
Girard, René. 1961. *Mensonge romantique et vérité romanesque*. Paris: Grasset
Glowczewski, Barbara. 1983. "Manifestations symboliques d'une transition économique: le juluru, culte intertribal du 'cargo' (Australie Occidentale et Centrale)," *L'Homme* 23: 7–35
Godelier, Maurice. 1977. "'Monnaie de sel' et circulation des marchandises chez les Baruya de Nouvelle-Guinée." In Maurice Godelier, *Horizon, trajets marxistes en anthropologie*. Vol. 2: 159–200. Paris: Maspero
———.1996. *L'énigme du don*. Paris: Fayard
Goodwin, Harold. 1984. *Cargo*. Scarsdale, N.Y.: Bradbury Press
Gordon, Sir Arthur Hamilton. 1879a. *Letters and Notes Written during the Disturbances in the Highlands (Known as the "Devil Country") of Viti Levu, Fiji*, 1876. Vols. 1 and 2. Edinburgh: Privately printed by R. and R. Clark
———. 1879b. *Paper on the System of Taxation in Force in Fiji: Read before the Royal Colonial Institute 18 March 1879*. London: Harrison and Sons
Gorz, André. 1980. *Adieux au prolétariat, Au delà du socialisme*. Paris: Editions Galilée
Gould, Richard A. 1980. *Living Archaeology*. Cambridge: Cambridge University Press
Gourguechon, Charlene. 1977. *Journey to the End of the World: A Three-Year Adventure in the New Hebrides*. New York: Charles Scribner's Sons
Grolier. 1969. *The New Book of Knowledge: The Children's Encyclopedia*. New York: Grolier
Guess, Raymond. 1981. *The Idea of Critical Theory: Habermas and the Frankfurt School*. Cambridge: Cambridge University Press
Guiart, Jean. 1951a. "Forerunners of Melanesian Nationalism," *Oceania* 22: 81–90
———. 1951b. "John Frum Movement in Tanna," *Oceania* 22: 165–175
Guinness, Patrick. 1994. "Local Society and Culture." In Hal Hill, ed., *Indonesia's New Order: The Dynamics of Socio-Economic Transformation*, 267–304. Sydney: Allen & Unwin

Gustafsson, Berit. 1995. "From God to Win: The Rise of a Melanesian Religious Movement Based on Christianity." In G. Aijmer, ed., *Syncretism and the Commerce of Symbols*, 60–83. Gotheburg: Institute of Advanced Studies in Social Anthropology

Habermas, Jürgen. 1983. *Philosophical-Political Profiles*. Trans. Frederick G. Lawrence. Cambridge, Mass.: MIT Press

Hamilton, John. 1983. "The Cargo-Cult Chief and the Letters from a God," *Brisbane Courier-Mail* 1 December: 1–2

Harris, Marvin. 1975. *Cows, Pigs, War and Witches: The Riddles of Culture*. New York: Vintage Books

Harrison, Simon. 1993. "The Commerce of Cultures in Melanesia," *Man* 28: 139–158

———. 2000. "From Prestige Goods to Legacies: Property and the Objectification of Culture in Melanesia," *Comparative Studies in Society and History* 42: 662–679

Hart, Stephen. 1996. "The Cultural Dimension of Social Movements: A Theoretical Reassessment and Literature Review," *Sociology of Religion* 57: 87–100

Hau'ofa, Epeli. 1975. "Anthropology and Pacific Islanders," *Oceania* 45: 283–289

Hefner, Robert. 2000. *Civil Islam: Muslims and Democratization in Indonesia*. Princeton, N.J.: Princeton University Press

———. 2002. "Global Violence and Indonesian Muslim Politics," *American Anthropologist* 104: 754–765

Heidegger, Martin. 1993. *Sein und Zeit*. Tübingen: Max Niemeyer Verlag

Heilbroner, Robert. 1962. *The Making of Economic Society*. Englewood Cliffs, N.J.: Prentice Hall

Helman, Sarit. 1988. "The Javanese Conception of Order and its Relationship to Millenarian Motifs and Imagery," *International Journal of Comparative Sociology* 29: 126–138

Hempenstall, Peter J., and Noel Rutherford. 1984. *Protest and Dissent in the Colonial Pacific*. Suva: University of the South Pacific

Hermann, Bernard, and Joël Bonnemaison. 1975. *New Hebrides*. Papeéte: Les Éditions du Pacifique

Hermann, Elfriede. 1987. "'Nem Bilong Kago Kalt Em I Tambu Tru!': Rezeption und Konsequenzen des Konzepts 'Cargo Cult' am Fallbeispiel der Yali-Bewegung in der Madang Province, Papua New Guinea." M.A. thesis, University of Tübingen

———. 1992a. "Die Konstruktion von 'cargo cult' und das ruinierte Ansehen eines Ngaing-Dorfes in Papua New Guinea." Paper presented at a colloquium of the Institute of Ethnology, University of Basel, January 1992

———. 1992b. "The Yali Movement in Retrospect: Rewriting History, Redefining 'Cargo Cult.'" In Andrew Lattas, ed., *Alienating Mirrors: Christianity, Cargo Cults and Colonialism in Melanesia*, 55–71. Oceania 63

———. 1993. "The Cultural Construction of 'Cargo Cults': Anthropological and Indigenous Reflections on the Yali Movement in Papua New Guinea." Paper presented at the symposium "Cargo, Charisma, and Capitalism," organized by Klaus-Peter Koepping and Gerrit Huizer at the conference of the Deutsche Gesellschaft für Völkerkunde, Leipzig, October

———. 1995. *Emotionen und Historizität. Der emotionale Diskurs über die Yali-Bewegung in einer Dorfgemeinschaft der Ngaing, Papua New Guinea*. Berlin: Dietrich Reimer

———. 1997. "Kastom versus Cargo Cult. Emotional Discourse on the Yali Movement in Madang Province, Papua New Guinea." In Ton Otto and Ad Borsboom, eds., *Cultural Dynamics of Religious Change in Oceania*, 87–102. Leiden: KITLV Press

———. 2002 "YALI." In John Ritchie and Diane Langmore, eds., *Australian Dictionary of Biography*. Vol. 16: 1940–1980, Pik–Z; p. 601. Carlton: Melbourne University Press

Heryanto, Ariel. 1988. "The Development of 'Development,'" *Indonesia* 46: 1–21

———. 1999a. "Where Communism Never Dies: Violence, Trauma, and Narration in the Last Cold War Capitalist Authoritarian State," *International Journal of Cultural Studies* 2: 147–177

———. 1999b. "The Years of Living Luxuriously. Identity Politics of Indonesia's New Rich." In Michael Pinches, ed., *Culture and Privilege in Capitalist Asia*, 159–187. London: Routledge

Hiatt, Lester R.1986. *Aboriginal Political Life*. Canberra: Australian Institute of Aboriginal Studies

———. 1996. *Arguments about Aborigines: Australia and the Evolution of Social Anthropology*. Cambridge: Cambridge University Press

Hobsbawm, Eric J. 1962. *The Age of Revolution*, 1789–1848. New York: New American Library

———. 1975. *The Age of Capital, 1848–1875*. New York: New American Library

———. 1996. *The Age of Extremes: A History of the World, 1914–1991*. New York: Vintage

Hobsbawm, Eric, and Terence Ranger. 1983. *The Invention of Tradition*. Cambridge: Cambridge University Press

Hogbin, Ian. 1958. *Social Change*. Carlton: Melbourne University Press

Höltker, Georg. 1941. "Die Mambu-Bewegung in Neuguinea. Ein Beitrag zum Prophetentum in Melanesia," *Annali Lateranensi* 5: 181–219

Holtzappel, Coen. 1997. "Nationalism and Cultural Identity." In Victor King and Michael Hitchcock, eds., *Images of Malay-Indonesian Identity*, 63–107. Kuala Lumpur: Oxford University Press

Hoskins, Janet. 1993. *The Play of Time: Kodi Perspectives on Calendars, History, and Exchange*. Berkeley: University of California Press

Howard, Michael. 1991. *Fiji: Race and Politics in an Island State*. Vancouver: University of British Columbia Press

Huizer, Gerrit. 1992. "Cargo and Charisma. Millenarian Movements in Today's Global Context." In Ton Otto, ed., *Imagining Cargo Cults*, 106–130. *Canberra Anthropology* 15

Human Rights Watch. 1999. *Indonesia: The Violence in Ambon*. March [www.hrw.org/reports/1999/ambon]

ICG. 2000. *Overcoming Murder and Chaos in Maluku*. Jakarta/Brussel: International Crisis Group (*ICG Asia Report* 10. December 19 [www.crisisweb.org])

———. 2002. *Indonesia: The Search for Peace in Maluku*. Jakarta/Brussel: International Crisis Group (*ICG Asia Report* 31. February 8 [www.crisisweb.org])

Illich, Ivan. 1971. *Deschooling Society*. New York: Harper and Row

Illouz, Eva. 1997. *Consuming the Romantic Utopia: Love and the Cultural Contradictions of Capitalism*. Berkeley: University of California Press

Inselmann, R. 1946. "'Cargo Cult' Not Caused by Missions," *Pacific Islands Monthly* 16: 44

Jaarsma, Sjoerd. 1997. "Ethnographic Perceptions of Cargo: Fragments of an Intermittent Discourse." In Ton Otto and Ad Borsboom, eds., *Cultural Dynamics of Religious Change in Oceania*, 67–85. Leiden: KITLV Press

Jarvie, I. C. 1964. *The Revolution in Anthropology*. London: Routledge & Kegan Paul

———. 1972. "Cargo Cults." In P. Ryan, ed., *Encyclopaedia of Papua and New Guinea*, 133–137. Melbourne: Melbourne University Press

Jebens, Holger. 1990. *Eine Bewältigung der Kolonialerfahrung: Zur Interpretation von Cargo-Kulten im Nordosten von Neuguinea*. Bonn: Holos (Mundus Reihe Ethnologie 35)

———. 2002 "Trickery or Secrecy? On Andrew Lattas' Interpretation of 'Bush Kaliai Cargo Cults,'" *Anthropos* 97: 181–199

Jebens, Holger, and Karl-Heinz Kohl. 1999. "Konstruktionen von 'Cargo': Zur Dialektik von Fremd- und Selbstwahrnehmung in der Interpretation melanesischer Kultbewegungen," *Anthropos* 94: 3–20

Johnston, Raymond L. 1980. *Nakanai of New Britain: The Grammar of an Oceanic Language*. Canberra: Australian National University (Pacific Linguistics Series B 70)

Jolly, Margaret. 1992. "Specters of Inauthenticity," *Contemporary Pacific* 4: 49–72

———. 1997. "Women-Nation-State in Vanuatu: Women as Signs and Subjects in the Discourse of *Kastom*, Modernity, and Christianity." In Ton Otto and Nicholas Thomas, eds., *Narratives of Nation in the South Pacific*, 133–162. Amsterdam: Harwood Academic Publishers

Jones, Charles. 1962. "The Millennial Dream as Poetry." In Sylvia Thrupp, ed., *Millennial Dreams in Action: Essays in Comparative Study*, 207–208. The Hague: Mouton

Jorgensen, Dan. 1994. "Locating the Divine in Melanesia: An Appreciation of the Work of Kenelm Burridge," *Anthropology and Humanism* 19: 130–137

Juillerat, Bernard. 1996. *Children of the Blood: Society, Reproduction and Cosmology in New Guinea*. Translated from the French by Nora Scott. Oxford: Berg

Kamma, Freerk C. 1972. *Koreri: Messianic Movements in the Biak-Numfor Culture Area*. The Hague: Martinus Nijhoff

———. 1976. *"Dit Wonderlijke Werk," het Probleem van de Communicatie tussen Oost en West Gebaseerd op de Ervaringen in het Zendingswerk op Nieuw-Guinea (Irian Jaya) 1855–1972: Een Socio-missiologische Benadering*. Oegstgeest: Raad voor de Zending der Nederlands Hervormde Kerk

Kapferer, Bruce. 1997. "Remythologizing Discourses: State and Insurrectionary Violence in Sri Lanka." In David Apter, ed., *The Legitimization of Violence*, 159–188. London: MacMillan and UNRISD

Kaplan, Martha. 1988. "The Coups in Fiji: Colonial Contradictions and the Postcolonial Crisis," *Critique of Anthropology* 8: 93–110

———. 1990a. "Christianity, People of the Land, and Chiefs, in Fiji." In John Barker, ed., *Christianity in Oceania*, 189–207. Lanham, Md.: University Press of America

———. 1990b. "Meaning, Agency and Colonial History: Navosavakadua and the *Tuka* Movement in Fiji," *American Ethnologist* 17: 3–22

———. 1995a. "Blood on the Grass and the Dogs Will Speak: Ritual Politics and the Nation in Independent Fiji." In Robert J. Foster, ed., *Nation Making: Emergent Identities in Postcolonial Melanesia*, 94–125. Ann Arbor: University of Michigan Press

———. 1995b. *Neither Cargo nor Cult: Ritual Politics and the Colonial Imagination in Fiji*. Durham, N.C.: Duke University Press

———. 2003. "Promised Lands: From Colonial Law-Giving to Postcolonial Takeovers in Fiji." In Donald Brenneis and Sally Merry, eds., *Law and Empire in the Pacific: Fiji and Hawai'i, 153–186*. Santa Fe, N.M.: School of American Research

Kaplan, Martha, and John D. Kelly. 1999. "On Discourse and Power: 'Cults' and 'Orientals' in Fiji," *American Ethnologist* 26: 843–863

Keen, Ian. 1997. "A Continent of Foragers: Aboriginal Australia as a 'Regional System.'" In P. McConvell and N. Evans, eds., *Archaeology and Linguistics: Aboriginal Australia in Global Perspective*, 261–274. Oxford: Oxford University Press

Keesing, Roger. 1978. "Politico-Religious Movements and Anticolonialism on Malaita: Maasina Rule in Historical Perspective," *Oceania* 48: 241–261; 49: 46–73

———. 1989. "Creating the Past: Custom and Identity in the Contemporary Pacific," *Journal of the Contemporary Pacific* 1: 19–42

———. 1992. *Custom and Confrontation: The Kwaio Struggle for Cultural Autonomy*. Chicago: University of Chicago Press

Kelly, John D. 1988. "Political Discourse in Fiji: From the Pacific Romance to the Coups," *Journal of Historical Sociology* 1: 4

———. 1998. "Aspiring to Minority and Other Tactics Against Violence in Fiji." In Dru Gladney, ed., *Making Majorities: Constituting the Nation in Japan, Korea, China, Malaysia, Fiji, Turkey, and the United States*, 173–197. Stanford, Calif.: Stanford University Press

———. 2003. "Gordon Was No Amateur: Imperial Legal Strategies in the Colonization of Fiji." In Donald Brenneis and Sally Merry, eds., *Law and Empire in the Pacific: Fiji and Hawai'i, 61–100*. Santa Fe, N.M.: School of American Research

Kelly, John D., and Martha Kaplan. 1990. "History, Structure and Ritual," *Annual Review of Anthropology* 19: 119–150

———. 1999. "Race and Rights in Fiji." In Joe Feagin and Pinar Batur-Van der Lippe, eds., *The Global Color Line*, 237–257. Stamford, Conn.: JAI Press

———. 2001. *Represented Communities: Fiji and World Decolonization*. Chicago: University of Chicago Press

———. Kelly, Raymond C. 1976. "Witchcraft and Sexual Relations: An Exploration in the Social and Semantic Implications of the Structure of Belief." In P. Brown and G. Buchbinder, eds., *Man and Woman in the New Guinea Highlands*, 36–53. Washington, D.C.: American Anthropological Association (Special Publication 8)

Kempf, Wolfgang. 1992. "'The Second Coming of the Lord': Early Christianization, Episodic Time, and the Cultural Construction of Continuity in Sibog." In Andrew Lattas, ed., *Alienating Mirrors. Christianity, Cargo Cults and Colonialism in Melanesia*, 72–86. Oceania 63

———. 1994. "Ritual, Power and Colonial Domination: Male Initiation Among the Ngaing of Papua New Guinea." In Charles Stewart and Rosalind Shaw, eds., *Syncretism/Anti-Syncretism: The Politics of Religious Synthesis*, 108–126. London, New York: Routledge

———. 1996. *Das Innere des Äusseren: Ritual, Macht und Historische Praxis bei den Ngaing in Papua Neuguinea*. Berlin: Reimer

Kierkegaard, Søren. 1987. *Either/Or*. Part 1. Princeton, N.J.: Princeton University Press

Kilani, Mondher. 1983. *Les Cultes du Cargo Mélanesiens: Mythe et Rationalité en Anthropologie*. Lausanne: Le Forum Anthropologique/Éditions d'en Bas

Kipp, Rita Smith. 1993. *Dissociated Identities: Ethnicity, Religion, and Class in an Indonesian Society*. Ann Arbor: University of Michigan Press

Klandermans, Bert. 1992. "The Social Construction of Protest and Multiorganizational Fields." In Aldon D. Morris and Carol McClurg Mueller, eds., *Frontiers in Social Movement Theory*, 77–103. New Haven, Conn.: Yale University Press

Knauft, Bruce. 1989. "Bodily Images in Melanesia: Cultural Substances and Natural Metaphors." In Michel Feher, ed., *Fragments for a History of the Human Body*, Part Three, 192–279. New York: Zone

Kocher Schmid, Christine, ed. 1999. *Expecting the Day of Wrath: Versions of the Millennium in Papua New Guinea*. Boroko: National Research Institute of Papua New Guinea, in association with the European Commission Programme "Future of the Tropical Forest Peoples" (NRI Monographs 36)

Koentjaraningrat, ed. 1993. *Masyarakat Terasing di Indonesia*. Jakarta: Departemen Sosial dan Dewan Nasional Indonesia untuk Kesejahteraan Sosial in collaboration with Gramedia Pustaka Utama

Koepping, Klaus-Peter. 1988. "Nativistic movements in Aboriginal Australia: Creative Adjustment, Protest or Regeneration of Tradition." In Tony Swain and Deborah B. Rose, eds., *Aboriginal Australians and Christian Missions*, 397–411. Adelaide: Australian Association for the Study of Religions

Kohl, Karl-Heinz. 1975. Review of Peter Worsley, *Die Trompete wird erschallen*. *Das Argument* 90: 325–327

Kolig, Erich. 1981. *The Silent Revolution: The Effects of Modernisation on Australian Aboriginal Religion*. Philadelphia: Institute for the Study of Human Issues

———. 1988. "Mission Not Accomplished: Christianity in the Kimberleys." In Tony Swain and Deborah B. Rose, eds., *Aboriginal Australians and Christian Missions*, 321–337. Adelaide: The Australian Association for the Study of Religions

———. 1989. *Dreamtime Politics: Religion, World View and Utopian Thought in Australian Aboriginal Society*. Berlin: Dietrich Reimer Verlag

Kopytoff, Igor. 1986. "The Cultural Biography of Things." In Arjun Appadurai, ed., *The Social Life of Things: Commodities in Cultural Perspective*, 64–91. Cambridge: Cambridge University Press

Koselleck, Reinhart. 1988 [1959]. *Critique and Crisis: Enlightenment and the Pathogenesis of Modern Society*. Cambridge, Mass.: MIT Press

Kramer, Fritz W. 1987. *Der rotes Fes: Über Besessenheit und Kunst in Afrika*. Frankfurt am Main: Athenäum

Kumar, Krishnan. 1995. *From Post-Industrial to Post-Modern Society: New Theories of the Contemporary World*. Oxford: Blackwell

Lacan, Jacques. 1966. *Ecrits*. Paris: Edition de Seuil

Lacey, Roderic. 1990. "Journeys of Transformation: The Discovery and Disclosure of Cosmic Secrets in Melanesia." In Garry W. Trompf, ed., *Cargo Cults and Millenarian Movements: Transoceanic Comparisons of New Religious Movements*, 181–211. Berlin: Mouton de Gruyter

Lal, Brij V. 1988. *Power and Prejudice: The Making of the Fiji Crisis*. Wellington: New Zealand Institute of International Affairs

———. 1992. *Broken Waves: A History of the Fiji Islands in the Twentieth Century*. Honolulu: University of Hawai'i Press

———. 2000. "Madness in May." In Brij V. Lal, ed., *Fiji Before the Storm: Elections and the Politics of Development*, 175–194. Canberra: Asia Pacific Press at the Australian National University

Lal, Brij V., and Tomasi Rayalu Vakatora, eds. 1997. *Fiji Constitution Review Committee Research Papers*. Vol. 1: *Fiji in Transition*; Vol. 2: *Fiji and the World*. Suva: School of Social and Economic Development, University of the South Pacific

Lattas, Andrew. 1991. "Sexuality and Cargo Cults: The Politics of Gender and Procreation in West New Britain," *Cultural Anthropology* 6: 230–256

———, ed. 1992a. *Alienating Mirrors: Christianity, Cargo Cults, and Colonialism in Melanesia*. *Oceania* 63

———. 1992b. "Introduction. Hysteria, Anthropological Discourse and the Concept of the Unconscious: Cargo Cults and the Scientisation of Race and Colonial Power." In Andrew Lattas, ed., *Alienating Mirrors: Christianity, Cargo Cults, and Colonialism in Melanesia*, 1–14. Oceania 63

———. 1992c. "The Punishment of Masks. Cargo Cults and Ideologies of Representation in West New Britain," *Canberra Anthropology* 15: 69–88

———. 1992d. "Skin, Personhood and Redemption: The Double Self in West New Britain Cargo Cults." In Andrew Lattas, ed., *Alienating Mirrors: Christianity, Cargo Cults and Colonialism in Melanesia*, 27–54. Oceania 63

———. 1993. "Sorcery and Colonialism: Illness, Dreams and Death as Political Languages in West New Britain," *Man* 28: 51–77

———. 1998. *Cultures of Secrecy: Reinventing Race in Bush Kaliai Cargo Cults*. Madison: University of Wisconsin Press

———. 1999. " 'Neither cargo nor cult ...,'" *Anthropological Forum* 9: 107–112

Laum, Bernhard. 1924. *Heiliges Geld: Eine historische Untersuchung über den sakralen Ursprung des Geldes*. Tübingen: Mohr Siebeck

Lawrence, Peter. 1954. "Cargo Cult and Religious Beliefs among the Garia," *International Archives of Ethnography* 47: 1–20

———. 1955. "The Madang District Cargo Cult," *South Pacific* 8: 6–13

———. 1964. *Road Belong Cargo: A Study of the Cargo Movement in the Southern Madang District New Guinea*. Manchester: Manchester University Press (1971, Prospect Heights, Ill.: Humanities Press)

Lawrence, Peter, and Mervyn J. Meggitt. 1965. "Introduction." In Peter Lawrence and Mervyn J. Meggitt, eds., *Gods, Ghosts and Men in Melanesia*, 1–65. Melbourne: Oxford University Press

Leadbeater, Charles, and John Lloyd. 1987. *In Search of Work*. Harmondsworth: Penguin

Leavitt, Stephen. 1995a. "Political Domination and the Absent Oppressor: Images of Europeans in Bumbita Arapesh Narratives," *Ethnology* 34: 177–189

———. 1995b. "Seeking Gifts from the Dead: Long-Term Mourning in a Bumbita Arapesh Cargo Narrative," *Ethos* 23: 453–473

———. 1995c. "Suppressed Meanings in Narratives about Suffering: A Case from Papua New Guinea," *Anthropology and Humanism* 20: 1–20.

———. 2000. "The Apotheosis of White Men? A Reexamination of Beliefs about Europeans as Ancestral Spirits." In Doug Dalton, ed., *A Critical Retrospective on "Cargo Cult": Western/Melanesian Intersections*, 304–323. Oceania 70

———. 2001. "The Psychology of Consensus in a Papua New Guinea Christian Revival Movement." In Holly Matthews and Carmella Moore, eds., *The Psychology of Cultural Experience*, 151–172. Cambridge: Cambridge University Press

Lévi-Strauss, Claude. 1962. *La pensée sauvage*. Paris: Plon (1966: *The Savage Mind*. Chicago: University of Chicago Press)

———. 1963. *Totemism*. Trans. Rodney Needham. Boston: Beacon Press

Li, Tania Murray. 1999. "Compromising Power: Development, Culture, and Rule in Indonesia," *Cultural Anthropology* 14: 295–322

Lifton, Robert. 1993. *The Protean Self*. New York: Basic Books

Lindstrom, Lamont. 1984. "Doctor, Lawyer, Wise Man, Priest: Big-Men and Knowledge in Melanesia," *Man* 19: 291–309

———. 1990a. "Knowledge of Cargo, Knowledge of Cult: Truth and Power on Tanna, Vanuatu." In G. W. Trompf, ed., *Cargo Cults and Millenarian Movements*. Transoceanic Comparisons of New Religious Movements, 239–261. Berlin: Mouton de Gruyter

———. 1990b. *Knowledge and Power in a South Pacific Society*. Washington, D.C.: Smithsonian Institution Press

———. 1993. *Cargo Cult: Strange Stories of Desire from Melanesia and Beyond*. Honolulu: University of Hawai'i Press

———. 1995. "Cargoism and Occidentalism." In James G. Carrier, ed., *Occidentalism: Images of the West*, 33–60. Oxford: Clarendon Press

———. 1996. "Cargo Inventories, Shopping Lists, and Desire." In William A. Haviland and Robert J. Gordon, eds., *Talking about People: Readings in Contemporary Cultural Anthropology*, 2nd ed. 35–39. Mountain View, Calif.: Mayfield

———. 1999. "Mambu Phone Home," *Anthropological Forum* 9: 99–105

———. 2000 "Cargo Cult Horror." In Doug Dalton, ed., *A Critical Retrospective on "Cargo Cult": Western/Melanesian Intersections*, 294–303. Oceania 70

Linnekin, Jocelyn. 1992. "On the Theory and Politics of Cultural Construction in the Pacific." In Margaret Jolly and Nicholas Thomas, eds., *The Politics of Tradition in the Pacific*, 249–263. Oceania 62

Locke, John. 1988. *Two Treatises of Government*. Edited by Peter Laslett. Cambridge: Cambridge University Press

Lommel, Andreas. 1970. "Changes in Australian Art." In Arnold R. Pilling and Richard A. Waterman, eds., *Diprotodon to Detribalization*, 217–236. East Lansing: Michigan State University Press

Lorens, Pita, and Bil Tomaseti (Tanimtok). 1986. *Rot Bilong Kago*. Pos Mosbi: Institut Bilong PNG Stadis

Lyotard, Jean-François. 1984. *The Postmodern Condition: A Report on Knowledge*. Trans. Geoff Bennington and Brian Massumi. Volume 10 in Theory and History of Literature series. Series edited by Wlad Godzich and Jochen Schulte-Sasse. Minneapolis: University of Minnesota Press

MacAndrews, Colin. 1986. *Central Government and Local Development in Indonesia*. Singapore: Oxford University Press

Mackie, Jamie, and Andrew MacIntyre. 1994. "Politics." In Hal Hill, ed., *Indonesia's New Order: The Dynamics of Socioeconomic Transformation*, 1–53. Sydney: Allen and Unwin

MacKnight, Campbell C. 1976. *The Voyage to Marege: Macassan Trepangers in Northern Australia*. Melbourne: Melbourne University Press

Maclean, Neil. 1994. "Freedom or Autonomy: A Modern Melanesian Dilemma," *Man* 29: 667–688

Maddock, Kenneth. 1969. "The Jabaduruwa." Ph.D. dissertation, University of Sydney

———. 1972. *The Australian Aborigines: A Portrait of Their Society*. Ringwood: Penguin

Mair, Lucy P. 1948. *Australia in New Guinea*. London: Christophers

Malchow, H. L. 1996. *Gothic Images of Race in Nineteenth-Century Britain*. Stanford, Calif.: Stanford University Press

Maloat, Paliau. 1985. *The Last Knowledge*. Leaflet signed by Paliau Maloat. O.B.E. The last Prophet of the World. Distributed by Makasol, Manus

Mandeville, Bernard. 1988. *The Fable of the Bees; Or, Private Vices, Public Benefits*. Edited by F. B. Kaye. 2 vols. Oxford: Liberty Fund

Manus District Annual Report. 1956/1957. *Manus District Annual Report*. Department of Decentralisation. National Archives of Papua New Guinea, Port Moresby

———. 1957/1958. *Manus District Annual Report*. Department of Decentralisation. National Archives of Papua New Guinea, Port Moresby

———. 1958/1959. *Manus District Annual Report*. Department of Decentralisation. National Archives of Papua New Guinea, Port Moresby

———. 1959/1960. *Manus District Annual Report*. Department of Decentralisation. National Archives of Papua New Guinea, Port Moresby

Marcus, George, and Michael Fischer. 1986. *Anthropology as Cultural Critique: An Experimental Moment in the Human Sciences*. Chicago: University of Chicago Press

Marx, Karl. 1970. *Capital*. Vol. 1. London: Lawrence & Wishart

McDowell, Nancy. 1988. "A Note on Cargo and Cultural Constructions of Change," *Pacific Studies* 11: 121–134

———. 2000. "A Brief Comment on Difference and Rationality." In Doug Dalton, ed., *A Critical Retrospective on "Cargo Cult": Western/Melanesian Intersections*, 373–380. Oceania 70

McGinn, Bernard. 1995. "The End of the World and the Beginning of Christianity." In Malcolm Bull, ed., *Apocalypse Theory and the Ends of the World*, 58–89. Oxford: Blackwell

McMichael, Philip. 1996. *Development and Social Change: A Global Perspective*. Thousand Oaks, Calif.: Pine Forge Press

Meggitt, Mervyn J. 1962. *Desert People: A Study of the Walbiri Aborigines of Central Australia*. Sydney: Angus and Robertson

———. 1966. *Gadjari among the Walbiri Aborigines of Central Australia*. Sydney: University of Sydney (Oceania Monograph 14)

Melucci, Alberto. 1989. *Nomads of the Present: Social Movements and Individual Needs in Contemporary Society*. Philadelphia: Temple University Press

Merleau-Ponty, Maurice. 1962. *Phenomenology of Perception*. Trans. Colin Smith. New York: Routledge

———. 1964. *The Primacy of Perception*. Trans. James M. Eddie, Arleen B. Dallery, et al. Edited by James M. Eddie. New York: Routledge

Merton, Thomas. 1968. *The Geography of Lograire*. New York: New Directions

———. 1979. *Love and Living*. New York: Farrar, Straus, Giroux

Middendorf, Heinrich. 1985. *Phänomenologie der Hoffnung*. Amsterdam: Editions Rodopi

Mimica, Jadran. 1988. *Intimations of Infinity: The Mythopoeia of the Iqwaye Counting System and Number*. Oxford: Berg

Minkowski, Eugène. 1970. *Lived Time: Phenomenological and Psychopathological Studies*. Evanston, Ill.: Northwestern University Press (1933: *Le temps vécu*)

Money, J. W. B. 1861. *Java; Or, How to Manage A Colony, Showing a Practical Solution of the Questions Now Affecting British India*. 2 vols. London: Hurst and Blacket

Montesquieu, Charles-Louis. 1993 [1724]. *Persian Letters*. London, New York: Penguin Books

Morauta, Louise. 1972. "The Politics of Cargo Cults in the Madang Area," *Man* 7: 430–447

———. 1974. *Beyond the Village: Local Politics in Madang, Papua New Guinea*. London: Athlone Press

Morphy, Howard. 1983. "Now You Understand: An Analysis of the Way Yolngu Have Used Sacred Knowledge to Retain Their Autonomy." In N. Peterson and M. Langton, eds., *Aborigines, Land and Land Rights*, 110–133. Canberra: Australian Institute of Aboriginal Studies

———. 1991. *Ancestral Connections*. Chicago: University of Chicago Press

———. 1998. *Aboriginal Art*. London: Phaidon

Morren, George E. B. 1981. "A Small Footnote to the 'Big Walk': Environment and Change Among the Miyanmin of Papua New Guinea," *Oceania* 52: 39–65

Morris, Aldon D., and Carol McClurg Mueller, eds. 1992. "Preface." In Aldon D. Morris and Carol McClurg Mueller, eds., *Frontiers in Social Movement Theory*, ix–x. New Haven, Conn.: Yale University Press

Mortimer, Rex. 1979. "The Colonial State: Paternalism and Mystification." In Azeem Amarshi, Kenneth Good, and Rex Mortimer, eds., *Development and Dependency*, 163–186. Melbourne: Oxford University Press

Mosko, Mark S. 1991. "Yali Revisited: The Interplay of Messages and Missions in Melanesian Structural History," *Journal of the Polynesian Society* 100: 269–298

Mühlmann, Wilhelm Emil. 1961. *Chiliasmus und Nativismus: Studien zur Psychologie, Soziologie und historischen Kasuistik der Umsturzbewegungen*. Berlin: Reimer

Mulvaney, D. John. 1989. *Encounters in Place: Outsiders and Aboriginal Australians, 1606–1985*. St. Lucia: University of Queensland Press

O'Flynn, Paul. 1983 "Production and Reproduction: The Case of Frankenstein," *Literature and History* 9: 194–213

Opeba, Willington Jojoga. 1981. "The Peroveta of Buna." In Garry W. Trompf, ed., *Prophets of Melanesia*, 127–142. Port Moresby: Institute of Papua New Guinea Studies

Oram, Nigel. 1992. "Tommy Kabu: What Kind of Movement?" *Canberra Anthropology* 15: 89–105

Ortner, Sherry B. 1991. "Reading America: Preliminary Notes on Class and Culture." In Richard G. Fox, ed., *Recapturing Anthropology*, 163–189. Santa Fe, N.M.: School of American Research Press

———. 1995. "Resistance and the Problem of Ethnographic Refusal," *Comparative Studies in Society and History* 37: 173–193

Otto, Ton. 1984. "Waarde, arbeid en betekenis: Antropologie en de kritiek op de economische ideologie." In T. Lemaire, ed., *Antropologie en ideologie*, 41–79. Groningen: Konstapel

———. 1990. "De antropoloog en het individu: Beschouwingen over ideologie en interculturele vergelijking." In R. Corbey and P. van der Grijp, eds., *Natuur en cultuur: Beschouwingen op het raakvlak van antropologie en filosofie*, 139–156. Baarn: Ambo

———. 1991. "The Politics of Tradition in Baluan: Social Change and the Construction of the Past in a Manus Society." Ph.D. dissertation, Australian National University. Canberra (reproduced by the Centre for Pacific Studies, University of Nijmegen)

———. 1992a. "Introduction: Imagining Cargo Cults." In Ton Otto, ed., *Imagining Cargo Cults*, 1–10. *Canberra Anthropology* 15

———. 1992b. "From Paliau Movement to Makasol: The Politics of Representation," *Canberra Anthropology* 15: 49–68

———. 1992c. "The Paliau Movement in Manus and the Objectification of Tradition," *History and Anthropology* 5: 427–454

———, ed. 1992d. *Imagining Cargo Cults*. *Canberra Anthropology* 15

———. 1997. "Social Practice and the Ethnographic Circle: Rethinking the 'Ethnographers Magic' in a Late Modern World." In E. Roesdahl, H. Thrane, and Ton Otto, eds., *Tre tiltrædelsesforelæsninger på Moesgård*, 53–96. Aarhus: Det Humanistiske Fakultet, Aarhus University

———. 1998a. "Local Narratives of a Great Transformation: Conversion to Christianity in Manus, Papua New Guinea," *Folk* 40: 71–97

———. 1998b. "Paliau's Stories: Autobiography and Automythography of a Melanesian Prophet," *Focaal* 32: 71–87

———. 1999. "Cargo Cults Everywhere?" *Anthropological Forum* 9: 83–98

Otto, Ton, and Ad Borsboom. 1997. "Cultural Dynamics of Religious Change." In Ton Otto and Ad Borsboom, eds, *Cultural Dynamics of Religious Change in Oceania*, 103–112. Leiden: KITLV Press

Pacific Island Monthly. 1946a. "Editorial Note," *Pacific Islands Monthly* 16: 44–45

———. 1946b. "How 'Cargo Cult' Is Born: The Scientific Angle on an Old Subject." Translated and condensed from a paper in *Nouvelle Revue de Science Missionaire* (Hoeltker, G.), *Pacific Islands Monthly* 17: 16, 70

———. 1947a. "Of Missionaries and 'Cargo Cult,'" *Pacific Islands Monthly* 18: 58

———. 1947b. "Of Pinnaces and Cargo Cult," *Pacific Islands Monthly* 17: 69

———. 1948. "Restless Sepik Natives, Adherents of 'Cargo Cult,'" *Pacific Islands Monthly* 17: 62

———. 1950a. "Case History of Yali. New Guinea's First Native Leader," *Pacific Islands Monthly* 20: 33–35

———. 1950b. "Sumit: Some Sidelights on Yali . Can He Be Regarded as 'Cargo Cult,' or Mischievous Influence?" *Pacific Islands Monthly* 21: 45–47

Panoff, Michel. 1977. "Energie et vertu: le travail et ses répresentations en Nouvelle-Bretagne," *L'Homme* 17: 7–21

Parkin, Michael. 2000. *Economics*, 5th ed. Reading, Massachusetts: Addison-Wesley

Pater, Walter. 1911. *Marius the Epicurean: His Sensations and Ideas*. London: Macmillan

Petri, Helmut, and Gisela Petri-Odermann. 1970. "Stability and Change: Present-Day Historic Aspects among Australian Aborigines." In R. M. Berndt, ed., *Australian Aboriginal Anthropology*, 248–276. Nedlands: University of Western Australia Press

———. 1988. "A Nativistic and Millenarian Movement in North West Australia." In Tony Swain and Deborah B. Rose, eds., *Aboriginal Australians and Christian Missions*, 391–396. Adelaide: Australian Association for the Study of Religions

Pletsch, Carl. 1981. "The Three Worlds; Or, the Division of Social Scientific Labor, circa 1950–1975," *Comparative Studies in Society and History* 23: 565–590

Pocock, J. G. A. 1971. "Time, Institutions and Action." In J. G. A. Pocock, ed., *Politics, Language and Time: Essays on Political Thought and History*. New York: Atheneum

Pos, Hugo. 1950. "The Revolt of 'Manseren,'" *American Anthropologist* 52: 561–564

Pouillet, André. 1992. "Une Suite à la Présence Américanie: L'Affaire John Frum," *Bulletin de la Société d'Études Historique de la Nouvelle Calédonie* 92: 37–44

Premdas, Ralph. 1980. "Constitutional Challenge: The Rise of Fijian Nationalism," *Pacific Perspective* 9: 30–44

Priday, H. E. L. 1950. "'Jonfrum' is New Hebridean 'Cargo Cult': Interesting History of this Native Movement on the Island of Tanna," *Pacific Islands Monthly* 20: 67–70 (6 January); 59–65 (7 February)

Prowse, D. R. 1946. "Patrol Report No. 3 of 1946, Saidor Sub-District, Madang District." Waigani: National Archives of Papua New Guinea

Read, K. E. 1958. "A 'Cargo' Situation in the Markham Valley, New Guinea," *Southwestern Journal of Anthropology* 14: 273–294

Reitano, F. V. 1949/1950 "Patrol Report No. 4 of 1949/50, Saidor Sub-District, Madang District." Waigani: National Archives of Papua New Guinea

Reynolds, Henry. 1981. *The Other Side of the Frontier*. Townsville: James Cook University

Ricklefs, Merle. 1981. *A History of Modern Indonesia, c. 1300 to the Present*. London: MacMillan

Rimoldi, Max, and Eleanor Rimoldi. 1992. *Hahalis and the Labour of Love: A Social Movement on Buka Island*. Oxford: Berg

Robbins, Joel. 1997. "'When Do You Think the World Will End?' Globalization, Apocalypticism, and the Moral Perils of Fieldwork in 'Last New Guinea,'" *Anthropology and Humanism* 22: 6–30

———. 1998a. "Becoming Sinners: Christianity and Desire among the Urapmin of Papua New Guinea," *Ethnology* 37: 299–316

———. 1998b. "Becoming Sinners: Christian Transformations of Morality and Culture in a Papua New Guinea Society." Ph.D. thesis, University of Virginia

———. 2001. "Secrecy and the Sense of an Ending: Narrative, Time and Everyday Millenarianism in Papua New Guinea and in Christian Fundamentalism," *Comparative Studies in Society and History* 43: 525–551

———. 2003. "On the Paradoxes of Global Pentecostalism and the Perils of Continuity Thinking," *Religion* 33: 221–231

———. 2004. *Becoming Sinners: Christianity and Moral Torment in Papua New Guinea Society*. Berkeley: University of California Press

Romein, Jan. 1971. "Het arbeidsbegrip in Oost en West." In Jan Romein, *Historische lijnen en patronen*, 446–473. Amsterdam: Querido

Rose, Deborah B. 1994. "Ned Kelly Died for Our Sins," *Oceania* 65: 175–186

Ross, T. J. 1972. "Introduction." In Roy Huss and T. J. Ross, eds., *Focus on the Horror Film*. Englewood Cliffs, N.J.: Prentice-Hall

Rowley, C. D. 1965. *The New Guinea Villager: A Retrospect from 1964*. Melbourne: F. W. Cheshire

Rutschky, Michael. 1992. "Nachrichten aus dem Beitrittsgebiet," *Merkur* 519: 465–480

Rutz, Henry. 1995. "Occupying the Headwaters of Tradition: Rhetorical Strategies of Nation Making in Fiji." In Robert J. Foster, ed., *Nation Making: Emergent Identities in Postcolonial Melanesia*, 71–93. Ann Arbor: University of Michigan Press

Sahlins, Marshall. 1972. *Stone Age Economics*. Chicago: Aldine

———. 1976. *Culture and Practical Reason*. Chicago: University of Chicago Press

———. 1981. *Historical Metaphors and Mythical Realities: Structure in the Early History of the Sandwich Islands Kingdom*. Ann Arbor: University of Michigan Press (ASAO Special Publication 1)

———. 1985. *Islands of History*. Chicago: University of Chicago Press

———. 1992. "The Economics of Develop-Man in the Pacific," *RES* 21: 12–25

———. 1993. *Waiting for Foucault*. Cambridge: Prickly Pear Press

Said, Edward. 1978. *Orientalism*. New York: Pantheon

Sarup, Madan. 1993. *An Introductory Guide to Post-Structuralism and Postmodernism*, 2nd ed. New York: Harvester Wheatsheaf

Scheurmann, Erich. 1997 [1920]. *Tuiavii's Way: A South Sea Chief's Comments on Western Society*. Adapted and translated into English by Peter C. Cavelti. Toronto: Legacy Editions

Schneider, David M. 1984. *A Critique of the Study of Kinship*. Ann Arbor: University of Michigan Press

Schwartz, Theodore. 1962. "The Paliau Movement in the Admiralty Islands, 1946–1954," *Anthropological Papers of the American Museum of Natural History* 49: 207–421

———. 1976. "The Cargo Cult: A Melanesian-Type Response to Change." In G. A. de Vos, ed., *Responses to Change: Society, Culture and Personality*, 157–206. New York: Van Nostrand

Schwimmer, Erik. 1979. "The Self and the Product." In S. Wallman, ed., *Social Anthropology of Work*, 287–315. London: Academic Press

Sejarah Perjuangan. 1989. *Sejarah Perjuangan Rakyat Irian Jaya, 1900–1969: Laporan Penelitian*. Jayapura: Universitas Cenderawasih dengan Badan Perencanaan *Pembangunan* Daerah Tingkat I Irian Jaya. Typescript

Sennett, Richard. 1998. *The Corrosion of Character: The Personal Consequences of Work in the New Capitalism*. New York: W.W. Norton

Shears, Richard. 1980. *The Coconut War: The Crises on Espiritu Santo*. Sydney: Cassell Australia

Shineberg, Dorothy. 1967. *They Came for Sandalwood*. Melbourne: Melbourne University Press

Sillitoe, Paul. 1998. *An Introduction to the Anthropology of Melanesia*. Cambridge: Cambridge University Press

Smith, Adam. 1976. *An Inquiry into the Nature and Causes of the Wealth of Nations*. Edited by R. H. Campbell, A. S. Skinner, and W. B. Todd. 2 vols. Oxford: Clarendon

Smith, Michael French. 1994. *Hard Times on Kairiru Island*. Honolulu: University of Hawai'i Press

Soeffner, Hans-Georg. 1997. *The Order of Rituals: The Interpretation of Everyday Life*. Trans. Mara Luckmann. New Brunswick: Transaction Publishers

Spivak, Gayatri Chakravorty. 1976. "Translator's Preface." In Jacques Derrida, *Of Grammatology*, ix–lxxxvii. Baltimore: Johns Hopkins University Press

———. 1985. "The Rani of Sirmur." In Francis Barker, Peter Hulme, Margaret Iversen, and Diana Loxley, eds., *Europe and Its Others*. Vol. 1. *Proceedings of the Essex Conference on the Sociology of Literature, July 1984*, 128–151. Colchester: University of Essex

———. 1993. *Outside in the Teaching Machine*. New York: Routledge

Stanner, William E. H. 1958. "On the Interpretation of Cargo Cults," *Oceania* 29: 1–25

———. 1965. "Religion, Totemism and Symbolism." In R. M. Berndt and C. H. Berndt, eds., *Aboriginal Man in Australia*, 207–237. Sydney: Angus and Robertson

———. 1966. *On Aboriginal Religion*. Sydney: University of Sydney (Oceania Monograph 11)

———. 1979. "The Dreaming." In William E. H. Stanner, *White Man Got No Dreaming: Essays, 1938–1973*, 23–40. Canberra: Australian National University Press

Steinbauer, Friedrich. 1971. *Die Cargo-Kulte: Als religionsgeschichtliches und missionstheologisches Problem*. Erlangen: Delph'sche Verlasgbuchhandlung

Stephen, Michele. 1997. "Cargo Cults, Cultural Creativity, and Autonomous Imagination," *Ethos* 25: 333–358

Stewart, Kathleen, and Susan Harding. 1999. "Bad Endings: American Apocalypsis," *Annual Review of Anthropology* 28: 285–310

Stewart, Pamela, and Andrew Strathern, eds. 1997. *Millennial Markers*. Townsville: Centre for Pacific Studies, James Cook University

———. 2000. *Millennial Countdown in New Guinea*. Ethnohistory 47

Strathern, Andrew J. 1996. *Body Thoughts*. Ann Arbor: University of Michigan Press

Strathern, Marilyn. 1987. "An Awkward Relationship: The Case of Feminism and Anthropology," *Signs* 12: 276–292

———. 1988. *The Gender of the Gift*. Berkeley: University of California Press

———. 1990. "Artefacts of History: Events and the Interpretation of Images." In J. Siikala, ed., *Culture and History in the Pacific*, 25–44. Helsinki (Finnish Anthropological Society Transactions 27)

Strethlow, Theodore G. H. 1947. *Aranda Traditions*. Melbourne: Melbourne University Press

Strelan, John. 1977. *Search for Salvation: Studies in the History and Theology of Cargo Cults*. Adelaide: Lutheran Publishing House

Stritecky, Jolene Marie. 2001. "Israel, America, and the Ancestors: Narratives of Spiritual Warfare in a Pentecostal Denomination in Solomon Islands," *Journal of Ritual Studies* 15: 62–77

Strozier, Charles. 1994. *Apocalypse: A Theory of Fundamentalism in America*. Boston: Beacon Press

Sumule, Agus. 2002. *Protection and Empowerment of the Rights of Indigenous People of Papua (Irian Jaya) over Natural Resources under Special Autonomy: From Legal Opportunities to the Challenge of Implementation*. Canberra: Resource Management in Asia-Pacific Program, Division of Pacific and Asian History, Research School of Pacific and Asian Studies, Australian National University (Resource Management in Asia-Pacific Working Paper 36)

Swain, Tony. 1993. *A Place For Strangers: Towards a History of Australian Aboriginal Being*. Cambridge: Cambridge University Press

Swain, Tony, and Deborah Bird Rose. 1988. "Introduction." In Tony Swain and Deborah B. Rose, eds., *Aboriginal Australians and Christian Missions*, 1–8. Adelaide: Australian Association for the Study of Religions

Tambiah, Stanley J. 1985. *Culture, Thought, and Social Action: An Anthropological Approach*. Cambridge, Mass.: Harvard University Press

Taussig, Michael. 1980. *The Devil and Commodity Fetishism in South America*. Chapel Hill: University of North Carolina Press

———. 1987. *Shamanism, Colonialism, and the Wild Man: A Study in Terror and Healing*. Chicago: University of Chicago Press

———. 1993. *Mimesis and Alterity: A Particular History of the Senses*. New York: Routledge

Tawney, R. H. 1938 (1922). *Religion and the Rise of Capitalism*. Harmondsworth: Penguin Books

Thomas, Nicholas. 1991. *Entangled Objects: Exchange, Material Culture, and Colonialism in the Pacific*. Cambridge, Mass.: Harvard University Press

Thomson, Donald F. 1933. "The Hero Cult, Initiation and Totemism on Cape York," *Journal of the Royal Anthropological Institute* 63: 453–537

Timmer, Jaap. 1998. "Lost Power, Concealed Knowledge, and the Return of the Kingdom among the Imyan of the Bird's Head of Irian Jaya." In J. Miedema, C. Odé, and R. A. C. Dam, eds., *Perspectives on the Bird's Head of Irian Jaya, Indonesia: Proceedings of the Conference, Leiden, 13–17 October 1997*, 79–116. Amsterdam: Editions Rodopi

———. 2000a. "Living with Intricate Futures: Order and Confusion in Imyan Worlds, Irian Jaya, Indonesia." Ph.D. thesis, University of Nijmegen

———. 2000b. "The Return of the Kingdom: *Agama* and the Millennium among the Imyan of Irian Jaya, Indonesia," *Ethnohistory* 47: 27–63

———. Forthcoming. *Narratives of Government and Church among the Imyan of Papua/Irian Jaya, Indonesia*. Canberra: State, Society and Governance in Melanesia Project, Research School of Pacific and Asian Studies, Australian National University (State, Society and Governance in Melanesia Discussion Paper)

Timmer, Jaap, and Leontine Visser. 2000. "Waiting for the Tide to Turn: Marginalization of the Tehit of Irian Jaya, Indonesia." In J. Fitzpatrick, ed., *Endangered Peoples: Struggles to Sustain Cultural Diversity, Oceania*, 197–212. Westport, Conn.: Greenwood

Tonkinson, Robert. 1970. "Aboriginal Dream-Spirit Beliefs in a Contact Situation." In R. M. Berndt, ed., *Australian Aboriginal Anthropology*, 277–291. Nedlands: University of Western Australia Press

———. 1974. *The Jigalong Mob: Aboriginal Victors of the Christian Crusade*. Menlo Park, Calif.: Cummings

———. 1978. "Aboriginal Community Autonomy: Myth and Reality." In M. C. Howard, ed., *Whitefella Business: Aborigines in Australian Politics*, 93–103. Philadelphia: Institute for the Study of Human Issues

———. 1982. "Outside the Power of the Dreaming: Paternalism and Permissiveness in an Aboriginal Settlement." In M. Howard, ed., *Aboriginal Power in Australian Society*, 115–130. Brisbane: University of Queensland Press

———. 1988a. "Egalitarianism and Inequality in a Western Desert Culture," *Anthropological Forum* 5: 545–558

———. 1988b. "'Ideology and Domination' in Aboriginal Australia: A Western Desert Test Case." In T. Ingold, D. Riches, and J. Woodburn, eds., *Hunters and Gatherers*. Vol. 1: *Property, Power and Ideology*, 170–184. Oxford: Berg

———. 1988c. "One Community, Two Laws: Aspects of Conflict and Convergence in a Western Australian Aboriginal Settlement." In B. Morse and G. Woodman, eds., *Indigenous Law and the State*, 395–411. Dordrecht: Foris

———. 1991. *The Mardu Aborigines: Living the Dream in Australia's Desert*. Fort Worth, Tex.: Holt, Rinehart and Winston (1978: *The Mardudjara Aborigines*. New York: Holt, Rinehart and Winston)

———. 1999. "The Pragmatics and Politics of Aboriginal Tradition and Identity in Australia," *Journal de la Société des Océanistes* 109: 133–147

———. 2000. "'Tradition' in Oceania, and Its Relevance in a Fourth World Context (Australia)," *Folk* 42: 169–195

Trigger, David S. 1986. "Blackfellas and Whitefellas: The Concepts of Domain and Social Closure in the Analysis of Race-Relations," *Mankind* 16: 99–117

———. 1992. *Whitefella Comin': Aboriginal Responses to Colonialism in Northern Australia*. Cambridge: Cambridge University Press

Trompf, Garry W., ed. 1990. *Cargo Cults and Millenarian Movements: Transoceanic Comparisons of New Religious Movements*. Berlin: Mouton de Gruyter

———. 1991. *Melanesian Religion*. Cambridge: Cambridge University Press

Trouillot, Michel-Rolph. 1991. "Anthropology and the Savage Slot: The Poetics and Politics of Otherness." In Richard G. Fox, ed., *Recapturing Anthropology*, 17–44. Santa Fe, N.M.: School of American Research Press

Tsing, Anna. 1993. *In the Realm of the Diamond Queen: Marginality in an Out-of-the-Way Place*. Princeton, N.J.: Princeton University Press

Turney, Jon. 1998. *Frankenstein's Footsteps: Science, Genetics and Popular Culture*. New Haven, Conn.: Yale University Press

Tuveson, Ernest. 1972. *Millennium and Utopia: A Study in the Background of the Idea of Progress*. Gloucester: Peter Smith

Uplegger, Helga, and Wilhelm Emil Mühlmann. 1961. "Die Cargo-Kulte in Neuguinea und Insel-Melanesien." In Wilhelm Emil Mühlmann, *Chiliasmus und Nativismus: Studien zur Psychologie, Soziologie und historischen Kasuistik der Umsturzbewegungen*, 165–189. Berlin: Reimer

Valentine, Charles A. 1955. "Cargo Beliefs and Cargo Cults Among the West Nakanai of New Britain." Unpublished manuscript

———. 1958. "An Introduction to the History of Changing Ways of Life on the Island of New Britain. Ph.D. dissertation, University of Pennsylvania

———. 1960. "Uses of Ethnohistory in an Acculturation Study," *Ethnohistory* 7: 1–27

———. 1961. *Masks and Men in a Melanesian Society: The Valuku or Tubuan of the Lakalai of New Britain*. Lawrence: University of Kansas Publications

———. 1963. "Social Status, Political Power, and Native Responses to European Influence in Oceania," *Anthropological Forum* 1: 3–55

———. 1965. "The Lakalai of New Britain." In Peter Lawrence and Mervyn J. Meggitt, eds., *Gods, Ghosts and Men in Melanesia: Some Religions of Australian New Guinea and the New Hebrides*, 162–197. Melbourne: Oxford University Press

Valentine, Charles A., and Bettylou Valentine. 1979. "Nakanai: Villagers, Settlers, Workers and the Hoskins Oil Palm Project (West New Britain Province)." In Charles A. Valentine and Bettylou Valentine, eds., *Going Through Changes: Villagers, Settlers and Development in Papua New Guinea*, 49–71. Port Moresby: Institute of Papua New Guinea Studies

van der Kroef, J. 1959. "Javanese Messianic Expectations: Their Origin and Cultural Context," *Comparative Studies in Society and History* 6: 299–323

Van Klinken, Gerry. 1999. "What Caused the Ambon Violence?" *Inside Indonesia* 60 (October–December)

———. 2001. "The Maluku Wars of 1999: Bringing Society Back In," *Indonesia* 71: 1–26

Van Langenberg, Michael. 1986. "Analysing Indonesia's New Order State: A Keywords Approach," *Review of Indonesian and Malaysian Affairs* 20: 1–47

Wagner, Hans. 1947. "Ulap-Station-Report 1947." Archiv der Evang.-Luth. Kirche in Bayern. Neuendettelsau. Unpublished Manuscript.

Wagner, Roy. 1975. *The Invention of Culture*. Englewood Cliffs, N.J.: Prentice-Hall (revised and expanded edition 1981: Chicago: University of Chicago Press)

———. 1979. "The Talk of Koriki: A Daribi Contact Cult," *Social Research* 46: 141–165

———. 2000. "Our Very Own Cargo Cult." In Doug Dalton, ed., *A Critical Retrospective on "Cargo Cult": Western/Melanesian Intersections*, 362–372. Oceania 70

Waiko, John D. 1973. "European-Melanesian Contact in Melanesian Tradition and Literature." In Ronald J. May, ed., *Priorities in Melanesian Development*, 417–428. Port Moresby: University of Papua New Guinea

Walter, Michael A. H. B. 1981. "Cult Movements and Community Development Associations: Revolution and Evolution in the Papua New Guinea Countryside." In Rolf Gerritsen, Ronald J. May, and Michael A. H. B. Walter, eds., *Road Belong Development: Cargo Cults, Community Groups and Self-Help Movements in Papua New Guinea*, 81–105. Canberra: Department of Political and Social Change, Research School of Pacific Studies, Australian National University (Working Paper 3)

Warner, W. Lloyd. 1937. *A Black Civilisation*. New York: Harper

Weber, Max. 1979. "Die protestantische Ethik und der Geist des Kapitalismus." In J. Winckelmann, ed., *Max Weber: Die protestantische Ethik: Eine Aufsatzsammlung 1*, 27–277. Gütersloh: Gütersloher Verlagshaus

Widlok, Thomas. 1992. "Practice, Politics and Ideology of the 'Travelling Business' in Aboriginal Teligion," *Oceania* 63: 114–136

———. 1997. "Traditions of Transformation: Travelling Rituals in Australia." In Ton Otto and Ad Boorsboom, eds., *Cultural Dynamics of Religious Change in Oceania*, 11–22. Leiden: KITLV Press

Wilde, Oscar. 1891. *The Picture of Dorian Gray*. London: Ward Lock and Co.

Williams, Francis Edgar. 1976a [1923]. "The Vailala Madness and the Destruction of Native Ceremonies in the Gulf Division." In Eric Schwimmer, ed., *Francis Edgar Williams 'The Vailala Madness' and Other Essays*, 331–384. London: Hurst & Co.

———. 1976b [1934]. "The Vailala Madness in Retrospect." In Eric Schwimmer, ed., *Francis Edgar Williams 'The Vailala Madness' and Other Essays*, 385–395. London: Hurst & Co.

Williams, N. M. 1986. *The Yolngu and their Land: a System of Land Tenure and the Fight for its Recognition*. Canberra: Australian Institute of Aboriginal Studies

Williams, Raymond. 1983 [1976]. *Keywords: A Vocabulary of Culture and Society*. New York: Oxford University Press

Winzeler, Robert. 1995. *Latah in Southeast Asia: The History and Ethnography of a Culture-Bound Syndrome*. Cambridge: Cambridge University Press

Wolf, Eric R. 1999. *Envisioning Power: Ideologies of Dominance and Crisis*. Berkeley: University of California Press

Wolin, Richard. 1994. *Walter Benjamin: An Aesthetic of Redemption*. Berkeley: University of California Press

Wood, Christopher. 1986. *Kago*. New York: Henry Holt

Woolmington, Jean. 1988. "'Writing on the Sand': The First Missions to Aborigines in Eastern Australia." In Tony Swain and Deborah B. Rose, eds., *Aboriginal Australians and Christian Missions*, 77–92. Adelaide: Australian Association for the Study of Religions.

Worsley, Peter. 1957. *The Trumpet Shall Sound: A Study of "Cargo" Cults in Melanesia*. London: MacGibbon and Kee (second, augmented edition 1968, New York: Schocken Books)

———. 1999. "'Cargo Cults': Forty Years On." In C. Kocher Schmid, ed., *Expecting the Day of Wrath: Versions of the Millennium in Papua New Guinea*, 145–155. Boroko (NRI Monograph 36)

Young, Michael. 1971. "Goodenough Island Cargo Cults," *Oceania* 42: 42–57

———. 1997. "Commemorating Missionary Heroes: Local Christianity and Narratives of Nationalism." In Ton Otto and Nicholas Thomas, eds., *Narratives of Nation in the South Pacific*, 91–132. Amsterdam: Harwood Academic Publishers

Contributors

Nils Bubandt is associate professor of anthropology at the University of Aarhus (Denmark). He received his Ph.D. from the Australian National University and since 1991 has been conducting extensive fieldwork in North Maluku, working on topics such as witchcraft and modernity, Christianity and conversion, rumor and violence. Since 1999, he has been following the communal riots in North Maluku, analyzing them in light of the political process of decentralization and neotraditionalism. His recent publications include "Malukan Apocalypse: Themes in the Dynamics of Violence in Eastern Indonesia," in I. Wessel, and G. Wimhoefer, eds., *Violence in Indonesia* (2001) and "Conspiracy Theories, Apocalyptic Narratives and the Discursive Construction of 'the Violence in Maluku,'" *Antropologi Indonesia* (2000).

Vincent Crapanzano is Distinguished Professor of Anthropology and Comparative Literature at the CUNY Graduate Center (New York City, USA). Among his many books are *Tuhami: Portrait of a Moroccan* (1980), *Hermes' Dilemma and Hamlet's Desire* (1992), and *Serving the Word: Literalism in America from the Pulpit to the Bench* (2000). His most recent book, *Imaginative Horizons: An Essay in Literary-Philosophical Anthropology*, based on the Frobenius Lectures he delivered in Frankfurt am Main, is being published by the University of Chicago Press.

Doug Dalton is professor of anthropology at Longwood University (Farmville, Virginia, USA). He lived and worked with Rawa-speaking people in the mountains of northeastern Papua New Guinea from 1982 to 1984 and continues to study and interpret their culture and experience in a variety of publications, papers, and presentations.

Elfriede Hermann has since the mid-1980s conducted multisited fieldwork in Madang Province of Papua New Guinea. Her research interests include social movements, ethnopsychology, gender, migration, ethnicity, interculturality, and transnationality. Among her publications are *Emotionen und Historizität. Der emotionale Diskurs über die Yali-Bewegung in einer Dorfgemeinschaft der Ngaing, Papua New Guinea* (1995) and (coauthored with Wolfgang Kempf) "Dreamscapes: Transcending the Local in Initiation Rites among the Ngaing of Papua New Guinea," in R. Lohmann, ed., *Dream Travellers: Sleep Experiences and Culture in the Western Pacific* (2003). She is currently studying self-differentiation and agency among the resettled Banaban community of Fiji, after having commenced continuing fieldwork with the latter in 1997.

Holger Jebens is research fellow at the Frobenius-Institute at the Johann Wolfgang Goethe-University (Frankfurt am Main, Germany) and managing editor of the journal *Paideuma*. On the basis of his fieldwork in Highland and Seaboard Papua New Guinea (1990–1991, 1995–1996, 1997), he has worked on topics such as religion, inter- and intraethnic conflict, identity, museology, and fieldwork methodology. Recent articles include "Trickery or Secrecy? On Andrew Lattas's Interpretation of 'Bush Kaliai Cargo Cults,'" *Anthropos* (2002), and "Starting with the Law of the *Tumbuan*: Masked Dances in West New Britain (Papua New Guinea) as an Appropriation of One's Own Cultural Self," *Anthropos* (2003). His recent book, *Pathway to Heaven: Contesting Mainline and Fundamentalist Christianity in Pairundu (Southern Highlands Province, Papua New Guinea)*, is being published by Berghahn Books.

Martha Kaplan is professor of anthropology at Vassar College (Poughkeepsie, New York, USA). She received her Ph.D. in anthropology from the University of Chicago. She has pursued field and archival research in Fiji for two decades and has published widely on topics in anthropological theory, ritual, history, and colonial and postcolonial societies. She is the author of *Neither Cargo nor Cult: Ritual Politics and the Colonial Imagination in Fiji* (1995) and the coauthor (with John D. Kelly) of *Represented Communities: Fiji and World Decolonization* (2001).

Karl-Heinz Kohl is professor of ethnology and director of the Frobenius-Institute at the Johann Wolfgang Goethe-University (Frankfurt am Main, Germany). He did intensive fieldwork among the Lamaholot-speaking population of East Flores and conducted several ethnographic research projects in eastern Indonesia, New Guinea, and Nigeria. Among his most recent books on the anthropology of religion are *Der Tod der Reisjungfrau. Mythen, Kulte und Allianzen in einer ostindonesischen Lokalkultur* (1998), and *Die Macht der Dinge. Theorie und Geschichte sakraler Objekte* (2003).

Stephen C. Leavitt is associate professor of anthropology at Union College (Schenectady, New York, USA). He was trained in psychological anthropology at the University of California, San Diego, and conducted twenty-six months of fieldwork among the Bumbita Arapesh in the East Sepik Province of Papua New Guinea in 1984–1986, at a time when local communities were undergoing a widespread Christian religious revival. His central research interests there include religious conviction and the narrative construction of personal experience. He is coeditor (with Gilbert Herdt) of *Adolescence in Pacific Island Societies* (1998) and has also written on Bumbita sexuality, mourning, self, and religious experience. In recent years he has conducted three research trips to the Rakiraki area of Fiji, focusing on local religious change.

Lamont Lindstrom is professor of anthropology at the University of Tulsa (Tulsa, Oklahoma, USA). He is the author of *Knowledge and Power in a South Pacific Society* (1990), *Cargo Cult: Strange Stories of Desire from Melanesia and Beyond* (1993), coauthor of *Island Encounters: Black and White Memories of the Pacific War* (1990, with Geoffrey M. White) and *Kava: The Pacific Drug* (1992, with Vincent Mark Merlin). He has also published on chiefs and governance, and language on Tanna (Vanuatu).

Ton Otto is professor of anthropology and ethnography at the University of Aarhus (Denmark). He has conducted extensive fieldwork in Manus and New Ireland (Papua New Guinea) on issues of social and cultural change. His publications include *The Politics of Tradition in Baluan: Social Change and the Construction of the Past in a Manus Society* (1991) and three coedited volumes: *Narratives of Nation in the South Pacific* (1997, with Nicholas Thomas), *Cultural Dynamics of Religious Change in Oceania* (1997, with Ad Borsboom), and *Perplexities of Identification: Anthropological Studies in Cultural Differentiation and the Use of Resources* (2000, with Henk Driessen).

Joel Robbins is associate professor of anthropology at the University of California (La Jolla, California, USA). He has published extensively on the anthropology of Melanesia and on issues of religion, ritual, and cultural change and is the author of *Becoming Sinners: Christianity and Moral Torment in a Papua New Guinea Society* (2004).

Jaap Timmer is a research fellow in the State, Society and Governance in Melanesia Project at the Research School of Pacific and Asian Studies, Australian National University (Canberra, Australia). He was educated at the University of Amsterdam (M.A., 1993), Leiden University, and the University of Nijmegen (Ph.D., 2000), and has a broad regional interest in Southeast Asia and the southwest Pacific, with particular emphasis on Netherlands New Guinea/Irian Jaya/Papua, the Malukus, and Papua New Guinea. His anthropological research interests include issues of identity, conflict, violence, religiosity, and millenarianism. In addition to his research, he works as a consultant for international nongovernmental organizations and government agencies on programs for emergency aid, conflict resolution, special autonomy, and development.

Robert Tonkinson is emeritus professor of anthropology and sociology at the University of Western Australia (Crawley, Australia) and editor of the journal *Anthropological Forum*. He has conducted extensive fieldwork since the early 1960s among Aboriginal people in the Western Desert of Australia and with Melanesians in the islands of Ambrym and Efate, in Vanuatu. The author of *The Jigalong Mob* (1974), and *The Mardu Aborigines* (1991), he has published on a wide variety of topics under the rubric of religion, change, Western impacts, the politics of tradition, social organization, and identity.

Index